OTHER THAN IDENTITY

C   KINDRED COLL

Other than identity

The subject, politics and art

edited by Juliet Steyn

MANCHESTER UNIVERSITY PRESS
MANCHESTER AND NEW YORK

distributed exclusively in the USA by St. Martin's Press

Copyright © Manchester University Press 1997

While copyright in the volume as a whole is vested in Manchester University Press, copyright in individual chapters belongs to their respective authors, and no chapter may be reproduced wholly or in part without the express permission in writing of both author and publisher.

Published by Manchester University Press
Oxford Road, Manchester M13 9NR, UK
and Room 400, 175 Fifth Avenue, New York, NY10010, USA

Distributed exclusively in the USA by
St. Martin's Press, Inc., 175 Fifth Avenue, New York, NY10010, USA

British Library Cataloguing-in-Publication Data

A catalogue record for this book is available from the British Library

Library of Congress Cataloging-in-Publication Data applied for

ISBN 0–7190–4462–6 *hardback*
ISBN 0–7190–4463–4 *paperback*

First published 1997

00 99 98 97   10 9 8 7 6 5 4 3 2 1

Typeset by Carnegie Publishing, Preston
Printed in Great Britain
by Redwood Books, Trowbridge

Contents

Part 3   Refiguring identity in art

Figures

Notes on contributors

RICHARD APPIGNANESI is Originating Editor and Art Director of Icon Books. He was Gulbenkian Foundation Fellow, Department of Portuguese and Brazilian Studies, King's College, London, 1993–4, and co-curator of the art exhibition *Pretext: Heteronyms*, Clink Street Studios, London (1995), and S. Michele, Rome, Italy (1997). Publications include the fiction trilogy *Italia Pervesa* (1985–6) and *Postmodernism for Beginners* (1995). He is currently writing a biography of Fernando Pessoa.

GLEN BOWMAN is a social anthropologist who chairs the interdisciplinary programme in Communication and Image Studies at the University of Kent. His research has focused on articulation of Palestinian identity in Israel and the Israeli-Occupied Territories. More recently he has examined religious, ethnic and secularist mobilizations of identity in the former Yugoslavia. Recent publications include 'Making space for "the Other": on the implications of the crisis of the subject for anthropological discourse' in *Anthropological Journal on European Cultures* (1996). The article 'Constitutive violence and rhetorics of identity: a comparative study of nationalist movements in the Israeli-Occupied Territories and Former Yugoslavia' is to appear in *Nationalism and Violence*.

ANDREW BENJAMIN is Professor in the Department of Philosophy at the University of Warwick and a visiting lecturer in philosophy, architecture and fine art in academic departments world-wide. His publications include *Translation and the Nature of Philosophy* (1989), *What is Deconstruction?* (with Christopher Norris) (1989), *Art, Mimesis and the Avant-Garde* (1991) and *Object. Painting* (1994). He has edited several collections including *Problems of Modernity: Adorno and Benjamin* (1989) and is Editor of the *Journal of Philosophy and the Visual Arts*.

HOWARD CAYGILL is Professor of Cultural History at Goldsmiths' College, University of London. He is author of *The Art of Judgement* (1989), *A Kant Dictionary* (1995) and *Walter Benjamin: the Colour of Experience* (1996).

ALAN CURRY lectures in Cultural Studies at the London Institute, Central St Martin's and Kent Institute of Art and Design. Recent art exhibitions include *Works Perfectly* (1994). He has been Artistic Director and performer, *Mombasa Road Show*, since 1982. Performances include *Diorama*, Regent's Park Ghost Club and Jeanette Cochrane Theatre, London.

KATY DEEPWELL is an artist, critic and lecturer. She edited *New Feminist Art Criticism: Critical Strategies* (1995) and recent publications include 'Feminist readings of Louise Bourgeois' in *Louise Bourgeois* (1996) and 'Hepworth and her critics' in *Barbara Hepworth Reconsidered* (1996). She is currently working on a book of selected essays on women and modernism for Manchester University Press.

JOHN GANGE lectures in Cultural and Critical Studies and Time-based Media at the Kent Institute of Art and Design. He has been a regular contributor to *Live Arts* magazine and is Production Editor of the journal *ACT*. He is currently completing a Ph.D. thesis on Georges Bataille and anti-aesthetics. He has published 'Photography and auto-fetishism' in *Pierre Molinère: comme je voudrais être* (1993).

JANET HAND is a writer, performer and lecturer. She founded the performance group *Anna O.* in 1988. She is now studying at the Centre for Psychoanalytic Research at Kent University. She currently teaches Critical Theory in Textiles at Goldsmiths' College, University of London and Art and Design at Central St Martin's. She has contributed to the journal *Hybrid* and *Live Arts* magazine and, most recently, to the book *Feminist Stages* by Lizbeth Goodman.

LEWIS JOHNSON teaches theories and histories of art in the Department of Visual Art at Goldsmiths College, University of London. He is currently engaged in research on the history and theory of installation art, and on time and vision. He has published on the history and theory of nineteenth and twentieth century art, and on contemporary art, in journals and in exhibition catalogues, recently on collaboration and photographic installation work. He is the author of *Prospects, Thresholds, Interiors* (1994).

JOAN KEY is an artist whose work is currently represented by Richard Salmon. Her work has been exhibited by *Rear Window* in their exhibitions *Affective Light* and *Pretext Heteronyms*. She has worked as a curator in collaboration with the Curwen Gallery. Recent publications include 'A body too much' in *New Feminist Art Criticism: Critical Strategies* (1995) and articles in the journals *ACT* and *Women's Art* magazine.

MARYSIA LEWANDOWSKA is an artist. She was born in Poland and moved to London in 1985. Her work is conceptually based and often engages and implicates photography through the context of display. Her most recent exhibitions include *Now/Here* at Louisiana Museum of Modern Art, Denmark, *Prospect '93* at the Frankfurter Kunstverein and *Wonderful Life* at the Lisson Gallery. Her work is included in the collections of the Arts Council of England, Fondation National d'Art Contemporain, Paris; Centre for Contemporary Art, Warsaw; and Saatchi, London. Since 1988 she has edited a series of books on contemporary visual culture, *Sight Works*. She teaches at Goldsmith's College, University of London, and at the Slade School of Fine Art.

CLAIRE PAJACZKOWSKA is Senior Lecturer in the School of History and Theory of Visual Culture, Middlesex University. Her most recent essays include 'Getting there' in *Travellers Tales* (1994), 'Assimilation, identity and entertainment: the Hollywood solution' in *The Jew in the Text* (1995), both written with Barry Curtis, and 'The penis and the phallus' in *What She Wants* (1994). Recent translations include *L'Image* by Jacques Aumont (1995) and *Le Discours vivant* by André Green (forthcoming).

ZIAUDDIN SARDAR, writer, broadcaster and cultural critic, is Consulting Editor of *Futures*, the journal of forecasting, planning and policy, and Visiting Professor of Science Policy at Middlesex University. Publications include *The Future of Muslim Civilisation* (1977), *Islamic Futures: the Shape of Ideas to Come* (1985) and, most recently, *Muhammad for Beginners* and *Cyberfutures: Culture and Politics on the Information Super Highway*. He is currently working on *Postmodernism and the Other* which examines the postmodern perceptions and treatment of non-Western peoples and cultures.

JULIET STEYN is Course Leader of the MA in Art Crticism and Theory at the Kent Institute of Art and Design. She is Commissioning Editor of the journal *ACT*. Recent publications include 'Charles Dickens' *Oliver Twist*: Fagin as a sign' in *The Jew in the Text* (1995). She was co-curator of the art exhibition *Pretext: Heteronyms*, Clink Street Studios, London (1995) and S. Michele, Rome, Italy (1997). *The Jews: Assumptions of Identity* will be published in 1998.

CHRISTOPHER WANT, art historian and theorist, is Deputy Course Leader of the MA in Art Criticism and Theory at the Kent Institute of Art and Design and lectures in Critical Theory at Goldsmiths' College, University of London. Publications include essays in *ACT* and *Art Monthly* and his forthcoming book *Kant for Beginners*.

Introduction

JULIET STEYN

The speculative and, for me, sometimes melancholic essays that have emerged as responses to the proposition, *Other than identity*, all testify to the complexity of questions which are bound to arise from a serious consideration of the theme of Identity, its determinations and figurations. Identity (which may be as much about the future and the past, as the present) touches each one of us, reverberating within and throughout individual, social, political and cultural domains. The relationship between these is contingent, or in prospect, not already accomplished or given. Identity can be described as a process which entails differentiation between the self, not-self and other.

Over the last twenty-five years in the English-speaking world, approaches to the study of the humanities have radically changed: the impact of critical theory, Western Marxism and psychoanalysis have dramatically affected the ways of thinking about culture and altered its parameters. This anthology, with its evident debts to post-structuralism, bears witness to this change. The multi-disciplinarity of this project makes it provocative and risky: no one reader is expected to know intimately the work of all the philosophers and artists considered in the collection. The issue at stake is Identity, and in several senses, its assumptions.

The ways in which identity can be thematized are multifold: it is made and un-made in many sites and crosses many paths. Here it is *supposed* as identity in the subject, in politics and in art. These themes cannot be kept strictly apart. Between essays, the reader may discern overlaps and digressions, agreements and contestations: any disparities are wilful and are presented so as to allow new configurations to emerge. The anthology is conceived as a heterogeneous association of voices resembling unheard conversations between disciplines. At a moment of negativity and pessimism, exemplified in the failure of Communism, they appear as testimonies to a range of possibilities, views and agendas. Let us approach them as manifestations which are not necessarily manifest and value them as offering different ways of speaking about ourselves which allow philosophy, politics and aesthetics other possibilities.

The cornerstone of the Western philosophical tradition has been the notion of a single unitary subject, construed as identical with itself. Identity becomes a question for ontology. Self-identity is a problem for philosophy and philosophy's definition of itself. Western philosophy, in its attempts to understand

and thereby to control the nature of the world, has tended towards systems of thought which have sought to represent totality. For Hegel, the cognitive process unfolds into the absolute idea. Subject and object are complete, identical. A concept and an object, a regulating idea and reality are linked. The particular is subsumed by the universal just as the concept is subsumed by the system. Adorno has called this constellation of thought *Identity Thinking*.[1] There is a tendency within identity thinking which inclines it towards totalizing structures and institutions. To name *identity thinking* risks presuming it in a pure or essential form, but not to name may be not to speak. So it may well be that *Other than identity* is caught in a paradox: it acknowledges the articulations of identity while presenting a challenge to their assumptions. Posited upon doubt, then, the only certainty that this collection can offer us is that we cannot think outside language which is not identical with certainty: language gives us thought which is itself shaped by language. The essays open to thought a range of ways to rethink Being, the Subject, the Other and language. Moreover, as Jean-François Lyotard declares:

> We have paid a high enough price for the nostalgia of the whole and the one, for the reconciliation of the concept and the sensible, of the transparent and the communicable experience. Under the general demand for slackening and for appeasement, we can hear the mutterings of the desire for a return of terror, for the realisation of the fantasy to share reality. The answer is: let us wage a war on totality; let us be witnesses to the unpresentable; let us activate the differences and save the honour of the name.[2]

The spectre of totalitarianism haunts Lyotard's text: his critique of totalizing systems and theory can stand as a critique of Fascism. Absorbed by its own fantasies of completeness, Fascism mobilized the identificatory emotions of the masses: it politicized desire and fear, negated them and obliterated others in a radical synthesis. It made itself subject in terms which were absolute. We may recall here, too, Walter Benjamin's stark observations to the effect that Fascism aestheticizes politics; Communism responds by politicizing art.[3] However, these remarks are not to be understood as merely commenting upon long past historical events but as having a continuing bearing upon history now: witness former Yugoslavia, where life-and-death struggles are mobilized and legitimated in the name of identity. The ghosts of the past and the future haunt every present. It is only in the traces and ruins of some other possible reality that we can perhaps escape the totalitarian power of the whole. Those that do not remember are compelled to repeat.[4] Remembering enables a going-beyond (in so far as a going-beyond necessitates a working through, a repetition).

The concern of this book is to disturb the identification of subject and identity: not to quest for anonymity or non-identity but rather to test the strictures and articulations of *identity thinking* and to destabilize the dialectical paradigm it presupposes.[5] As long as the logic of identity remains, we can only ever move endlessly from the same (the already assigned) to identity, inevitably and always under the authority of the same, and of the foregrounding of the problematic of identity.

Rethinking identity entails a demand: to split the traditional link between self and identity. Identity is presented as akin to culture, which allows identity but is not a guarantor of the subject. Likewise the assumptions of the subject are no guarantors of subjectivity. Nowadays it has become commonplace in cultural theory to describe ourselves as 'split', in between, fragmented, ceaselessly losing our identity, destabilized by changes in our relationships to the other.[6] However, in Julia Kristeva's terse words, 'the discovery of the other in me does not make me schizophrenic'.[7] Human beings, as speaking beings, are heterogeneous by nature (and perhaps none more so than Fernando Pessoa with his creation of 'Heteronyms', other writers with their own separate and distinct identities, existences and languages). Plurality, a recognition of the otherness of the self, as well as others, is essential to human consciousness and creativity. We can still speak of a Subject, however provisional, as long as language creates the identity of the speaker and ascribes to it an interlocutor and a referent.

The essays in this anthology evoke the Subject in a number of different ways: as a reaffirmation of the self offering the promise of reconstitution; as a presence which constantly attests to and assumes new configurations; as a figuration of appearance and disappearance; as provisional and yet achieved in the allusive space between absence and presence, and, as a subject in excess of itself, an expenditure of forces that is utterly impersonal.

Any presentation of an other is itself a political representation which sets up the drive for a liberating, emancipatory politics which can be figured as an overcoming. The politics of overcoming can also produce a solution: mastery and suppression. In the ambiguous dialectic of the Enlightenment, reason is both the instrument by which humankind frees itself from nature and the very means through which others are subjugated – subject to and subjects of.[8] A particular problem we now face is a loss of faith in the political processes of democracy, unleashing xenophobic outbursts. Today, Jacques Rancière suggests:

> racism is the hatred of the other that comes forth when political procedures of social polemics collapse. The political culture of conflict may have had disappointing outlets. But it was also a way of coming to terms with something that lies before and beneath politics: the question of the other as a figure of identification for the object of fear.[9]

The discourses of Emancipation, under the banners of citizenship and reason, admitted the possibility of civilizing the fear of the other and the feared other. None the less the negative connotations attributed to others do not arise purely out of ignorance or individual opinions, which are presumed to be easily changed by education and more positive attitudes to cultural diversity. The rational spawns the irrational and vice versa. Identification occurs through desire and denial, affirmation and negation: love and hate occupy the same psychic sphere and are forces which bind the self with the other. Our attitudes towards others are often plagued by feelings of ambivalence: 'In the undisguised antipathies and aversions which people feel towards strangers ... we may recognize the expression of self-love – of narcissism', explains Freud.[10] Ambivalence is the unknown component of the known. Identity is imbued with projections of the Other as an erotic object and semiotic space. Embroiled in the figurations of identity is also an implication of an-other *erotics* with attendant probings of seduction and narcissism and their effects.

Identity can also function as a powerful myth which fuses people together, creating a seemingly unstoppable force which emanates from mobilizing fundamental forces and beliefs of people, articulating a deep, manifest and embodied identity.[11] Often the most belligerent affirmations of cultural difference (identity) are most evident where the possibility of loss is imminent. It appears that there can be no creation of an 'us' without the designation of a 'them', which can slip easily into enemy, scapegoat or feared other. Nevertheless the processes of identification are not monolithic. Identities are formed by and validated in representation, and anything identified as identity is already in a position that acknowledges the possibility that it is other than its representation.

> One
> and the same
> has lost us, one
> and the same
> has forgotten us, one
> and the same has –

Paul Celan's verse prompts a heterogeneity of possible interpretations which invite us to speculate upon the representable, the certain, the unpresentable and provisional.[12] The poem could refer to God, or to the *identity thinking* of total systems. Or again it might also prompt us to recall the primary bond between mother and child and thus the primal anxiety of separation upon which culture is founded. Unity figures in the past tense: as a representation of a distant memory which trauma has disturbed. Both the dread and the possibilities of unity haunt the universal. Having represented a unity but refused an ending, Celan also refuses to represent a closure, or indeed a 'finite totality'. We are prompted to remember that there is something other which might yet be named. In the unbreachable space between identity and otherness the horizons of the universal may be expanded and reaffirmed. Hence the project of the Enlightenment might begin anew.

This anthology has been conceived of so as to offer a reworking of the terms in which identity can be thought, precisely so as to avoid the seductions and entrapments of *identity thinking*. By proposing a move beyond a single 'yes' which can only function in opposition to 'no', those perspectives offering identity as either affirmation or negation of the subject and its identity can be re-evaluated. *Other than identity* indicates what might be other in identity and in thought. It does not provide a brief for the ecstasies of eclecticism, relativism or even cynicism, but is marked by a desire for identifying different ways of thinking being. The subject is rediscovering itself in its obliteration. The essays at once offer a mitigation or a defence of otherness and at the same time point to the thought of alterity as potentially horrifying, because it is thought that is other than thought and identity which is other than identity. The representation of alterity prevents complete identification and totalization. That which has been traditionally thought of as aesthetics is reaffirmed as a site in which the limits of the thinkable are at work and might be rephrased and represented.

Finally, perhaps *Other than identity* would have been a melancholic project had its demand been to witness the failure of culture to give us ethics, politics or truth. But, after all, maybe its demand has not been about judgement but rather a stricture about what is entailed in making judgements. The need to rethink identity continues, lest a politics of total identification and a recurring history of annihilation is forever precipitated and determined.

Notes

1 T. Adorno, *Negative Dialectics* (trans. E. B. Ashton), New York and London, 1973. For an account of Adorno and *identity thinking*, see David Held, *Introduction to Critical Theory: Horkheimer to Habermas*, London: Routledge, 1973, p. 202.

2 Jean-François Lyotard, *The Post Modern Condition: A Report on Knowledge* (trans. Geoff Bennington and Brian Massumi), Manchester: Manchester University Press, 1989, pp. 81–2.

3 Walter Benjamin, 'The work of art in the age of mechanicl reproduction', *Illuminations* (trans. Harry Zohn), London: Fontana, 1973, p. 244.

4 George Santayana's observation has now become a commonplace of cultural criticism. It originally appeared in *Life of Reason*, 1905, cited in *The Oxford Dictionary of Modern Quotations*, ed. Tony Augarde, Oxford: Oxford University Press, 1991, p. 190.

5 Jean-Luc Nancy argues that the critique or deconstruction of subjectivity is one of the great enterprises of contemporary philosophical work ('Introduction', *Who Comes After the Subject*, eds E. Cadava, P. Connor and J.-L. Nancy, New York and London: Routledge, 1991, p. 4.

6 For an extended critique of current uses of theories of 'schizophrenia' and celebrations of the 'split' subject, see Fredric Jameson, 'Postmodernism and consumer society', in *Postmodern Culture*, ed. Hal Foster, London: Pluto Press, 1985, *passim*.

7 Julia Kristeva, *In the Beginning was Love: Psychoanalysis and Faith* (trans. Arthur Goldhammer), New York: Columbia University Press, 1987, p. 55.

8 T. Adorno and M. Horkheimer, *Dialectic of Enlightenment* (trans. John Cumming), London: Verso, 1989, remains a seminal work on this theme.

9 Jacques Rancière, 'Politics, identification, and subjectivization', *October*, 61, 1991, pp. 63–4.

10 Sigmund Freud, 'Group psychology', in *Civilisation, Society and Religion*, Harmondsworth: Penguin, 1987, p. 141

11 My particular use of the term 'myth' here has a debt to Philippe Lacoue-Labarthe, *Heidegger, Art and Politics: the Fiction of the Political* (trans. Chris Turner), Oxford: Basil Blackwell, 1990, p. 94.
12 Paul Celan, 'Zürich, the Stork Inn', from *Paul Celan: Selected Poems* (trans. Michael Hamburger), Harmondsworth: Penguin, 1990, p. 163.

PART I

Refiguring identity in the subject

Figuring self-identity: Blanchot's Bataille

With the self the problem of identity will necessarily be at work. Indeed, any conception of the self already presupposes a necessarily reciprocal conception of identity, even if that necessity remains unstated as such. Moreover, a fundamental component marking the reciprocity between self and identity is the residual presence of authenticity; rather than authenticity being merely a contingent possibility it will always have to have been present as an ineliminable potential. It is thus that to write of the self – offering the self an identity – is already to raise the possibility that what is being addressed is the self as it actually is; the authentic self. (Even though the ontology in question will need to be taken up, this *address* will need to be understood as an ontological rather than a straightforwardly empirical claim.) There is therefore a complex demand within which both the self and identity will inevitably figure in relation to the possibility of the authentic. As what determines any conception of the relationship between identity and the self will involve a commitment to a form of authenticity, taking up the question of identity will give rise to specific demands. (Here the demands pertain to what it is that is designated by certain terms; i.e. how, given the absence of any determining form of essentialism, are identity, authenticity, etc. to be understood?) It is thus that what is demanded opens up the recognition of limits. It is these limits which must be established and explored. Returning to the subject – to the self – is to return to the question of what allows for *self-identity*. (The latter term – *self-identity* – being the site in which the interrelation between self and identity is announced as a question to be answered. It will be an answer that allows for the interplay of self, identity and authenticity to be at work.) In this instance these questions will acquire specificity by concentrating the site of their work within the writings of Maurice Blanchot and Georges Bataille; in particular in Blanchot's own estimation of Bataille as it comes to be formulated in *L'Entretien infini*.[1] Integral to the undertakings of both Blanchot and Bataille is authenticity. Part of the challenge here will be to identify the nature of this authenticity and the role it plays in their work.[2]

Here, therefore, what will be taken as central is the task of tracing the relationship between Blanchot and Bataille as it is presented in Blanchot's text *L'Affirmation et la passion de la pensée négative*;[3] one of his most sustained and explicit encounters with Bataille's thought. What is at work in this interpretive site moreover what is implicated in responding to the difficulty of what comes to be presented within this engagement – needs to be given a provisional formulation. The site's insistence needs to be broached. As will emerge, thinking complexity will have to have been at work from the start. While it will be essential to stay with the text's work, work will always allow for a translation into concerns which already figure within the necessity of the interrelation between self and identity. It is this complex relation that is captured by the formulation *self-identity*. It signals both that the act of translation will have already been at work in itself, and because the formulation *self-identity* – what the term marks out – can be taken as already carrying over and therefore being a translation of that necessity.

Towards the site

While it may appear far too elementary a beginning, it is clear from the start that once the determinations of identity are no longer assumed as given and that as a consequence identity can endure as a question, then what will figure in such a questioning are the already predetermined possibilities of identity thinking. In other words what will figure are the already given forms in which identity will have been thought. (The difference here is, of course, between figuring and determining.) Once the pregiven forms in which identity is given no longer dominate – a position acquired because they endure within questioning – then what follows from this repositioning is itself inevitably structured by repetition. Only certain repetitions of identity are possible. At the extreme – a limit defining the moment at which possibility and impossibility merge while holding themselves apart – will be that form of repetition in which what is given comes to be repeated again for the first time. While it is not argued for as such by Blanchot, the concern exemplified in his writings with modes of thinking which are themselves located at the limit and demanding alterity within thinking and thus an-other form of description, can be situated within this possibility. Singularity will be located within the primordiality of repetition. Once again the site of this possibility – a possibility that is given by allowing repetition an inherent and sustaining complexity – is the self. Once given, the self opens out by having to bring with it that which takes place with the thinking of that self; in sum the interplay of *self-identity*.[4]

    With the project of the self – the self as a projected being, bringing the question of its being, of being a subject and thus of (its) subjectivity into play – the question that comes to insist will concern the philosophical formulation adequate to this project; the identity in question. Despite the hold of tradition, adequation need not be understood as part of a search driven by an essence that will need to be named. Allowing for the abeyance of essential thinking means that the self will come to be confronted with precisely those determinations in which it finds itself at work. In not being able to extricate itself, the self *is* – it is what it is – within these determinations: the self is in its becoming. There is no one thing that is determined – there is not even one body on which these determinations come to be acted out – since determinations become and thus become part of the continuity of the 'thing' – and therefore of the 'things' – becoming itself; a discontinuous continuity. Countering that which is given by the determining effect of a series of interrelated and ineliminable connections will involve, almost of necessity, the projection of other possibilities. A fundamental part of the alterity that will be at work here is that the self, and with it its identity, will be necessarily positioned beyond the hold of that which would be given as complete and thus held within a self-completing finality. It will be in this precise sense that there will be another possibility for thinking the self and thus for thinking its subjectivity. Once again thinking will turn on the question of identity; of *self-identity*. With this opening what arises – emerging with an almost insistent necessity – is an-other possibility for thinking. Here what alterity would entail is a turn in thought; a movement away from the repetition of the traditional forms in which the interplay of self and identity is enacted and thus a turn towards another possibility. (It is precisely this turn, and with it a move towards that conception of the self in which the self is what it is in the continuity of its becoming itself, that will allow for the more traditional conceptions of self to be understood as strictly ephemeral. Moreover it is a move in which the ephemeral is taken as natural.) In this particular turn the possibility of singularity will come to be announced. These concerns are not distanced from Blanchot's own. As always, the central difficulty will be how such an undertaking is formulated. Part of the problem is style. How is that which resists an already present determination in advance to find a determinant form? With this question style is freed as much from the claims of generality as it is from the hold of meaning. With this freedom it is able to form an integral part of the work's work and thus becomes linked to signification.

A text – one structured in terms of a dialogue that defeats the tradition of dialogue – that takes as its central concern the possibility of a 'change of epoch' begins with an interchange setting up the conditions in terms of which change may admit of being thought: '"Will you allow as a certainty that we are at a turning point [*un tournant*]?" "If it is a certainty it is not a turning"' (pp. 394/264).

Here with this strange question and its equally problematic response – partially reproduced here – Blanchot begins another complex deliberation on the possibility of change by inscribing into the difficult complex relation in which such a possibility is to be thought what amounts to a form of the question of recognition. What does the recognition of 'a turn' (*un tournant*) – a recognition in which such a possibility begins to have a type of reality – entail? The problematic nature of recognition is itself already at work within Blanchot's own interpretations of both philosophical and literary texts. What returns within those interpretations is the possibility of attributing a singular force to a particular writer. With such an attribution interpretation and experience become involved. With that emergent relation, questions that pertain to the self can no longer be held apart from ones that pertain to identity. In this complex site the possibility of singularity is given; it is the site in which the interconnection between self and identity is dramatically staged. The demands raised by singularity pertain to thinking as much as to identification: indeed the two are, once what is at stake is the actuality of a turn, inter-articulated. Singularity and the turn are inherently connected; thinking the likelihood of the latter's occurrence will mean however that the former – singularity – will itself have to become rethought and thus repositioned in the process. 'Un tournant' hinges on the real emergence of an-other singularity.[5] The possibility of this move – and here possibility means no more than thinking this move philosophically – will depend upon a reinscription and thus a reworking of repetition. In the same way that philosophy will open itself, thereby showing that it is not one thing – philosophy is not the same as itself – repetition, in becoming subject to the process that its name identifies, will also exempify a plurality that pertains at the origin: i.e. they will show themselves in terms of the anoriginal presence of the plural event.[6]

With Blanchot, Bataille

There are two moments within this text – *L'Affirmation et la passion de la pensée négtive* – that can be taken as guiding that which is central to its work. By staging its concerns they repeat the problematic presence of the turn. One occurs at the end; the other is in the centre of the text. Both announce its strategy and furthermore both indicate the gravity of what is at stake. And yet neither is straightforwardly programmatic. (Indeed both question the possibility of a programme.) The text's final lines rehearse the singularity that Blanchot attributes to the work of Bataille. Utilizing Nietzsche's words spoken of Zarathustra, Blanchot reiterates his initial judgement of *L'Expérience intérieure* that 'This work is entirely apart [*Cette œuvre est tout à fait à part*]' (pp. 313/211). The question that arises, inescapably, within this description is how the 'à part' is to be understood. Before returning to a consideration of this question, what must be noted is the other strategic description which Bataille has identified as 'inner experience'. It is a state of affairs that has been redescribed by Blanchot in terms of what he calls in this text 'l'expérience-limite'. Blanchot's term translates the one used by Bataille. Once again, terminologically, *self-identity* translates some of their concerns: 'The problem brought forth by the limit experience is the following: how can the absolute (in the form of totality) still be gotten beyond [*dépassé*]?' (pp. 307/207).

What links these two passages is whatever it is – the still intangible quality – that is designated by the terms 'à part' and 'dépassé'. Both hinge on the possibility that there can be a type of singularity; the reality of the singular. The question concerns, of course, the precise nature of this singularity. In other words because the singular cannot be simply posited, it has to concern the question of identity and with it the thinking of that identity; the singular has to be thought. For both Blanchot and Bataille this reality – the particularity of thinking involved – can be articulated in relation to the self. The reason for this relation is not difficult to identify. It is there, for Bataille, in the name 'Hegel'. Indeed it is possible to argue that Bataille's undertaking in *L'Expérience intérieure*, as well as in a number of his other writings, involves a specific encounter with Hegel. Part of what drives it is the desire to allow chance, particularity and the singular a form that had not already been announced within Hegel's own system. More accurately it was an encounter that would allow for that working of these terms in which their presence was neither subdued by, nor incorporated into, the systematic work of system.

Equally Blanchot's concern to mark the movement in which the limit no longer delimits what is possible has to be understood as a sustained, even though unstated, encounter with Hegel: Hegel as the philosopher of the absolute. Blanchot's engagement with Hegel is also one that is concerned to hold open the possibility of the singular. However, it is a conception of singularity that is linked to authenticity, pertaining as much to the self as to language. Authenticity will be the attribution to language of a primordial quality that is language's own. The thinking of that quality gives rise to a philosophical task which at the moment that it announces a potential relation to Heidegger, for whom the complex interplay of language and authenticity – a play, as for Blanchot, at its most intense within poetry – dissociates itself by refusing any incorporation into his construal of ontological difference and thus the thinking of Being proper to that project. Bataille was also concerned to link authenticity to poetry. It should not be surprising that poetry marks the divide between Heidegger on the one hand and Blanchot and Bataille on the other.[7]

In Blanchot's engagement with Mallarmé, for example, there is equally an engagement with Hegel. Here the relation concerns Blanchot's take on what could be described as Mallarmé's own self-avowed relation to Hegel. While the relation is explicitly stated by Mallarmé, for Blanchot it is only really there in the use of one vocabulary rather than another. In other words, Mallarmé's Hegelianism is merely intentional. In response to this use of language, Blanchot argues the following (it is a position that splits language by introducing different possibilities of thinking and in so doing robs language of the question of the essence): 'His Hegelian vocabulary would merit no attention, were it not animated by an authentic experience, and this experience is that of the power of the negative.'[8] The central element of this formulation is the reference to authenticity. With authenticity the work of system has become displaced. It is there only in the letter. Authenticity is linked to what in this formulation is described as 'the power of the negative'. Prior to a certain vocabulary there is the productive work of the negative, prior, therefore, to a certain instantiation there is another element at work; what is at work is not itself immediately *workful*. It is an element that touches on authenticity and thereby raises the possibility that singularity and the question of value will always have to be worked through this authentic and productive element. In allowing for its effective presence, what is indicated is the presence of language as that which has a primordial determination. It is thus that with the continuity of language's own instantiation what is held open as a continual possibility is either the affirmation or the sublimation of this primordial status. (Here the problem of action comes to be rewritten in relation to an acting out of the authentic.) While this does not, in itself, give rise to a simple either/or, it comes to be the way of distinguishing philosophically between Hegel (or Heidegger) and Bataille on the one hand, and, perhaps, also in poetry between Rilke and Mallarmé, on the other. Authenticity will be connected to a form of affirmation and affirmation will be connected to a founding claim about the nature of poetic language. And yet what is marked by the formulation – poetic language – must at the same time guard the poetic and open itself out in terms of what is being formulated within. What does poetic language stand for? How is authenticity to be understood here? As will emerge, part of the answer to these questions lies in affirmation. However not in affirmation *tout court* – it is not as though there is an essence of the affirmative – but in the particular thinking of affirmation that is proper to 'inner experience' and thus proper to what Blanchot identifies as 'limit-experience'. As such the status of the authentic is reinforced while at the same time it takes on an inherent complexity. Authenticity will emerge within that site in which experience and the ontological – the ontology of *anoriginal* complexity – are effectively present. Authenticity guards their connection: in a certain sense it also names it.

While writing of the poetry of René Char and in the process of offering a general description of poetic language Blanchot situates the poetic work as that which is in a continual state of struggle with its genesis. One description of that situation involves the allocation of a specific centrality to 'struggle' (*lutte*):

> the work [*l'œuvre*] is, therefore, the intimacy within the struggle of irreconcilable and inseparable moments [*moments irréconciliables et inséparables*], communication torn between the measure [*la mesure*] of the work by which it empowers itself and the excessiveness [*la démesure*] of the work which desires impossibility, between the form in which it seizes itself and the limitless wherein it refuses itself, between the work as commencement and the origin from which there is never work, where eternal unworking [*désœuvrement éternel*] reigns.[9]

While what is being gestured at here is foundational, it is so only to the extent that it will have to be a foundation without foundation; in other words an-other foundation. The founding presence of a productive symmetry is not identified. It is as though the contrary is the case, since what is being allowed is that which could be described as the founding presence of a dissymmetry there *ab initio*.[10] Part of the force lies in its comprising the 'irréconciliable' as well as the 'inséparable' where both have always already been there. Moreover the advent of the work – its having been enacted as a work – neither forces nor denies this founding complex relation. Indeed, as Blanchot suggests in the same text, 'in the movement of its genesis, every poetic work is the return to this initial contestation [*contestation initiale*] and by the same token, in so far as it is work, it does not cease to be the intimacy of its eternal birth'.[11] However, there is more than the simple presence of a 'désœuvrement éternel'. What is significant is that the actual work of poetry is, in its particularity – here the work of Char, though equally the work of Mallarmé – linked to the enacting of this complex relation; its being presented. As has already been intimated, if the detail were to be filled in what would need to be taken up is the reason why, for Blanchot, this state of affairs is not the work of Being as identified by Heidegger – and with it more specifically the revealing and concealing of Being – which is evidenced for him in the work of poetry, and in particular in the poetry of Hölderlin.[12] Rather than attempt here to track the specific detail of this question, what is vital to pursue are the terms in which it would be thought; through which it would, moreover, have to be thought. The apparently forced nature of this construction is an attempt to display the almost material quality of thought. At work here is neither simply the figure of thought nor a relativity introduced by an interpretive equivocation that was semantic in origin. It is rather that with Bataille's work, what is essential is the thinking that is given within it, and therefore which gives it. It is this which must guide any reading of Blanchot's explication of what it is that is at work in Bataille's conception of 'inner experience'.[13]

Blanchot has staged the location of singularity in relation to Hegel. The force of this staging lies in the fact that for Hegel singularity – thought as contingency, the particular, chance, etc. – only has this status on the level of appearance. In fact there is a more primordial belonging to the whole or to the universal.[14] As such, the possibility of the actually singular, the truly contingent, etc., is marked by a logical impossibility. (It is, however, a logic that in being inter-articulated with 'culture'(*Bildung*) has explicit and implicit political consequences.) Blanchot is causing Bataille – as Bataille himself allowed[15] – to intervene at this precise point. What must be pursued, therefore, are two inter-related modes of approach. The first concerns the detail of Blanchot's explication of Bataille; the second is to incorporate that detail in a mode of thinking that will allow the possibility of the singularity proper to that thinking, itself, to be presented. Having noted the nature of what is involved here it is essential to pursue these two paths.

Blanchot's own approach works to bring them together. He can be read as addressing this twofold in so far as what guides his approach is that rather than taking 'inner experience' as having no more than the quality of 'a strange phenomenon', or as being no more than the expression of 'an extraordinary mind', there is the insistence on its maintaining its power to interrogate (pp. 302/203). This repositioning is significant, as it moves the singular away from the domain of the individual, thereby opening up as a question the nature of the singularity involved. The particular individual has become the particular within thought. As an opening it is already implicated in the next stage. Rather than simply questioning, what Blanchot means by the 'power to question/power of questioning [*pouvoir d'interrogation*]' is that which causes a pre-given identity to open itself up as a question; it becomes the question of its identity. What Blanchot calls 'l'expérience-limite' is that complex relation that 'man encounters when he has decided [*il a décidé*] to put himself radically in question' (pp. 302/ 203). While it may need to be taken up in greater detail at a later stage, the importance of this formulation is twofold. In the first place it implicates subject and object in the same activity; secondly, it indicates that what is at work here is a decision – 'il a décidé' – and thus an acting out. Action here is unthinkable outside of its relation to authenticity. Moreover, the questioning, once it begins to take place, will involve the abeyance of conventional and therefore traditional forms of identity thinking. As a result, this will demand an-other thinking of identity. It is thus that this particular concepton of questioning splits the traditional linkage of self and identity – finality has become open-ended – and therefore the presence of this split will already have been incorporated into the more general strategy of thinking the 'à part' and thus of taking up the possibility of an actual turning. The question of acting is becoming one of responding to an enacting. These are already present implications.

The negativity that ensues once the question of *self-identity* comes to be posed radically will always allow itself a type of completion. The power of the negative – be it the negation of nature, animal or machine – can render the subject the same as itself. The self, thus formed, takes on the form of the absolute. And yet, for Blanchot reading Bataille, the action in which the self constructs itself, within this particular determination of 'the power of the negative' (negativity entailing positivity) can never be absolute. Even with the absolute there is a passion; negative thought's passion. What passion marks out here is a continually productive potential. In spite of a possible assertion of absolute identity, despite a claimed consciousness of the 'all', negative thought is still able to hold these claims, and yet, and at the same time,

> is still capable of introducing the question that suspends it, and, faced with the accomplishment of the all [*le tout*], still capable of maintaining the other exigency [*l'autre exigence*] that again raises the issue of the infinite [*l'infini*] in the form of contestation [*contestation*] (pp. 304/205).

The question here concerns what is to be understood by the 'autre exigence'? It may be that the answer – and in this instance the answer would gesture towards that which was involved in thinking the particularity of this complex relation – lies in the presence of a link between the terms 'l'infini' and 'contestation'. Recalled here is the earlier allusion to 'contestation' – identified by Blanchot in writing on Char – that marked the origin and the genesis of the work of poetry.

It is vital in this instance to guard both the presence of the complete and the incomplete. The force of holding to their necessarily separate though conjoint presence – thereby allowing that an already present irreducibility pertains at the same time – is that by trying to work outside of exclusion and inclusion, their co-presence needs an explanation in which the ontology and the temporality proper to the work of a founding irreducibility will have to hold sway. (Again it will be an argument admitting of a necessary, if in this instance subsequent, generality.) Suggesting that even with the 'all' (*le tout*) there is still that which is outside it, is not to claim that the all is incomplete and that it may be completed; it is neither sundered from within nor yet to be realized. It is rather that even with it there is still that which cannot be incorporated; nor will it ever be able to be incorporated. With this 'all', with its enduring quality, what is meant by 'inside' and 'outside' will have to be reworked. What will emerge here is the possibility of thinking a conception of spacing and thus of positioning, that is already differentiating itself from the work of tradition. Once more it may be that the 'à part' is already in play. Even though the 'all' is still able to be thought from where it is, thought still endures as an important question. Blanchot formulates this complex play of limits within which the 'all' is delimited in the following way:

> The limit experience is the experience of what is outside the all [*hors de tout*] when the all [*le tout*] excludes every outside; the experience of what is still to be attained when all is attained [*lorsque tout est atteint*] and of what is still to be known when all is known [*lorsque tout est connu*]: the inaccessible, the unknown itself [*l'inaccessible même, l'inconnu même*] (pp. 304–5/205).

What is involved here is an experience. What this experience will have to demand is a description adequate to it. (Again, this marks out the presence of the two paths.) As experience is central – at least explicitly – what must be recognized is that what is being described pertains to the subject of experience; namely, the self. Blanchot is arguing that this conception of negativity – the negative understood as productive – forms an essential part of human being. The possibility in Blanchot's own terms is the 'right' (*droit*) of being able to indulge in a radical questioning in which both self and the totality of other things is put into question, deriving from 'an essential lack'. For Bataille there is a point at which the negativity exists outside the possibility of an automatically productive relation, which amounts to a conception of negativity in which there is a type of surplus. As such it is a 'negativity without employ'. It is this conception of negativity that is linked to 'inner experience'. This explains why for Blanchot 'the inner experience is the manner in which this radical negation, which has nothing more to negate [*qui n'a plus rien à nier*], is *affirmed* [*s'affirme*]' (pp. 305/205–6). Mirrored in the form of a negation that 'n'a plus rien à nier' is the presence of an outside that is only present when the presence of all outsides has been excluded, or with the presence of that which is still to be known when all is known. The latter is the 'unknown' (*inconnu*) itself. The identity proper to the 'unknown' is the important question here. Its significance lies in the fact that, for both Blanchot and Bataille, the 'unknown' is not the mere negative counter to the known. The reality of each has to be thought outside a relation that pairs them within an all-including – and thus exclusive – binary opposition. Again, the demand is for that which is already at work.

An important move is taking place here. Negation, understood as an act in which a particular complex relation is denied – a negation in which a positivity emerges – has given way to a negativity that does not result in a positivity. And yet this negation – named thus far as 'désœuvrement' – has a productive potential. It is a potential that is harboured within its impossibility; the impossibility of maintaining itself. Returning to Blanchot's treatment of Mallarmé in *L'Espace littéraire*, this productive element is contrasted to varying formulations of the work of the negative. What emerges is an ineliminable presence that 'when there is nothing [*il n'y a rien*], it is this nothing itself which can no longer be negated, which affirms, keeps on affirming, and states nothingness [*dit le néant*] as being, as the unworking of being [*le désœuvrement de l'être*]' (pp. 138/110). Even though this formulation maintains a positive description of 'nothingness' (*néant*), there is no attempt to hypostasize it. The question that emerges is, how does nothingness not come to be incorporated into the language of traditional ontology? It is this question that is directly addressed by Blanchot in *L'Entretien infini*. Here the risk is described as that which would lead to 'substantializing the "nothing" [*substantialiser le 'rien'*]' (pp. 309/208). Faced with this risk, there is a different form of presence. The presence in question is an enacting of the negative in which its productive potential does not – in the strict sense of the term – reside in its own negation. It is thus that Blanchot has linked the presence of negation to affirmation. It is a presence thought within and as affirmation. And yet, at the same time it is a presence that while maintaining its negativity is linked within a contestation – and here it will be necessary, still, to return to the initial complexity of this site, as provided, for example, in the poetry of René Char – to the generative and the productive. What this particular complex relation gives to thought is that which exists 'as though' (*comme*) it were an-other conception of the origin. (The origin, therefore, and with it the possibility of thinking at the origin – an original form of thinking – has been neither destroyed nor denied. It is rather that the origin has been retained in being reworked. This is the ineliminable though implicit work of repetition.) With this other origin, what takes place is an-other form of giving and therefore a different gift, demanding different responses:

> What it gives is the essential gift [*le don essentiel*], the prodigality of affirmation; an affirmation for the first time, that is not a product (the result of a double negation), and that thereby escapes all the movements, oppositions and reversals of dialectic reason, which, having completed itself before this affirmation, can no longer reserve a role for it under its reign (pp. 310/209).

Present with this affirmation is neither inside nor outside. And yet what must endure is the question of the nature of this affirmation. What is the nature of this 'event'; one which Blanchot correctly describes as 'hard to circumscribe' (pp. 310/209)? With the affirmation of pure negativity – a negativity existing in itself at the limit of negation – it is not negativity which is expressed. It is its power which is at work. Bataille's 'inner experience' is this affirmation. It is the purity of an act – a self-affirming of affirmation – that does not let itself either be taken up or taken over by universality. For Bataille, it is the moment at which chance emerges as itself. In being itself it announces its own impossibility. Prior to broaching that impossibility – a state of affairs succinctly captured by Blanchot's expression that 'Such an affirmation cannot be maintained [*une telle affirmation ne saurait se maintenir*]' (pp. 311/209) – it is essential to stay with the detail of the particular presentation of affirmation. At stake in any presentation of this affirmation is singularity itself. It would be thus that Blanchot's description of Bataille's work as 'à part' is a state of affairs that has already been thought within Bataille's own conception of 'inner experience'; a thinking that receives its own translation with 'limit-experience'.

The particularity of 'l'expérience intérieure' – always present as 'l'expérience limite' – is that in striving for its own singularity it becomes for Blanchot 'experience itself [*l'expérience même*]'. What this particular equation – or translation – means is presented in terms of particularity. Again, it is the detail that is significant:

> Thought thinking that which will not let itself be thought! Thought thinking more than it can think, in an affirmation that affirms more than can be affirmed. This more is the experience [*l'expérience*]: affirming only by an excess of imagination and, in this surplus, affirming without anything being affirmed – finally affirming nothing. An affirmation by way of which everything escapes and that, itself escaping, escapes unity (pp. 310–11/209).

What is at work here? The question pertains to a possibility for thinking. And yet it is neither thinking in itself nor the simple reality of experience. What appears in the above is 'l'expérience-limite' when understood as experience itself. The purity of experience cannot be disassociated from thought. It is essential to note the phrasing involved. Experience emerges with thought's own proper excess. What is being worked through here – in both senses of the expression *worked through* – are limits. It is thus that an integral part of what occurs in this passage is the attempt to present both the singular as well as the productive. Both are incorporated in what has already been identified as a reworking of the origin, marked out here by the insistence on an excess, a 'more' (*plus*) which is there, in addition, as well as at the point of departure. Part of the difficulty with a passage that seems to promulgate a giving that has neither a unified source nor a unity of product nor, finally, a unity of arrival, is that the subject of such an experience – given that what is involved here is, minimally, experience – seems to be elusive. This is the precise point that is recognized by Blanchot.

An affirmation which holds to a pure negativity brings with it another risk. In this instance it would involve the utilization of this form of recognition in order to rob human being of the right to the form of questioning that characterizes 'l'expérience intérieure'. And yet for Blanchot the possibility of such a claim already indicates the position of the 'imposture'. Returning here is the problematic of the decision which has now become split. This does not admit of an automatically ethical dimension, since it is not a split between decisions taken in good faith and those taken in bad faith, but in terms of the nature of their proximity to the authentic. While this works to preclude a number of possibilities it leaves open the question of the subject. In the next line Blanchot addresses this question directly:

> the self [le moi] has never been the subject of this experience: 'I' ['je'] will never arrive at it, nor will the individual, this particle of dust that I am, nor even the self of us all [le moi de tous] that is supposed to represent absolute self-consciousness (pp. 311/209).

Before taking up the positive description which emerges here, it is essential to note the critical force of this passage. What is being suggested is that differing conceptions of the self are inadequate to the reality of 'l'expérience-limite', and as such the limit of their capacity to think the self – to think that which has been designated thus far as *self-identity* – is given by the reality of the human situation. Once more *self-identity* comes to be bound up with the insistent presence of authenticity. Again it will be an authenticity that pertains as much to thinking as it does to the corporeality and the materiality of experience. In other words, if an-other subject is to be thought it will have to be thought within that conception of identity that it will also enact. Here the demand is an insistence on thinking the 'à part' by means of a thinking that is itself already 'à part'. In part, what is at work in this complex relation is itself the result of an experience. Reading or interpreting this complex relation falls within the purview of experience. As such it would be an experience that holds itself apart from the everyday repetition that characterizes experience. It is an experience, therefore, precisely to the extent that it is not an experience. It may be that Blanchot has already gestured towards this position in one of his most enigmatic of lines, 'The experience of non-experience' (pp. 311/210). And yet this will be to translate this line, moving it from its given place, allowing it thereby a different repetition. What must be taken up, therefore, if only initially, is that which is translated.

The question then is, to use Blanchot's own formulation, who is the subject of this experience? What is its identity? Who is the subject of the experience of affirmation: of 'inner experience'? The question turns on the subject of those experiences which limit and delimit. The 'self' (*moi*), as has been noted, is not the subject in question. In response to the question of the subject – of who the subject is – Blanchot's own response is 'Only the ignorance that the I-who-dies [*le Je-qui-meurs*] would incarnate by acceding to the space where in dying it never dies in the first person as an "I" [*comme 'Je'*]' (pp. 310/209–10). In dying, the 'I' will never die as the traditional subject. Dying, therefore, becomes a translation of the 'limit-experience'. (The ineliminable presence of the reciprocity that is at work here must be noted.) As such, dying is, therefore, both the same as dying – the physiological state – as well as marking that which cannot be reduced to physical mortality. Dying is both. It names the experience that is not experienced. Again it is essential to pursue Blanchot's own formulation of what pertains to this experience:

> An experience that is not lived [*qui n'est pas un événement vécu*], even less a state of our self; at most a *limit experience* wherein, perhaps, the limits fall, but that reaches us only at the limit: when the entire future has become present [*tout l'avenir devenu présent*] and, through resolution of the decisive Yes [*Oui décisif*], there is affirmed the ascendency over which there is no longer any hold (pp. 311/210).

It is clear that with expressions of the form 'tout l'avenir devenu présent' dying is intimately connected to this complex relation. And yet once the 'Oui décisif' is involved – an affirmation, affirming affirmation itself, already described as that which is posited outside of the hold of dialectic – the opening up of dying begins to take place. Dying allows, in other words, for its own translation. It is the place of this translation that will have to be pursued here.[16] Blanchot has already indicated that affirmation in this sense 'ne saurait se maintenir' (pp. 311/209). Here the impossibility is located as the interplay of two nights. The first allows for an absorption and a form of completion. It is the night of prose. The second is 'l'*autre* nuit' (pp. 311/210).

Human being is already situated in relation to the event of death. Its relation is to that event, which will not be lived as such. It is precisely the nature of this situation that allows for a turning away from death. And yet – and here the play of translation begins to open out – how is the inexorable move towards death able to be endured? Part of this question's force lies in the failure of the night to yield the comfort of seclusion. What fails is the possibility of a night invaded with a clear beauty that will tranquilize and numb the sway of death. It is, however, the very recognition of this position that is found in the 'other' night. Blanchot describes this 'night' as 'false, vain, eternally restless and eternally falling back into its own indifference [*indifférence*]' (pp. 312/210). This is the night confronted by the self in its relation to death. How could this be desired? It is, however, a desire that emerges in the face of death. Consequently it is a desire for the prolongation of negativity without positivity. With the possibility of the continuity of folding back into 'indifférence' – the self's own proper indifference – a relation to death is established that is no longer trapped in the oscillation between self and other. Maintained is a desire for work's absent presence, once work is understood as that which moves from the incomplete to the complete. Desire here is characterized as that which has to sustain itself as desire. Desire is 'indifférence', an identification that continues to be recast:

> a desire for the impossibility of desire, bearing the impossible, hiding it and revealing it, a desire that, in this sense, is the blow of the inaccessible, the surprise of the point that is reached only in so far as it is beyond reach, there where the proximity of the remote offers itself only in its remoteness (pp. 312/210).

The complexity of this desire is to be located neither in its apparent objectlessness – it has an object – nor in its logic – desire is only possible as a desire without end. Its complexity lies in the position of the subject – the self of desire – as dispersed within it. (The question, as always, pertains to how this dispersal is to be thought. Questions of this form will always insist once essentialism no longer dominates thinking.) When, a few lines earlier, Blanchot writes that the subject is 'without horizon', not only should this be read as a counter (successful or not) to Heidegger's 'Sein zum Tode' ('Being towards death'), it should, perhaps more emphatically, be taken as a repositioning of the subject within *this* desire.[17] Before pursuing the final stages of the commentary on this passage, it is essential to reintroduce part of what emerged in Blanchot's confrontation with the poetry of René Char.

At that moment the poetic work was described as a 'struggle' between two moments. The nature of these moments is fundamental. As would be appropriate, they cannot be reconciled and yet at the same time they are 'inseparable'. A founding dissymmetry therefore marks out the work's work. Communication arises because of this dissymmetrical relation. What characterizes the inseparability in question is firstly, the co-presence of that which enacts the work and that which seeks enactment; secondly the simultaneity of what limits the work and the refusal of limitation itself; finally between the work as the self-identical point of departure and that which resists departure or enactment. This last element is not the negation of work but rather, as has already been cited, 'l'origine à partir de quoi il n'y a jamais œuvre'. It is in this space that 'règne le désœuvrement éternel'. Poetry's own work as poetry is the continuity of its return to this conflictual site. The importance of the link between work and 'désœuvrement' is what it allows to be shown as poetry's own work – the work of the work – the inevitability of their co-presence within that work. The insistent question here is the nature of that presence. Co-presence is ineliminable. Firstly, form demands it, and secondly, it arises with the recognition of the power of the negative. The continual holding back from presence is that which allows for presence. Once again the experience of this occurs with the limit, at the limit. Here there is an insistence that always works to open up a conjectured closure. The experience is the experience within excess; the reading of that which refuses any simple incorporation into a tradition and thus of being interpreted while allowing for both incorporation and interpretation; affirming the always 'more';

confronting that which discloses itself most intimately at its point of furthermost inaccessibility. The unmasterability of what emerges here – almost the affirmation of an effective impotence – is productive beyond measure. At an earlier stage in *L'Entretien infini* one of the voices that speaks within the complex dialogues that, in part, form an essential component of the work's work announces this point. The importance of this particular reiteration of the relation between work and 'désœuvrement' is that it comes to circumscribe what is described there as the 'important literary work'. It is work in which the possibility of a turning plays an insistent and productive role:

> I would even say that every important literary work is important to the extent that it puts more directly and more purely to work the meaning of this turn; a turning that, at the moment when it is about to emerge, makes the work pitch strangely. This is a work in which worklessness [*le désœuvrement*], as its always decentred centre, holds sway: the absence of work [*l'absence d'œuvre*] (p. 45).

Having chartered the encounter that thought ('la pensée') may have had at the limit, Blanchot asks how could it be that thought could return from that encounter with 'if not a new knowledge, at least what thought would need in order to hold itself, at the distance of a memory, in its keeping?' (pp. 312/210). The response given to this question is both elusive and dense. It will hinge on allowing the term 'la parole' far greater range than the passage initially allows. The response is staged in the text so that the answer is held back until the last. As a beginning it is announced that the answer to this question is 'inattendue'. He then suggests that no existing thing can attain it in its own name, nor can existence itself contain it, with its harbouring of both universal and particular. Finally it is said, the answer to the question is given – 'la parole l'accueille'. Speech welcomes it. More than that, however, speech holds on to what escapes the hold of existence (the latter being the tradition of ontology): 'it is from this always foreign and always furtive affirmation – the impossible and the incommunicable – that it speaks, finding there its origin, just as it is in this speech [*cette parole*] that thought thinks more than it can think' (pp. 312/210). The question arising here is what is meant by 'la parole'. It is essential to note that Blanchot has spent the first third of *L'Entretien infini* addressing this question. The radical reworking of 'la parole' has necessitated a continual opening up of the term's own possibilities in order that it incorporate the 'exigency of discontinuity'. The need for the incorporation lies not within the limit but with that which always exceeds it. (Almost definitionally what exceeds has to be *encountered* – its insistence is marked by a necessity – for the very reason that it cannot be incorporated.) The site of the exigency – the locus of its effectivity – is between being and nothingness. It is the third genre, 'a nothingness more essential than Nothingness itself'. Traditionally a name for that which would fill this gap and thus stem the exigency would be 'synthesis'. And yet even though synthesis is another possibility for a third term, and despite its attempt to expunge this nothingness by eliminating the space between any two terms, for Blanchot, both these possibilities involve an inescapable futility. It cannot achieve its own because even in achieving it spacing endures. As Blanchot writes: 'synthesis maintains it by accomplishing it, realises it in its very lack, and this makes of this lack a capacity, another possibility' (pp. 8/7). Speech, via its connection to questioning and discontinuity, enacts the work of the negative. Pursuing this will involve linking these concerns to the self and thus to identity. There are two specific moments in the text at which these elements are all interconnected. It will thus be that what will emerge is the force of Blanchot's evocation of 'la parole' and, more significantly, 'la parole' as it is identified by Blanchot at work in Bataille.

The first moment occurs at the end of an attempt to work through the demands of discontinuity. The second forms part of the undertaking to formulate what is called 'l'homme sans horizon'. This particular endeavour is one of a number of Blanchot's encounters with the work of Emmanuel Levinas. In both passages the location of 'la parole' takes place. Here speech comes to be trans-formed. And yet the transformation brings with it the claims of a type of reality, since what is thought to inhere in the possibility of actual speech – its presence within the act of communication – is that which is already there and which is shown in the transformative act.

> When we speak of man as a non-unitary possibility, this does not mean that there would remain in him some brute existence, some obscure nature, irreduc-ible to unity and to the labour of dialectical work. It means that, through man, that is, not through him but through the knowledge he bears, and first of all through *the exigency of speech* [*l'exigence de la parole*] that is in advance always already written, it may be that an entirely different relation announces itself – a relation that challenges the notion of being as continuity or as a unity or gathering of beings; a relation that would except itself from the problematic of being and would pose a question that is not one of being. Thus, in questioning, we would leave dialectics, but also ontology (pp. 11/9–10; my emphasis).
>
> Man without horizon, and not affirming himself on the basis of a horizon – in this sense a being without being, a presence without a present, thus foreign to everything visible and to everything invisible – he is what comes to me as *speech* when to speak is not to see [*vient à moi comme parole, lorsque parler, ce n'est pas voir*]. The Other speaks to me and is only this *exigency of speech* [*exigence de la parole*]. And when the Other speaks to me, speech is the relation of that which remains radically separate, the relation of the third kind affirming a relation without unity, without equality (p. 98; my emphasis).

The detail of these passages opens up the concerns which have been central to this specific enterprise; namely connecting the possibility of thinking the 'à part' to the concepts and categories that mark the limits of experience, writing and interpretation. Here connection takes the form of an inter-articulation. As will emerge, that which is designated by singularity, thought necessarily within the play of limits, gives rise to a conception of the singular that maintains and is maintained by the primordiality of relation. One name that this particular relation can be given is 'experience'.

Initially the first passage does no more than hold open an opportunity. The importance of what it stages, however, is found in its location: the site of this opening. Here it is in the self, as a fundamental part of what it is, that marks out the self as itself. It brings with it that which is amenable to discontinuity. This is not to say that the self is incomplete. It is rather that the demand of discontinuity, the demand that is located neither in the position of the subject nor that of the object, but which inheres in the continuity of its demand and in that continuity comes to position itself as always discontinuous; this demand that can only ever be formulated in terms of the power of the negative – again it is a negativity without positivity – is that to which the subject subjects itself. Thus, were this aspect of the subject's existence to be taken up as a questioning addressing the authentic subject, then the resources of what Blanchot identifies as 'ontology' and 'dialectic' would be inadequate for the task. Moreover, it would be a questioning which, once it began, would, in virtue of that beginning, indicate that 'we' would have left these two dimensions of thought. The claim is, therefore, to think that which is proper to the self – a propriety announced as much in the 'power of the negative' as in the 'exigence de la parole' – is already to think in the abeyance of the hold of philosophy's own traditional counters of thought. Again the importance of this position is that it links possibility of thinking the 'à part' – and therefore of thinking *à part* – to an implicit conception of authenticity. It is thus that such a mode of thinking takes on a necessity and thus acquires its own exigency. Possibility and necessity define the place of action.

In regard to the second of these passages, the limit of unity at work occurs not because of the impossibility of unity but because of the recognition that, even with it, there is still a demand. In the case of the Other holding the Other outside a relation of the Same – a positioning that is necessary if the identity of the Other is to be maintained – this means that not only is the category of the Same no longer pertinent to think the presence and the demand of the other, but that the demand that exceeds unity in providing unity entails that neither the One nor Unity are themselves appropriate to think the position of the self. The self – and here again what needs to be evoked is a conception of the authentic – is most properly itself in the position of a unity that still accedes to another demand and in acceding it becomes; in becoming it is itself.

In this passage there is also a direct allusion to an earlier text in *L'Entretien infini*, one in which Blanchot holds speaking and seeing apart and thus opens up a space in which to rework their particularity and their relation. ('*Parler, ce n'est pas voir*' (pp. 34–45/25–32).) In this instance the importance of this text is that it reinforces the complexity at work in this allusion to 'la parole'. At that moment 'la parole' takes on a number of different qualities. An integral part of the text's concern is to position 'la parole' outside of an opposition between revealing and concealing. (Part of the force of this text lies in the way in which Heraclitus comes to be deployed against Heidegger.) One of the formulations used is a possible equation between 'la parole' and the 'dream'. (It may be possible to argue here that 'dream' translates part of that which is at work within 'speech'.) The significance of the connection is that it allows for a formulation of that which, while present, is present in such a way that neither revealing nor concealing would lend themselves to a description of the way in which this form of presence would work. The further significance occurring with the dream is located in the manner in which seeing is both raised and differed. This occurs in the way in which seeing is differentiated from the seeing that takes place with the dream. (Once again what is occurring here is the affirmation of the inherent plurality within terms. Seeing is not just seeing, even though it is also seeing. The same point has already been noted with dying.)

> To see in a dream is to be fascinated, and fascination arises when, far from apprehending from a distance, we are apprehended by this distance, invested by it and invested with it. In the case of sight, not only do we touch the thing, thanks to an interval that disencumbers us of it, but we touch it without being encumbered by this interval. In the case of fascination we are perhaps already outside the realm of the visible–invisible (pp. 41–2/30).[18]

The dream opens up through the link to fascination, a presencing that demands a thinking in which what is present allows itself neither the full nor the empty word, but a being held in which distance comes close, but only by continually distancing itself; in being neither close nor distant. In being neither invisible nor visible, the co-presence of the neither/nor, far from being the presence of paradox, betrays the presence of what has already been identified as the 'third genre'. The further consequence is that what is significant here – significant in the precise sense that it allows for an increasing generality – is that which could be provisionally designated as the logic of the neither/nor. Identifying the work of a logic such as this within Blanchot's writings is, perhaps, a commonplace. Its importance in this instance is what it indicates in terms of founding a description adequate to what it marks out.

A similar complex relation is announced in the passage in which 'l'homme sans horizon' is positioned in relation to 'la parole'. The self in that position was described as 'étranger à tout visible et à tout invisible'. The Other comes to the 'self' (*moi*) as 'la parole' to the extent that it holds to a position and is thus positioned by the logic of the neither/nor. The address of the other is neither a pure relation nor completely separate; it is what has already been identified as 'le rapport radicalement séparé'. The importance of Levinas here does not reside in Blanchot's attempt to utilize Levinas – indeed, as a corollary, a reading of Blanchot that was fuelled by assimilating him to Levinas's own project would be equally mistaken – but rather to identify in Levinas's work that moment at

which a thinking that no longer let itself be assimilated to either the tradition
of 'ontology' or 'dialectic' held sway. It is with the thinking appropriate to
Levinas's conception of the Other and the demand that the other has on 'me'
that Blanchot can identify the work of the exigency that he has discovered
elsewhere. What is at play, therefore, is a commonality of project. It is the
possibility of attributing this commonality – an attribution, as with that which
it identifies, that must operate beyond the hold of essentialism, even beyond an
attempted reclaiming of essentialism – that allows Blanchot's work and the work
of others a critical element. Indeed, it can be argued that with the identification
of critique – critique being a complex relation to a tradition of thinking, poeti-
cizing etc. – it is possible to rethink the question of value. Value is perhaps
already implicit in Blanchot's use of the term 'important', as well as in the
already noted allusions by Blanchot and Bataille to authenticity.

When, in the text under consideration – *L'Affirmation et la passion de la
pensée négative* – Blanchot evokes 'la parole' which he distinguishes from mere
speech, it is not

> just any speech. It does not contribute to discourse, it does not add anything
> to what has already been formulated; it would wish only to lead what, outside
> community, would come to 'communicate' itself if, finally, when 'everything'
> [*tout*] was consummated, there was nothing more to say: saying at this point
> the ultimate exigency [*disant alors l'exigence ultime*]' (pp. 312/210–11).

Again what is being offered here is that which endures and thus which insists
at the moment of finality, and thus with the enacted moment of the all ('le tout').
It is at that point that the exigency and thus the demand is at its most insistent.
At the next stage, almost the moment at which work begins, dying has to have
been forgotten; the conception of 'la parole' has to be dismissed almost in order
that its own demands will have taken place. The continuity of a demand must
become discontinuous with the response to that demand. Desire, perhaps the
correct name for a demand without end, must play out in relation to the incomplete. Beginning to complete is most profoundly to begin to forget that desire
is an insistent point of departure. Writing takes place within this form of
forgetting, and yet with it writing – be it in the form of poetry or what Blanchot
has already identified as 'important literature' – returns and continues to return,
and thus in returning continues to work through its own contested beginning.
Speech understood in the sense outlined above becomes another expression of
a founding exigency and, as such, becomes another translation of/for those terms
which have already been identified as enacting this complex relation. Bataille's
work, at least the Bataille about whom Blanchot is writing, marks and affirms
this founding complexity. Finally, the centrality of experience lies in its purity.
When Blanchot claims in regard to exigency that 'Experience is this exigency
[*L'expérience est cette exigence*]' (pp. 313/211), what is being advanced is a
relation that, once given, comes to be effaced in the project that seeks to establish

that to which it gives rise. This movement has to be thought outside the hold of either melancholia or nostalgia.

Self-identity

Blanchot begins writing about Bataille in *L'Entretien infini* by raising the problem of commentary. Part of the problem touches on fidelity, another on what happens to words and phrases once they are cited. What is the nature of the change that will be involved in the process – perhaps more emphatically in the reality – of citation? The fear expressed by Blanchot is that words may change their 'meaning' (*sens*) or become immobilized. There is a straightforward sense in which this risk must endure in the process of commentary, and while it may not be able to be overcome absolutely, its nullifying effect can be obviated, in part, once thinking – or rather the demand for a particular form of thinking – is allowed to dominate. What emerges with the encounter between Blanchot and Bataille is a challenge which works at the limit of the possible. Within the context of what specifically is taking place it works within and as a result of the process of interpretation. The exigency at play here is the text's difficult insistence that it be experienced and thus that it be understood. It may be that Blanchot's own text *L'Affirmation et la passion de la pensée négative* positions itself in relation to an interpretive tradition such that its being read gives rise to the same complex relation – the demand of a limit experience – that it is seeking to enact. While this may give rise to a form of singularity, it marks out the primordiality of relation. Relation insists, as has already been indicated, because what is involved is an experience. This means here that experience no longer repeats experience's own conventions. There is a different constraint involved. (Freedom lies in the possibility of moving to an-other constraint.) Affirmation, therefore, can be linked to the possibility of the singular that arises while maintaining the ineliminable presence of relation. Moreover, it is the co-presence of the two – singularity and relation – that establishes the work's critical dimension. The singularity of Blanchot's own undertaking must be maintained at the same time as its concerns must allow for that which they have already staged; namely their own translation. It is in this context that it is possible to return, once more, to the reiteration of self-identity; the reiteration is the continuity of its own translation.

The premise that has guided this commentary is that the reciprocity that marked *self-identity* is such that reworking the self – developing or allowing a different conception of self to emerge – necessitated, whether it was recognized or not, another thinking of identity. Identity, therefore, is always at work. With Blanchot's reading of Bataille the demand to which it gives rise is to be situated within the recognition of this reciprocity. At a number of important points in Blanchot's treatment of the self, it was conceded that the resources of both 'ontology' and 'dialectic' were unable to think a non-unitary conception of the subject. Such a conception of the subject cannot just be posited as though it existed in itself. Responding to the demand of its presence will necessitate the possibility of this other thinking. And yet, that on its own is not sufficient. What has to be clarified is the nature of the alterity involved. If the demand is for another thinking – and even if that demand were explicable in terms of an exigency that is itself to be explained in terms of its connection to authenticity – this still does not account for the nature of the alterity at work. Here the possibility of otherness has emerged because of the presence of limits. Limits provide the possibility of understanding expressions such as 'à part' and 'dépassé'. In both instances, the limit is given by a specific relationship which obtains between that which is given in order that thinking take place (and this point will be true by extension for the tradition of interpretation and writing) and that which occurs because of the varying forms of exigency that have been located thus far. The relationship exists between the tradition of ontology and dialectic – this needs to be understood as the tradition of philosophy – and what has already been identified as the 'power of the negative'. (The specificity of the last and the consequences of its specificity will always have to be maintained.) In sum, this relationship is a falling apart; a relation of non-relation. The dispersal of the subject – an affirmation of the anoriginal presence of the non-unitary – cannot be thought within the tradition. While this marks the limit of philosophy, it only marks it to the extent that it is a limit to be overcome. It does not call for the end of philosophy, but for that very possibility in which philosophy is able to take up identity in the abeyance of the work of tradition. It is this that will allow thinking another possibility. Furthermore, the reason why this other repetition is neither idealist nor purely speculative is twofold. In the first place, it arises out of – and thus with – the experience of the limit. Secondly, it is linked to claims about the self and language that are determined on the one hand by authenticity and on the other by the possibility of language having a primordial quality, where that quality is to be thought outside of the hold of essentialism.

Finally, therefore, self-identity will make a demand upon identity thinking, once the non-unitary nature of the self has to be affirmed. It will be with this affirmation that the tradition of philosophy will have to give itself over to the possibility of another repetition. The force of this conclusion will reside in the recognition that such a repetition – its actual possibility – is that which has already been given by 'l'expérience-limite'.

Notes

1 This chapter is taken from a seminar given in the Department of Philosophy at the University of Warwick on Blanchot and Bataille. The topic of the seminar concerned the possibility of singularity in thinking. It orientated around a specific claim – a claim discussed in this chapter – made by Blanchot about Bataille. In writing of

L'expérience intérieure and quoting Nietzsche Blanchot asserts that 'This work is entirely apart [*Cette œuvre est tout à fait à part*]'. The question is how to think this 'à part' philosophically. Here the problem concerns the relationship between the self and identity. Both are at work in what can be provisionally designated as self-identity. While it has been in part redrafted this chapter has maintained the slower speed proper to pedagogy.

2 In *Blindness and Insight* (London: Methuen, 1983) Paul de Man notes that 'the disappearance of the self becomes the main theme of Blanchot's criticism' (p. 105). The importance of the claim about Blanchot is not diminished by the undertaking of this chapter. It is rather that de Man's claim needs to be interpreted as arguing that what characterizes Blanchot's criticism – and this will be true also of his *récits* – is the disappearance, or rather the abeyance, of the notion of self (or subject) as that which is self-identical and thus as always present to self. What this recognition gives rise to is the possibility – perhaps also the need – to develop that mode of philosophical thinking which is in itself appropriate to a reworking of the self.

3 In *L'Entretien infini*, Paris: Gallimard, 1969, pp. 300–13, translated by Susan Hanson as *The Infinite Conversation*, Minnesota: Minnesota University Press, 1993, pp. 202–11. All future references to this text and to the book in general will be given to these editions with the French text followed by the English. Translations have occasionally been modified.

4 Even though it does not concern itself with either repetition or the self, Daniel Wilhelm's interpretation of Blanchot also takes Blanchot's concerns with limits – the texts tracing their own limits – as one of its guiding motifs. See his *Maurice Blanchot: la voix narrative*, Paris: Union Générale d'Editions, 1974, p. 50.

5 While Hegel is central to these procedures it remains the case that behind Blanchot's preoccupation with 'le tournant' is equally a concern with Heidegger. (The French translation of Heidegger's 1962 work *Die Kehre* was, after all, *Le Tournant*.) It may be that the absolute incorporates both the Hegelian and Heideggerian project in the direct sense that both necessitate inclusivity. The problem of the absolute – thought as an inclusivity which gives particularity both its form and its possibility – is co-present in both and thus responding; a response conditioned by the possibility of an overcoming is a movement conditioned as much by one as by the other.

6 I have formulated the anoriginal construal of the event more fully in *The Plural Event: Descartes, Hegel, Heidegger*, London: Routledge, 1993, especially pp. 1–22.

7 While the detail cannot be pursued here, both Blanchot and Bataille work with a conception of authentic poetry. Furthermore, it is also worth noting that in an interview Derrida used literature, and in particular poetry, to plot the nature of the difference between his work and Heidegger's. Blanchot's name – its being the name of/for a certain type of literature – is deployed in setting up this position:

> while I owe a considerable debt to Heidegger's 'path of thought' we differ in our employment of language, in our understanding of language. I write in another language – and I don't simply mean in French rather than in German – even though this 'otherness' cannot be explained in terms of philosophy itself. The difference resides outside of philosophy, in the non-philosophical site of language; it is what makes the poets and writers that interest me (Mallarmé, Blanchot etc.) totally different from those that interest Heidegger (Hölderlin and Rilke). In this sense my profound rapport with Heidegger is also and at the same time a non-rapport ('Deconstruction and the Other', in *Dialogues with Contemporary Continental Thinkers*, Richard Kearney (ed.), Manchester: Manchester University Press, 1984, p. 110).

8 M. Blanchot, *L'Espace littéraire*, Paris: Gallimard, p. 137; translated by Ann Smock as *The Space of Literature*, Lincoln, Neb.: University of Nebraska Press, p. 109. Further references given in the text. Translations have again been modified. For a detailed discussion of Blanchot's complex relationship to Mallarmé see Leslie Hill, 'Blanchot and Mallarmé', in *Modern Language Notes*, 105, 1990, pp. 889–913. Hill's discussion of the role of 'désœuvrement' in Blanchot's work and the philosophical problems of taking up and describing that work needs to be studied in great detail. See in particular pp. 902–3 and 904–5.

9 M. Blanchot, *La Bête de Lascaux*, Montpellier: Fata Morgana, 1982, p. 35 (my translation).

10 The importance of a founding dissymmetry is treated by Blanchot in great detail in the opening of *L'Entretien infini* (see especially pp. 5–11/3–10).

11 *La Bête de Lascaux*, p. 36 (my translation).

12 It is interesting in this regard that one of Blanchot's most sustained encounters with Heidegger occurs in *L'Entretien infini*, in another text on René Char. See especially pp. 441/299–300. Perhaps it is not surprising in this regard that the French poet to whom Heidegger thought himself closest was Char. It would be of interest in this regard to pursue the detail of Char's own 1966 text 'Réponses interrogatives à une question de Martin Heidegger', in *Artine et autres poèmes*, Lausanne: Cercle du Livre Précieux, 1967.

13 Almost as an act of interpretive respect it will be essential to follow the detail of Blanchot's many critical encounters with attempts to think absolute inclusivity. The refusal, staged throughout his writings, of this type of thinking draws him ever closer to Bataille. See especially the important footnote in *L'Entretien infini*: pp. 32–4/439, n. 3.

14 I have analysed the way in which this relation and thus the impossibility of particularity – chance – works in Hegel in *The Plural Event*, pp. 83–112.

15 At this point it would be essential to pursue this possibility in Bataille's pivotal text. 'Hegel, la mort et le sacrifice' in *Œuvres Complètes*, T. XII, Paris: Gallimard, 1988, pp. 326–45; translated by Jonathan Strauss as 'Hegel, death, and sacrifice', in *Yale French Studies*, 78, 1990, pp. 9–28.

16 For a sustained and philosophically important discussion of the role of death in Blanchot, see Simon Critchley, '*Il y a* – a dying stronger than death (Blanchot with Levinas)', in *The Oxford Literary Review*, 15 (1–2), 1993.

17 For a good overview of this aspect of Heidegger's thought that takes authenticity into consideration, see Lawrence Vogel, *The Fragile 'We': Ethical Implications of Heidegger's 'Being and Time'*, Evanston, Ill.: Northwestern University Press, 1994, p. 28–48.

18 It would be worth pursuing in this regard the important discussion of fascination in *L'Espace littéraire*; see pp. 25–31/30–4.

Composite: 1 to 9

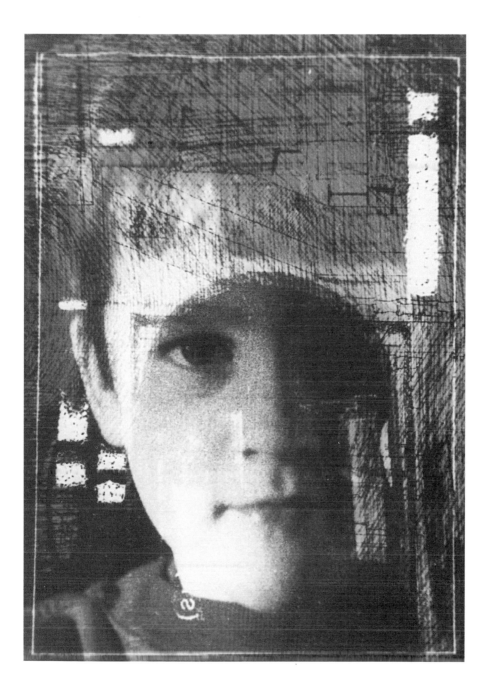

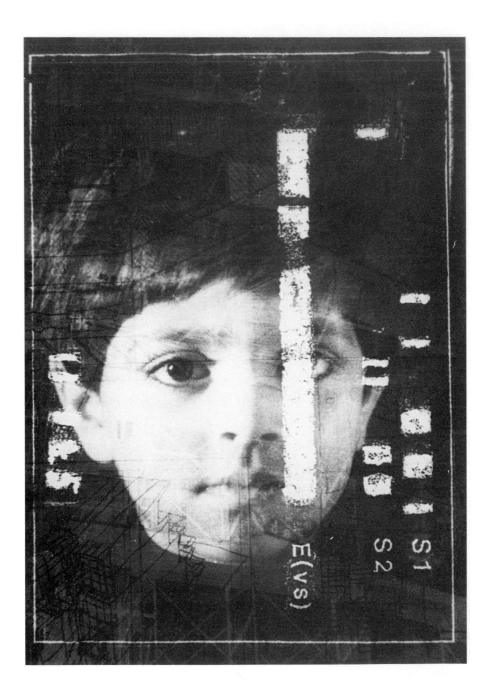

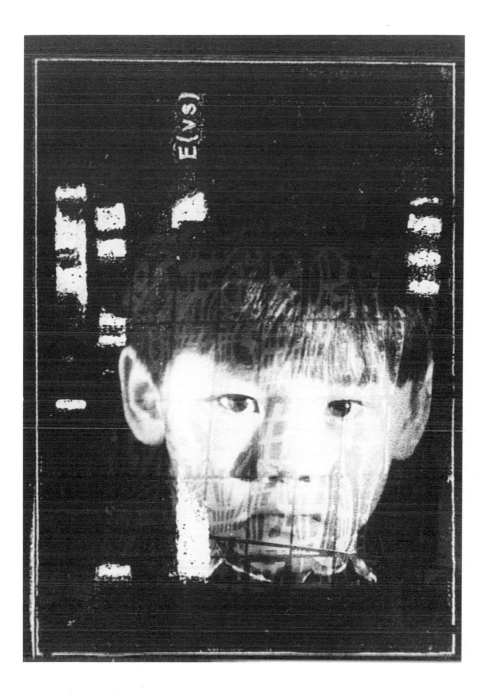

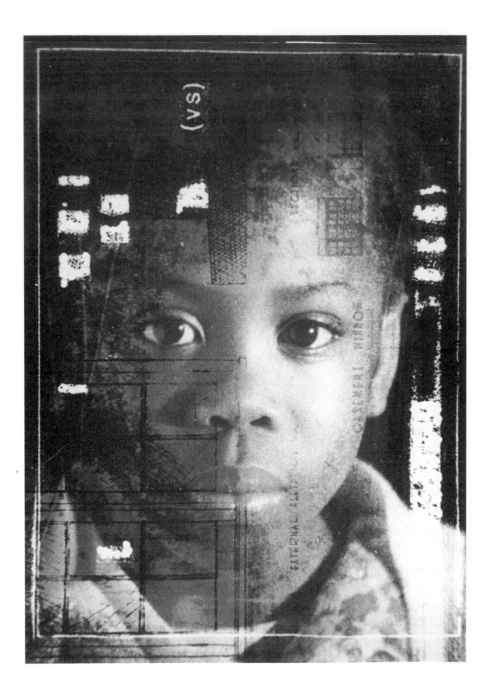

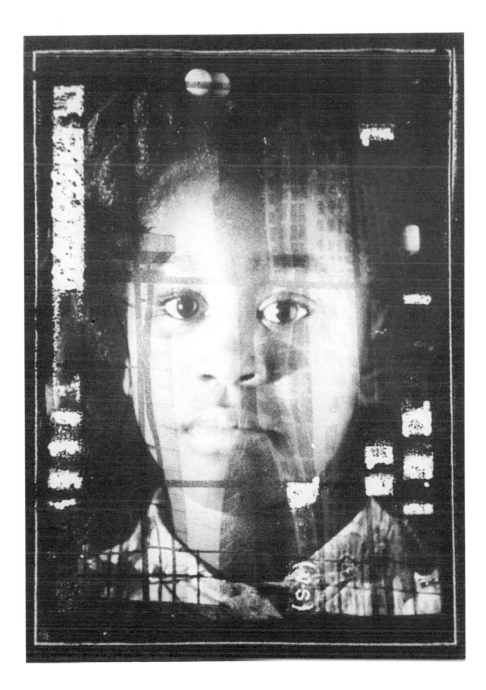

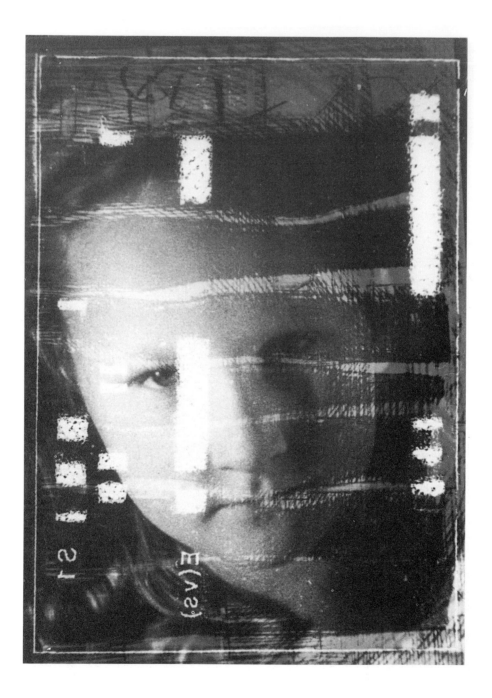

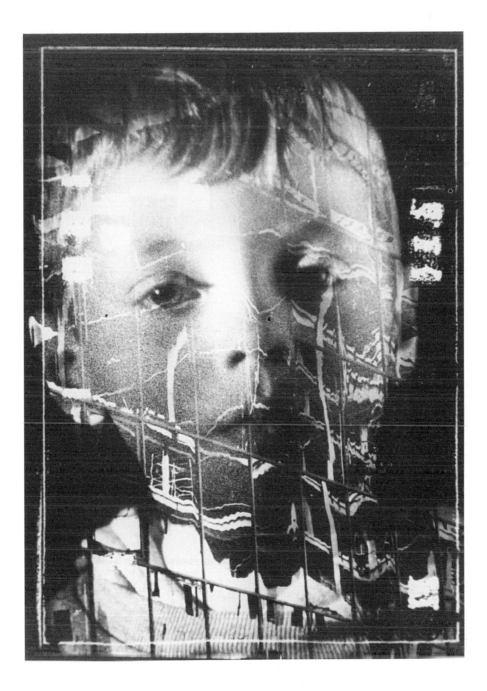

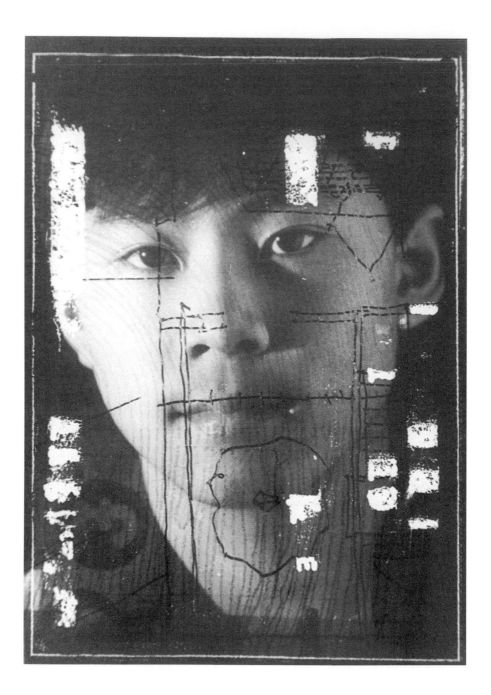

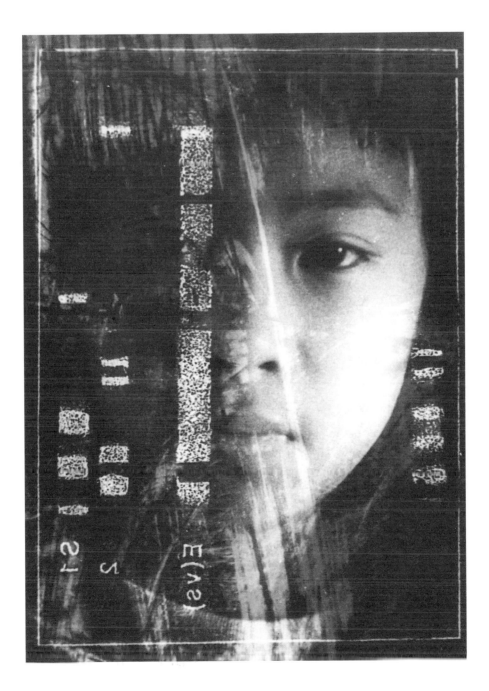

Fernando Pessoa: missing person

To create, I've destroyed myself; I've so externalized myself on the inside that I don't exist on the inside except externally. I'm the living stage where various actors act out various plays (Bernardo Soares).[1]

Prefaces and indexes to a Portuguese avant-garde

1912. A 24-year old, unknown Fernando Pessoa publishes some articles which cause a stir.[2] He surveys the uncertain terrain of Portuguese letters and concludes, much to his readers' surprise, that the time is ripe for the messianic entry of a 'supra-Camões'. No one at the time could have guessed what the upstart young poet intended by a supra-Camões. Did he propose himself as rival to Luis Camões, author of the monumental national epic, *The Lusiads* (1572)? He had in mind not a single individual poet of genius but a *set* of them, soon to burst on the scene.

Preface: *Ultimatum*

1917. In the one and only issue of *Portugal Futurista*, seized by the police, the mad, monocled naval engineer trained in Glasgow, Alvaro de Campos, proclaims a new science of art in his *Ultimatum* manifesto. With megaphonic Nietzschean bravura, and typically Futurist bombast, Campos sweeps away the *passéistes* who encumber the European scene. A few examples ...

> Out! Out!
> Out, you, George Bernard Shaw, vegetarian of the paradox, charlatan
>   of sincerity, frigid tumour of Ibsenism ...
> Out, you, H. G. Wells, gesso conceptualist, pasteboard corkscrew for the
>   bottleneck of Complexity! ...
> Out, you, Yeats of Celtic fog skulking round a signpost without
>   directions, sack of putrescences, beachcombing the shipwreck of
>   English Symbolism! ...[3]

Campos then proceeds to amputational acts of 'sociological surgery'. In philosophy, the abolition of the concept of absolute truth. In art, the total abolition of the concept that an individual has the right or duty to express what he feels. Only the individual who feels for *various others* has such a right of expression.

The scientific aim envisaged is an original modern aesthetic, 'The Malthusian Law of Sensibility'. Campos defines this as a 'survival of the fittest', a drastic population-control economy by which the sensibility of an epoch, normally represented by some thirty or more poets, must find future expression in (say) two or so poets, each endowed with fifteen or twenty personalities. The *Ultimatum* forecasts a protocol agreed between a minimum elite of avant-gardists.

Campos's manifesto-preface does not name these supra-individual poets. Are they the supra-Camões Fernando Pessoa prophesied? *Portugal Futurista* does include two sets of poems by Pessoa, one of these, 'Fictions of the Interlude', of a post-Symbolist, mock-Dada nature.[4]

A clue as to the identity of these supra-individuals is found in an undated prefatory memoir by Campos on his 'master', Alberto Caeiro:

> My master Caeiro was not a pagan; he was paganism. Ricardo Reis is a pagan, Antonio Mora is a pagan, I'm a pagan, and even Fernando Pessoa would be a pagan if he weren't a cat's cradle of snarled up yarn inside ...[5]

Sarcasm in this vein will persist in Campos's future dealings with Pessoa, although he admires Pessoa's poetry.

Years later, in an unpublished preface to Pessoa's collected poetry, Campos renders accurate but ironic account of his colleague's style of writing:

> To determine a state of soul, though it be inexistent, in verses that translate it impersonally; to describe emotions unfelt with the emotion itself with which they were felt – this is the privilege of those who are poets, for, if they weren't no one would believe them. I am too much the friend of Fernando Pessoa to say well of him without myself feeling unwell: truth is one of the worst hypocrisies to which friendship obliges one.[6]

Campos sums up: 'For the rest, the only preface needed to a work is the brain of whoever reads it.' He echoes the motto to an arcane work of suicidal depersonalization, Mallarmé's *Igitur*: 'this Story addresses itself to the reader's Intelligence which itself puts things on stage.'

Fictions of the Interlude: index and preface

Circa 1915–16. Pessoa contemplates a publisher's index of texts under the title, *Fictions of the Interlude*.[7]

General preface

1 Alberto Caeiro (1889–1915) – *The Keeper of Sheep* and other poems and fragments.
2 Ricardo Reis: *Odes*.
3 Antonio Mora: *Alberto Caeiro and the Revival of Paganism*.
4 Alvaro de Campos: *Arch of Triumph*, poems.
5 Vicente Guedes: *The Book of Disquietude*.

This impresario's list, one of countless in Pessoa's literary remains, goes in company with a trial preface addressed to us in the classical second-person plural, not commonly in use today.

> The attitude you should adopt towards these published texts is that of someone not given this explanation, who would have read them, having purchased them, one by one, off the counter of a bookshop. None other ought to be the state of mind of the reader. When reading *Hamlet*, you do not first begin by settling once for all in your mind that such a story never took place. You would thereby poison your own pleasure, which you go in search of in this text. Who reads ceases to live. So do now as you would have done. Cease living, and read. What is life?
>
> But here, more intensely than would be the case with the dramatic offering of some poet, you must reckon with the distinct reality of the supposed author. The right to believe in my explanation cannot come to your aid. You must assume, upon reading it, that I lied; that you are about to read the works of diverse poets or writers, that you shall garner from them emotions and instructions, in which I, save as publisher, neither figure nor partake. Who can say that such an attitude might not be, in the final account, the most correctly proper to the unknown reality of things?
>
> In my own personal work, there are elements that might seem to reveal similarities to what is in these works. Do not be surprised. These are legitimate literary influences – mine on theirs, or theirs on mine. There is neither similarity nor coexistence between the personalities.
>
> Each of these personalities – take heed – is perfectly at one with itself, and, where there is a work chronologically arranged, as with Caeiro and Alvaro de Campos, the moral and intellectual person of the author is perfectly delineated.
>
> . . .
>
> Do I feign? I do not feign. If I desired to feign, why should I preface it? These things occurred, I guarantee it; but occurred where, I do not know, yet so it did, inasmuch as anything takes place in this world, in real houses, whose windows open on landscapes really visible. Never was I actually there – but then, am I the one writing?
>
> . . .
>
> Do not tell me I am the medium of spirits alien to this Earth. With the Earth I deal, and with its blue circuit. The horizon has included so much as I include; the rest is bad dreams, to each his own.

What is one to make of the 'publisher's confession'? You might in a flash of *déjà vu* have imagined yourself a Danish reader of the 1840s, directed to a Copenhagen bookshop on the gnomic instruction of a certain S. Kierkegaard, the polemicist whose attacks on Hegelianized Christendom were published under multiple and bizarre pseudonyms, Victor Eremita, Johannes de Silentio, Anti-Climacus, and so on. Everyone knew that Kierkegaard was the author of these outrages against commonsense, and we too, with the same flat-footed, literal assurance, could recognize that the books on Pessoa's index are all 'his own' or those of his so-called *heteronyms*. Our perception of the truth would have lost, not gained a hold on truth.

I have postponed till now and, as it were, distanced from the reader the well-known enough revelation that Pessoa 'wrote' his heteronyms, Alvaro de Campos, Alberto Caeiro, Ricardo Reis, and indeed many others. I have done so for maximum high relief to emphasize that Fernando Pessoa is himself no other than another heteronym. In this century of prodigious fictions, Fernando Pessoa (1888–1935) can be said to have written the most singular one. I would even hazard to say that he bequeathed the most unusual novel of modern times, but this I cannot say, on two counts. First, it is illegitimate to say Pessoa *himself* wrote all his *œuvre*; and second, we are faced with an *unfinished œuvre*, an extensive conglomerate of fragments of every genre, that may always disguise from us the true nature and coherence of the 'master-narrative' it envisions.

One might rightly say of Pessoa's work as Duchamp in 1923 said of his *Large Glass*, that it was 'finally unfinished'. I recall too that Duchamp in his *Green Box* notes expunged the word 'painting' or 'picture' and replaced it with *delay*, implying a meditation on movement and a philosophizing on 'movements' in art.[8] So too, the parallel drawn with Kierkegaard is interesting and telling, but runs short of the extreme *de*-personalisation that Pessoa's heteronyms effected, an adventure in extra- and inter-subjective plurality unprecedented in literature. The writers named in Pessoa's index are not merely pseudonyms but genuine others, with distinct independent creative lives of their own, with idiosyncratic styles, and what is more, with different dates of birth and even deaths sometimes forecast by horoscopes. For this, Pessoa coined the term heteronym; and I propose *extraneity* as a more appropriate qualitative term than depersonalisation.

Imagine a mirror smashed into many pieces, each of which reflects not Pessoa's own but some aspect of another disjunctive personality. Only one of these *is* Pessoa. Seventy-two such heteronymic possibilities are said recoverable, according to the latest count by scholars burrowing into Pessoa's *espolio*, his legendary trunk of *inédits* found after his death, an archive of 27,543 unpublished bits of paper, placed, or more often than not, misplaced by previous investigators, in 343 envelopes.[9] The heteronyms apparently propagated in myrmidon-fashion, like the self-replicating fractals of Chaos theory. Perhaps only the cyber-resources of computerization will ever put this Humpty Dumpty together again.

Last preface: death

'I don't evolve', Pessoa confessed to a friend at the end of his life, 'I VOYAGE'.[10]

Explaining himself always risked proliferating more self-contradictions, and hence more authorships in already over-populated indexes of authors. Therefore, in respect of Pessoa himself as heteronym, untruavity is a sort of geometry which describes him at all points equidistant from the genesis of his 'others'. His prefaces are each and all origins that trace back to infancy a mediumistic habit of *autoscopy* which augments fictive beings of photographic faithfulness to life. The result is that Fernando Pessoa, unlike any other writer, does not obey a normal consecutive order of composition. At any one time in his life, were he asked, 'What are you writing now?', he would have to answer truthfully, '*All* of it'. An eerie simultaneity occurs between his own signed (orthonymic) works and those of his heteronymic coterie:

> The human author of these books does not recognize any personality of his own within himself. When on occasion he perceives a personality emerging from inside himself, no sooner does it appear than he promptly sees it is a being different from anyone he is; a mental offspring, perhaps, and with hereditary features, but with the differences of one who is Other.
>
> That such an attribute in a writer could be said a form of hysteria, or a so-called dissociation of personality, the author of these books does not contest, nor does he support it. Little good would it do him, slave as he is to the multiplicity of his being, to concur with this or that theory on the written remains of that multitude.[11]

On the eve of his death – when else? – Pessoa attempted to cast a final retrospective preface, in a sense akin to a horoscope, which would specify the precise moment of appearance of at least three heteronyms. So important was this singular Eureka point of origin that we find many variant drafts of it in Pessoa's *espolio*, until he settled on the letter sent to his friend Adolfo Casais Monteiro, dated 13 January 1935:

> ... it was the 8th of March, 1914 – I went over to a high desk and, taking a sheet of paper, began to write, standing, as I always write when I can. And I wrote thirty-odd poems straight off, in a kind of ecstasy whose nature I cannot define. It was the triumphal day of my life, and I shall never be able to have another like it. I started with a title – 'The Keeper of Sheep'. And what followed was the apparition of somebody in me, to whom I at once gave the name Alberto Caeiro. Forgive me the absurdity of the phrase: my master had appeared to me. This was the immediate sensation I had ...
>
> I jerked the latent Ricardo Reis out of his false paganism, discovered his name, and adjusted him to himself, because at this stage I already *saw* him. And suddenly, in a derivation opposed to that of Ricardo Reis, there arose in me impetuously a new individual. At one go, and on the typewriter, without interruption or correction, there arose the 'Triumphal Ode' of Alvaro de Campos – the Ode along with his name and the man along with the name he was ...
>
> I fitted it all into moulds or reality. I graded their influences, recognized their friendships, heard, inside me, their discussions and divergencies of criteria, and in all this it seemed to me that I, the creator of it all, was the least things there. It is as if it all happened independently of me. And it is as if it still happens like that ...[12]

Is this truth or fiction? Neither, since Alberto Caeiro already claims an origin in another earlier text, and one that places him *before time*:

> Night and Chaos are part of me. I date back to the silence of the stars. I am the effect of a cause of the Universe's time ... In my everyday presence, epochs prior to Life take part, times more ancient than the Earth, the hollows of Space before the world was ... There is not a single atom of the most distant star that does not collaborate in my being ...[13]

This is anamnesis of a god-like anthropic sort, a species of metempsychotic recollection in which a beginning recedes to abysmal infinity. 'In the Beginning, Genesis I, I', the Zohar says, is 'the mystery of *eyn sof*, the Infinite ... Beyond this point nothing can be known. Therefore it is called *reshit*, beginning – the first word by means of which the universe has been created.'[14]

Jakob Boehme, the seventeenth-century mystic shoemaker, would have recognized Caeiro's words as the Unground of Freedom:

> Seeing then the first will is an ungroundedness, to be regarded as an eternal nothing, we recognize it to be like a mirror, wherein one sees one's own image; like a life, and yet it is no life, but a figure of life and the image belonging to life ... Thus we recognize the eternal Unground out of nature to be like a mirror. For it is like an eye which sees, and yet conducts nothing in the seeing ...[15]

Pessoa's extraneity can only allow him to locate himself by reference to what is *originally* distanced, a situation which does nevertheless permit him to calibrate differences. At an extreme, he is transposed into Maria José, a tubercular hunchback pining away at her window in hopeless love for the neighbouring locksmith. Or we discover Alvaro de Campos, in a moment of Whitmanesque intoxication, celebrating her who is most distant from *him*, the axe-wielding Temperance feminist, Carrie Nation.[16]

Examples abound, but the originl distanced point of reference is the 'master', Alberto Caeiro, the keeper of sheep who begins his first poem by telling us, 'I never kept sheep.' The 'sheep' are his poems, transparent as the Zen act of unpremeditated seeing. He is the 'only poet of Nature', and yet nature appears only in Franciscan penury, stripped to the essentials as in Heidegger, a matter simply of nouns bereft of adjectives – trees, a hill, water, flowers, the sun –

> I look and I am moved,
> Moved as water flows when the ground slopes,
> And my poetry is natural, like the rising of the wind ...[17]

Caeiro is *seeing*, in Boehme's words, 'like an eye wherein Nature is hidden'.

From an Unground of Freedom, the others emerge and are centrifugally parted from Pessoa: Reis, the monarchist, is exiled in Brazil, Antonio Mora, the neo-pagan philosopher, is incarcerated in a Cascais madhouse; and Caeiro himself dies young in 1915 – all, except one, Alvaro de Campos, who returns from engineering work in Barrow-in-Furness to retirement in Lisbon. 'Only Alvaro de Campos ever knew me personally', Pessoa said.

Is there a centripetal force that could bring all these creatures back to their origin – and include Pessoa himself who is equally estranged from it?

In search of a grand narrative

Pessoa almost single-handedly invented modernism in retrograde Portugal – a soloist modernism that he populated with an imaginary Portuguese 'race of modernist poets' – Pessoa, dreamer of others' lives who smoked too much and drank too much, and whose hopes and liver finally gave out.

> Sometimes, when I'm actively engaged in life and am as sure about myself as other people are, my mind is beset by a strange sensation of doubt: I don't know if I exist, it seems I might be in someone else's dream, I have almost the carnal impression that I could be the character in a novel, moving within the reality constructed by a *grand narrative*, in the long waves of its style.[18]

Who is this speaking? Not Pessoa, but his near kin, the 'semi-heteronym' Bernardo Soares, assistant bookkeeper at the Lisbon firm of Vasques & Co., whose diary records a life of solitary uneventfulness which is an ironic simulacrum of Pessoa's own as translator of commercial correspondence in various Lisbon maritime firms. Soares replaces Vicente Guedes, indexed *circa* 1915 as author of *The Book of Disquietude*, described in earlier notes as 'dandy of the spirit whose autobiography is that of someone who never existed'.[19] Soares imposed himself on Pessoa as 'centripetally' nearer than Guedes to Pessoa's own 'disquietude'. But then, how near is even the nearest to someone who has already warned us, 'I was never actually there'?

From start to finish in his *œuvre*, Pessoa continually drew up plans of a final reunion, a discussion *en famille* with his unruly coterie of heteronyms. Whilst still an adolescent at high school in Durban, South Africa, and writing in English, Pessoa already 'prefaces' a meeting of his then companions at a place he poignantly names 'Moment House'.[20] Later, perhaps in 1916, the rendezvous switches to the Cascais madhouse and an interview with its inmate, Antonio Mora, at which the coterie is presumed to make an appearance.

Could such tangential and jealously independent destinies ever be relied on to keep an appointment? 'Duty, what a prolix nuisance!' exclaims Alvaro de Campos as he goes to see a friend off at the train station and thinks delightedly of the train's derailment.[21] Even Pessoa himself, in a late poem of 1935, 'Liberty', says, 'Ah, how delightful not to do one's duty!'[22]

So, although the coterie's individual existences are guaranteed, and they can each occupy the same 'real' time but not the same place as Pessoa, their chances of ever coming together are unlikely, except by pure accident of one day meeting in the street. Again, one thinks of Duchamp's *delays*, movement deferred, or indeed a rendezvous deliberately postponed and forgotten on the part of the heteronyms, which is a prerogative of autonomy.

Built into Pessoa's hopeless quest for a meta-narrative grail is this strange potential of occlusion and *oblivion*, a forerunner I might say of Jean-François Lyotard's idea that *forgetting* is a 'lethal function of narrative knowledge'. 'The narrative's references may seem to belong to the past, but in reality it is always contemporaneous with the act of recitation.'[23] In short, the Pessoan *œuvre* is doomed to the endless contemporaneity of the moment, *this*, the *next*, and so on.

To know oneself a fiction, even if the knower in this case is indeed a fiction, like Soares or any other others in their own lucubrations on self-reality, does not in the least release one from paralogism, the unconscious fallacy of thinking oneself right in being anything. A plurality of disintegral subjects without hope of congregation – this is Pessoa's dilemma; but at stake here is the predicament of the subject *forwarded* to postmodernity, recognizable in the contest between those of the French breed who would celebrate schizophrenia, affirm the decentred self and the illusion of a self, and those of the Frankfurt School who more traditionally defend psychic autonomy.[24]

'My dream has failed even in the metaphors and figurations', says Bernardo Soares.[25] An important clue, but what does he mean by this, the figurative dreamer so contiguous to Pessoa himself? Let us see where the clue might take us.

'I': a metaphysical reverie

In the world's structure, dream loosens individuality like a bad tooth (Walter Benjamin).[26]

I rise from the chair with a monstrous effort ['says Soares'], but I have the distinct impression of carrying it with me, and heavier too, because it is the seat of subjectivity.[27]

Descartes: the dream of ego rationality

Pessoa was always the hyper-rationalist, often censured, it seems, by Alvaro de Campos for his 'mania to prove things'. He copiously annotated the philosophers in the early years prior to the heteronymic Eureka of 1914.

A note in English, *c.* 1908, takes issue with Descartes' *cogito, ergo sum*. In arriving at the proof of his own existence, Descartes conveniently forgot to extend the principle, which had guided him so far, to existence and being itself. A perfectly human error, Pessoa concedes; but when I say 'I exist' the word *exist* has no explicatory signification, since it is in itself intangible.[28]

Descartes did not submit everything to the acid test of doubt merely to arrive at the self-certainty of a rational subject, but in order to establish the ground of empirical science itself, the certainties of which are absolute and cannot be doubted.

An apparently benign empirical realm without prejudice or preconception arises from ego-centric rationality, the projection of a pure mathematical universe which runs in direct line from Descartes to Einstein, who also stated a belief that the abstract mind alone is capable of any solution. Indeed it is, says Adorno, as he grimly concluded that 'Auschwitz confirmed the philosopheme of pure identity as death.' Adorno goes too far? Possibly. But 100 per cent rationality does look suspiciously like totalitarian sanity.

Cartesian doubt excludes the possibility of madness, one's own, of course, but moreover has no place for the unconscious, that banished force which if acknowledged can disrupt the formation of the 'I'-thesis (from the Greek *tithemi*, 'I place'). Lacan questions the formulation of place in Descartes, *ubi cogito, ibi sum*, 'where I think, there I am':

> Certainly this formulation limits me to being there in my being only insofar as I think I am in my thought ... It is not a question of knowing whether I am speaking about myself in conformity with what I am, but rather that of knowing whether, when I speak of it, I am the same as that of which I speak ...[29]

The conscious *cogito* is a mirage which makes one certain of being oneself even in one's uncertainties. Hence, for Lacan, it must be replaced by another more complete formula: 'I think about what I am, there where I do not think that I am thinking' – that is, at the level of the unconscious: '... the conscious *cogito* is supplemented by an unconscious subject who may be the subject saying "I think" or "I am", but never both at once, since the question of the subject's being is posed at the level of the unconscious'.[30]

Lacan's shadowy duel of subjects had already taken expression in the curious idea Bernardo Soares has of dream: 'I am not asleep. I inter-am.'[31] And this incidentally would give us insight into the sub-textual meaning of Pessoa's title, *Fictions of the Interlude*. 'I inter-am', *entresou* in Portuguese, could be variously translated as *I* – 'between', 'amid', 'among' – *am*. The 'I' which is so to speak 'intervalled', and implicitly plural, is the 'interlude' of fiction.

Kant: 'how many numbers am I?'

> That which is conscious of the numerical identity of itself at different times is in so far a *person* ... (Kant, *The Critique of Pure Reason*).[32]

The joke is – grown tiresome for being so oft-repeated – that *pessoa* in Portuguese means 'person'. The one thing he assures us he is not.

> I envy – but I'm not sure I envy – those for whom a biography could be written, or who could write their own. In these random impressions, and with no desire to be other than random, I indifferently narrate my factless autobiography, my lifeless history. These are my Confessions, and if in them I say nothing, it is because I have nothing to say (Bernardo Soares).[33]

Pessoa begins from a peculiarly *a*-human thesis-formation – the refutation of biography. 'I have no biography, because I am not my biography.' Pessoa's answer to biography is hyper-rationalist. These are not literally Pessoa's own words, but they are a reasonably accurate condensed version of his entire *œuvre*. Such a thesis would be embraceable, if one were prepared to seccde from the ambitious fallacy that 'I am' the empirical sum total of my experiences.

In a note, *circa* 1907, Pessoa asserts that for him Kant's *Critique of Pure Reason* is the only considerable theory in the history of philosophy. What then is Kant's guarantee of self-identity which Pessoa might have found appreciable?

> ... in the whole time in which I am conscious of myself, I am conscious of this time as belonging to the unity of myself; and it comes to the same whether I say that this whole time is in me, as individual unity, or that I am to be found as numerically identical in all this time.[34]

I am assured of being 'numerically me', but the question is, 'what about the *others*?

> But if I view myself from the standpoint of another person ... it is this outer observer who first represents *me in time*, for in the apperception *time* is represented, strictly speaking, only *in me*. Although he admits, therefore, the 'I', which accompanies, and indeed with complete identity, all representations at all times in *my* consciousness, he will draw no inference from this to the objective permanence of myself.[35]

Kant describes the 'I' as a game of monadic solitaire, a pessimist interpretation that verges on withdrawing reality from the thinking subject, except as convenient unit of grammar.

> The identity of the consciousness of myself at different times is therefore only a formal condition of my thoughts and their coherence, and in no way proves the numerical identity of my subject. Despite the logical identity of the 'I', such a change may have occurred in it as does not allow the retention of its identity, and yet we may ascribe to it the same-sounding [*gleichlautende*] 'I' ...[36]

Compare this with Soares's diary entry, 18 May 1930: 'To live is to be other. It's not even possible to feel, if one feels as one felt yesterday.'[37]

Elsewhere in a note *circa* 1910–15, Pessoa glosses on this Kantian predicament.

> Consciousness is not Reality. Consequently, Consciousness does not exist. We cannot affirm that it exists, because to so affirm is to affirm that it is Objective, and it is, essentially, Pure Subject.
>
> ...
>
> The fictitious subject is the Subject that perceives itself Object, which can be Object of itself and not Pure Subject. This is the first fiction ...[38]

The presence of Hegel?

Hegel is rarely ever mentioned by Pessoa. Such a neglect, or indeed outright hostility, would accord fittingly with a pluri-existential condition, as it also did for Kierkegaard, upholder of an absurdist faith in combat with Hegel's idealist absolutism. And it is in agreement with the *Ultimatum* of Alvaro de Campos which 'amputates' the Hegelian dogma of Absolute Truth. An idea of conditional truth is entirely consistent with avant-garde modernism and does not need to await on the misprisions of 'post'-modernity. Modernist as it might be, then, to throw out Hegel's absolutism, it is also archetypical to retain the essential feature of Hegel's *Selbstentfremdung*, 'self-estrangement' or 'alienation'. Alienation, as demonstrated in Hegel's *Phenomenology of Mind*, is the central process in the growth of self-consciousness. Consciousness divides itself into subject and object, and thereby mind 'estranges' or 'objectifies' itself in thought in the realization of self-consciousness.

Rightly, one might observe that heteronymic extraneity is an endlessly multiplied variation on this theme – except, of course, that the realization of self-consciousness is indefinitely deferred. *Delayed*, in Duchamp's terminology.

We arrive with Hegel at hyper-Cartesianism: doubt can be redeployed as self-estrangement in a dialectical cortège leading to positive self-consciousness. Self-consciousness would be realizable, if, but only if, each moment bears the entire weight of the consciousness that is being realized, otherwise, as Pessoa acknowledges, the movement towards self-consciousness risks bogging down in the Sophist paradox of Zeno which famously denied motion:

> In each instant that passes *an eternity elapses*, seeing that each instant, infinitely divisible, is infinite ideally, that is, eternal ... If we *advance* to the infinite, we do not advance really, but are *essentially* stationary.[39]

Consciousness is not simply 'in motion' as a synchronous line carried forward, but at any moment is *also* a diachronical axis describing all the planes of that consciousness – or none of it. It is not hard to see how this simultaneous vertical and horizontal 'cross' of consciousness we bear, resembles and prefigures the semantic diagram of Saussure's diachronic *parole* and synchronic *langue*. The elements of philosophic discourse are breaking down into constituents of grammar.

Tedium and nausea

Pessoa considered an alternative formula (*circa* 1924):

> ... for a being to perceive itself most *possible* for itself ... it must perceive as most absolutely and purely possible its *Relation*.

Relation is the liminal distinction of Identity:

> For it [identity] to be distinct from itself without being others ... it must neither be others nor itself, but must be the Essence of others and of itself, for only in this way, by being the essence of itself, can it distinguish itself from itself ... and distinguish itself from others by the selfsame process by which it distinguishes itself.[40]

Relation is the conscious element of *limit* between identities. Relational distinction is not the stuff of congregation. It is not the amalgam of a meta-narrative. On the contrary, it is the corrosive fluidity of *dis*-sociation. Prolonged reflection on 'liminalities' afflicts all of the coterie with vertiginous seasick pessimism – always with the exception of Alberto Caeiro who subsists on a limpid empiricism of ascetic unimpeachability 'To think is to destroy', says the diarist Soares, and he is the best recorder of tedium and nausea which the bad habit of thinking produces. What is tedium, really? It must not be confused either with the torpor of bordeom or the *acedia* which gives birth to mystics and saints.

> ... tedium is indeed the carnal sensation of the unending vacuity of things. But tedium, even more than this, is bordeom with other worlds, whether real or imaginary; indisposition at the thought of having to keep living, albeit as another, in another way, in another world; weariness not only of yesterday and today but also of tomorrow and of eternity, if such exists, or of nothingness, if that's what eternity is ... the vacuity of the soul that feels the vacuum, that feels itself the vacuum, and that is nauseated and repelled by itself therein ... Tedium is the physical sensation of chaos, a chaos that is everything.[41]

'There is as if a rheumatism in all my being', as Soares puts it, simply. A sense of *mal-estar*, being unwell, of cramps, of seeming to carry with him the heavy chair of subjectivity – all plain terms of discomfort that translate the motionless infinitude of consciousness. 'If the heart could think, it would stop', comments Soares. And 'to stop', *parar*, is the inactive predicate that sends Alvaro de Campos, the most fidgety, hyperactively travelled of the heteronyms, into paroxyms of fury.

Ah, a Sonnet ...

> My heart's a crazy admiral
> who's packed in his seafaring trade
> reliving it, as time goes by
> in housebound pacing, to and fro ...
>
> In such motion (stuck in my chair
> I travel, just to think of it)
> forsaken seas are telescoped
> on muscles wearied by inaction.
>
> Yearnings in the arms and legs.
> Yearnings in the brain outward bound.
> Great rages squalled from weariness.
>
> But – that's a good one! – I began by
> talking of my heart – now where the devil am I
> with an admiral instead of a feeling?[42]

Ricardo Reis, with his Stoic calm and neo-classical style, also contemplates cessation:

> Whatever stops is death, and is our death
> If it stops for us. That every shrub now
>   Withering, takes with it
>   Part of my present life.
> In everything I saw, part of me remained.
> With all I saw that moves I too move.
>   Nor does memory distinguish
>   What I saw from what I was.[43]

Solipsism

No one, I suppose, genuinely admits the real existence of another person. We may concede that the person in question is alive and that we think and feel as he does, but there will always be an anonymous element of difference, a materialized disadvantage. There are historical figures and mental images in books that are more real to us than the incarnate indifferences that talk to us over shop counters, or happen to glance at us in trams, or brush against us in the dead happenstance of pedestrian-filled streets. The rest are no more for us than scenery ... (Bernardo Soares).[44]

It was inevitable, having begun with the Cartesian assurance of an 'I', that we would end up in solipsism. Is it perhaps less a problem of metaphysics than of 'grammatical judgment', as Wittgenstein hygienically urges us to think? Solipsism is tautology, but tautologies fascinated Wittgenstein, because they often reveal the semantic knots tied by philosophers:

When philosophers use a word – 'knowledge', 'being', 'object', 'I', 'proposition', 'name' – and try to grasp the *essence* of the thing, one must ask oneself: is the word ever actually used in this way in the language-game which is its original home? – What *we* do is to bring words back from their metaphysical to their everyday use.[45]

Bringing back words to their everyday use, their original home, is precisely Caeiro's business as shepherd, and there are moments when the 'Nature' poems of this pagan pastoralist look like the anti-metaphysical hooliganism of Wittgenstein. Zen masters tend to slap more than utter:

> I don't know what Nature is: I sing it.
> I live on a hilltop
> In a solitary whitewashed cabin.
> And that's my definition.[46]

But what of solipsism, then? To untie the knot of its apparent existential proposition – that I can only be certain of my own existence but of no one else's – Wittgenstein must argue that the 'I' is not something to be encountered in the world. A statement like 'I can't feel your pain' is not asserting anything that could be found in the world but what is entailed in the rules-for-use that govern the meaning of terms like 'pain', 'experience', 'sense-data'. We are apt to confuse 'grammatical judgments' with information, and thereby generate philosophical puzzles.[47] Wittgenstein does not deny my everyday right to say 'I', but the subject of grammatical judgements is often in peril of being fiction.

Wittgenstein's grammatical judgements are not unlike Heidegger's 'Dasein designations', or C. S. Peirce's 'indexical symbols', or what linguists call 'shifters'. These all refer to so-called indices, such as 'here', 'there', 'now', but especially to personal pronouns, 'I', 'you' and so on. Of particular interest to us as clue-hunters is Roman Jakobson's assertion that pronouns are the last elements acquired by infants and one of the first lost in aphasia.[48] Aphasia – impairment of speech or language-understanding due to brain insult – has proven itself attractive to pioneer neurologists, Freud and Jakobson himself. We shall consider Jakobson's linguistic study of aphasia in a moment, but first let us journey to it via the 'blind Narcissus':

> The happiest moments of my life were dreams, and dreams of sadness, and I saw myself in their ponds like a blind Narcissus who enjoyed the freshness as he bent over the water, aware of his reflection in it by way of a prior, nocturnal vision, confided to his abstract emotions and experienced in the corners of his imagination with motherly attention in its self-adoration (Bernardo Soares).[49]

One could not imagine a better symbolization of occlusion, of oblivion and forgetting than a blind Narcissus. Any possibility of a meta-narrative is foreclosed by this negative image of an unsighted self-reflective I. Echo, we are told, was the nymph in love with Narcissus but disregarded by him. A blind Narcissus would therefore be 'echoed' by a mute Echo, no sound, or language severely impaired as by aphasia. I note that *occlusion* has some curious additional sense, in dentistry of the position of the teeth when the jaws are closed, in phonetics of the momentary closure of the vocal passage.

'... the dreamer reveals certain characteristics', Pessoa says, and by dreamer he means the patient of extraneity: 'Asexuality or parasexuality is the obvious one: it is the most flagrant form of his incapacity to wrestle with the normality and reality of things.'[50] Narcissus is already asexually drowned in his own self-love; but a *blind* Narcissus, well, he might of necessity be tempted to fall in love with a mute Echo, Silence. Refutation of biography necessarily required Pessoa's condemnation to asexual, virginal bachelorhood – or at least so the myth of him goes – like one of Duchamp's *célibataire* from *The Bride stripped bare by her bachelors, even*. Sterility is the price of occlusion, the uneventful momentousness of consciousness *only*, duplicated as misogyny and misanthropy, the *noli me tangere* of Christ appearing to Mary Magdalene at the sepulchre, or Alvaro de Campos in 'Lisbon revisited' (1923): 'Don't take my arm! I hate that when people take my arm ... oh, what a bore people wanting me to be one of them!'[51]

There is in fact an apostrophe to silence, glacial mute Echo, 'Our Lady of Silence', composed by Soares (or is it evidence of his more decadent and displaced predecessor, Vicente Guedes?):

> My dreaming of you implies no fascination with your sex, with what lies beneath the ethereal garments you wear as the Madonna of inner silences. Your breasts are not the kind one would imagine kissing. Your body is all soulish flesh, but it is body, not soul … My horror of real women endowed with sex is the road that brought me to you.[52]

Hostility to woman in modernism, hypertrophic in Strindberg's work, can be seen replaced by her gradual erasure as abstraction gathers momentum and we pass from Picasso's *demoiselles* to Duchamp's 'transsexual' Rrose Sélavy and finally to her total disappearance from the metaphysical space of Beckett's *Waiting for Godot*.

Turning now to Jakobson, I need hardly mention that his study of aphasia inspired him to an essay on the rhetorical figures of metaphor and metonymy that became a seminal classic of semiotics. He distinguished two types of aphasic disturbances, in which either the patient's capacity for the selection and substitution of words is deficient or their combination is impaired. These two potentials of language capacity correspond to the tropes of metaphor and metonymy. Jakobson noted that an aphasic who suffers from a substitution (metaphor) deficit will respond with metonymic expressions, while the one with a combination or contiguity (metonymic) problem replies with metaphors. Jakobson concluded that metaphor and metonymy are not associated forms of figurative speech, but distinct independent axes of the language system.

'The aphasic defect in the "capacity of naming" is properly a loss of metalanguage': Jakobson is here referring to Carnap's idea that 'to speak *about* an *object language*, we need a *metalanguage*'. In everyday speech, we perform this intellectual shift from 'object language' to 'metalanguage' virtually unconsciously when we interpret words and sentences by means of synonyms, circumlocutions and paraphrases. For instance, a speaker checks on his listener by asking, 'Do you follow that?', and if the listener replies, 'What do you mean by …?', the speaker will replace the questionable sign with another or shift the entire code to make the message intelligible. This is precisely what the aphasic has lost, 'equational predication', the metalinguistic recognition that 'bachelor' and the circumlocution 'unmarried man' are equivalent. 'Such an aphasic', Jakobson says, 'can neither switch from a word to its synonyms and circumlocutions, nor to its *heteronyms*, i.e. equivalent expressions in other languages. Loss of a polyglot ability and confinement to a single dialectical variety of a single language is a symptomatic manifestation of this disorder.'[53]

We begin to see now where Pessoa's own use of heteronyms is tending: to a 'fiction' polyglotism, a plurality of code-shifters, at the opposite extreme of the aphasic, but also removed from normal everyday metalinguistic usage.

'Heteronymia' is a condition of metalanguage that reflects both normality and pathology, and is threatened both by a 'supra'-normality (tedium) and a 'supra'-aphasia (blind Narcissus solipsism).

Jakobson's discovery led him to classify a variety of artistic phenomena on the basis of discourse which tends to develop either through metaphor-similarity or metonymic contiguity. Epic tends to metonymy; lyric poetry is metaphoric. Realist novels are metonymic; drama metaphoric. Cubism is metonymic; Surrealism metaphoric. Condensation and displacement, in Freud's interpretation of dreamwork, are metonymic; identification and symbolization are metaphoric. Cinema is essentially metonymic, but the film techniques of Chaplin's dissolves, or jump-cuts and montage are metaphoric; that of Griffith's close-ups, representing the whole by the part, is synecdochic and hence metonymic.

We are better placed now to understand the role that 'prefaces' and 'indexes' could play in generating a meta-narrative, no matter how fragmentary, postponed or resistant to credence this would appear. We could figure this as a chiastic order:

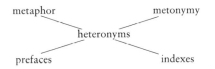

There is something 'wrong' with this chiasm. In good semiotic practice, as Barthes reminds us, the prefaces should really figure in the line of metaphor, since they are a kind of 'literary criticism', and all such discourse of a didactic nature, and even the metalanguage of semiotic analysis itself, is *metaphoric*. Here, instead, the 'didactic' prefaces are 'displaced' (as in Freud's interpretation of dreamwork) to metonymy; and the realistically populated indexes, with their Griffith's-like synecdochic close-ups of authors, end up in the wrong line of metaphor.

What has happened? I have assigned an *aphasic role* to heteronyms, literally as a 'shifter', but one that will employ collateral substitutions of metaphor and metonymy, according to whatever is 'deficient', as the condition of aphasia itself might prescribe.

I am taking *au pied de la lettre* Kristeva's avowed preference for *transposition* over intertextuality, which, as she says, better specifies the 'passage from one sign system to another', in the sense that mimetic articulation tends always to be 'plural, shattered, capable of being tabulated'.[54] Pessoa demarcated this 'field of transpositions' long before Kristeva systematized it on the example of Mikhail Bakhtin and other pioneering semioticians.

The modernist handling of the unconscious in fiction has incurred excessive debts to polyvalent analogy, overloading it and breaking it down. Metaphor and metonymy have not proven so distinctly compartmental, as Jakobson supposed, but are critically unstable at this point of overload. That crisis point is not reached at the end but is already at the beginning, the 'distanced origin', that which is precedent to the 'I' thesis-formation and before its 'place' (Greek *tithemi*, 'I place'), a place which is no place, the unconscious or *chora*, a term Kristeva borrows from Plato's *Timaeus* and which permits her to describe the unconscious itself as semiotic. *Chora*, for Plato, is a receptacle and amorphous space, unstable, uncertain, ever-changing, unnameable: 'This, indeed, is that which we look upon as in a dream and say that anything that is must needs be in some place and occupy some room ...' (*Timaeus*, 52a–52b).[55] So then, this is the unacknowledgeable pre-condition of the Cartesian *cogitatio*, with its rationalist boast, 'where I think, there *I am*'. There? Where is there? 'As in a dream' we say that anything that is (I) must needs be in some place (there). There-ness could not even be said without forgetting that I issue semiotically from the unconscious, the unruly, disorderly space 'when deity is absent' and outside the law, *an*-archic, the watery and fiery 'wet nurse of Becoming', as Plato calls the *chora*.

Attack on metaphor

We have seen Alvaro de Campos ballooning a metaphor – 'my heart is a crazy admiral' – to bursting point. A sudden awakening to reality befalls him with a bang, a metonymic close-up of the poet in denuded abnegation: 'what the devil am I doing with an admiral!' Campos has violated the golden rule of his master Caeiro: a thing is simple, single and a real sensation. Not a metaphor.

Uncharacteristically, one might think, Bernardo Soares attacks another and far better-known diarist, Henri-Frédéric Amiel (1821–81), for his lyrical statement, 'a landscape is a state of soul', a metaphor in the weak form of unaffirmed simile:

> ... the phrase is a flawed gem of a feeble dreamer. The moment the landscape becomes a landscape, it ceases to be a state of the soul. To objectify is to create, and no one would say that a finished poem is a state of thinking about writing one. Seeing is perhaps a form of dreaming, but if we call it seeing instead of dreaming, then we can distinguish between the two ... It would be better to say that a state of the soul is a landscape, for the phrase would contain not the lie of a theory but the truth of a metaphor.[56]

Soares pinpoints, as Barthes does, the metaphorical content underlying a *thematic* theory. And in so doing, he is reconciled with the master Caeiro:

> As for myself, I write out the prose of my poems
> And I am satisfied,
> Because I know I can understand Nature from the outside;
> I don't understand it from the inside
> Because Nature hasn't any inside;
> It wouldn't be Nature otherwise.[57]

Metonymy is a figure of contiguity, in the line of the diachronic syntagm, *parole*.

By the combinatory way of fragmentation, it refers to an attribute, adjunct, cause or effect of the thing meant rather than the thing itself. Realistic prose is metonymic, and in a passage of visionary clarity, Soares tells us why he prefers prose to verse:

> I consider verse to be an intermediate stage between music and prose ... Prose embodies all art – partly because words contain the whole world, and partly because free words contain all possibilities of saying and thinking. In prose, by way of transposition, we are able to render everything: colour and form, which painting can only render directly, in themselves, without an inner dimension; rhythm, which music can only render directly, in itself, without a formal body nor even that second body which is the idea; structure, which the architect must form out of given, hard, external things, and which we build with rhythms, indecisions, durations and fluidities; reality, which the sculptor must leave in the world, with neither aura nor transubstantiation; and poetry, finally, in which the poet, like the initiate of a secret order, is the servant (albeit voluntary) of a hierarchy and a ritual. I contend that in a perfect, civilized world there would be no other art but prose.[58]

'Prose', in this vision, is a de-materialization not of art only but of the world. It is Mallarmè's 'Prose' for des Esseintes –

> at hearing all the sky and map
> always in my steps attested,
> by the wave even that ebbs away,
> that this country never existed.[59]

And yet, what Soares is saying in the passage is a *theory*, and as such at bottom ineluctably metaphoric.

A considerable amount and perhaps most appreciable of the Pessoan *œuvre* is poetry, but this would overlook the sheer mass of prose, the essayistic inquiries into sociology, philosophy and the occult, detective stories, diaries, letters, dramas, even some advertising copy and a tourist guide. Every genre is touched on, an encyclopaedic universalism, like the commodious embrace of James Joyce's *Ulysses*. Much of the prose has been left 'unindexed', which means we cannot be sure of attributing its parts to the *right* authors, even those usually ascribed to Pessoa 'himself'. The task of 'finally' editing Pessoa's *œuvre* is unenviable, and perhaps untenable. But this should no longer disguise from us the point of it. *All* of it is in sum an overcharged, polyvalent analogy that collapses the unstable compartment wall between metaphor and metonymy and sets them at liberty as interchangeable tonalities. It is this, the occult key signatures of *transposition* from one sign system to another, which, if ever decoded, would reveal the canon of the heteronymic meta-narrative.

Pessoa's instruction is clear enough. All forms of fiction, poetry included, are the concessionaries of a meta-language that *does not exist*, save by being 'pointed to', and should not be confused with *information*. There is no narrative 'knowledgc', and therefore – contrary to Lyotard's opinion – it cannot have the 'lethal function' of oblivion; instead, its function is the *re-creation* of memory, in both senses of the term.

I shall end with a violated metaphor: the sender's message is metonymically parcelled to us.

This

They say I fake or lie
In all I write. Not so.
In simple truth I feel
With the imagination only.
The heart is not my tool.

All I dream or endure,
What fails me or expires,
Is the likeness of a terrace
On something else again.
Comely is this something else.

That's why I write whereof
I've not set foot,
Free of what I'm bound to,
Seriously bent on nothing.
Feel? Let the reader feel!

(Fernando Pessoa, April 1933)[60]

Notes

1 Bernardo Soares, the semi-heteronym of Fernando Pessoa, is the diarist author of *The Book of Disquietude* (*Livro do Desassossego*), although the several competing English-language editions of the book based on Portuguese versions credit Pessoa with the authorship. This is a confusion unfortunately become established, contrary to Pessoa's stated aim of independent authorships, not only for this but all other heteronymic titles.

   Quotations from the Soares book in my essay are from the translation by Richard Zenith, Manchester: Carcanet Press, 1991, hereafter abbreviated RZ. This is the best, most complete English translation available, but as Zenith himself acknowledges, a 'true' version of the book is impossible because the final order of its fragments can never be certain.

2 Sixty years after Pessoa's death, a complete critical edition of his *œuvre* is still not in sight, and given the disputes over it, a consensus one is unlikely.

   For convenience sake, I have used the paperback edition of Pessoa's 'complete' works organized by Antonio Quadros, Publicacões Europa-America, Portugal, hereafter abbreviated as AQ plus the volume title. For this reference, Pessoa's 1912 articles in the journal *A Águia*, reprinted in AQ, *Textos de Intervenção Social e Cultural*, pp. 17–64. Translations are mine unless otherwise stated.

3 AQ, *Textos de Intervenção, Ultimatum*, p. 86ff.

4 Reproduced in the reprint of *Portugal Futurista*, Lisbon: Contexto Editora, 1981.
5 AQ, *Textos de Intervenção*, p. 213.
6 *Ibid.*, p. 245.
7 *Ibid.*, pp. 182–4 for the index and preface that follows.
8 Reprinted in *Marchand du Sel, écrits de Marcel Duchamp*, Paris: Collection '391' Le Terrain Vague, 1958.
9 Excellent collections of these unpublished fragments from the *espolio* are being published by Teresa Rita Lopes and her team of researchers: see her two-volume *Pessoa por Conhecer*, Lisbon: Editorial Estampa, 1990, hereafter abbreviated TRL.
10 AQ, *Escritos Intimos*, letter of 20 January 1935 to A. C. Monteiro, p. 233.
11 AQ, *Textos de Intervenção*, p. 189.
12 Translated by Jonathan Griffin from his Introduction to *Fernando Pessoa, Selected Poems*, Harmondsworth: Penguin Books, 1988, a currently available selection of translations.
13 TRL, II, fragment 325, p. 360.
14 *Zohar*, ed. Gershom G. Scholem, London: Rider and Company, 1977.
15 Jakob Boehme, *Six Theosophic Points*, trans. J. R. Earle, Michigan: Ann Arbor Paperback, 1958.
16 For these two references see TRL, II, fragments 215, p. 256 and 263, p. 306.
17 Translated by Edwin Honig and Susan M. Brown, in *Poems of Fernando Pessoa*, New York: The Ecco Press, 1986, p. 17, hereafter abbreviated EH.
18 RZ, p. 170.
19 TRL, II, fragment 184, p. 228.
20 *Ibid.*, fragment 124, p. 170.
21 AQ, *Poesias de Álvaro de Campos*, p. 140.
22 EH, p. 159, for an English translation.
23 J.-F. Lyotard, *The Postmodern Condition: a Report on Knowledge*, Manchester: Manchester University Press, 1992, p. 22.
24 From Fredric Jameson's foreword to J.-F. Lyotard, *The Postmodern Condition* pp. ix-x.
25 AQ edition of *Livro do Desassossego*, I, p. 216.
26 From 'Surrealism: the last snapshot of the European intelligentsia', 1929, in *New Left Review*, 108, March–April 1978, p. 48.
27 AQ, *Livro*, p. 294.
28 For this and Pessoa's subsequent notes on philosophy see AQ, *A Procura da Verdade Oculta*, pp. 41–2 and *passim*.
29 Quoted from *The Language of the Self by Jacques Lacan*, translated by Anthony Wilden, A Delta Book, New York: Dell, 1975, pp. 182–3.
30 *Ibid.*, p. 183.
31 AQ, *Livro* p. 186.
32 Translated by Norman Kemp Smith, New York and London: Macmillan & Co., 1964, p. 341.
33 RZ, p. 13.
34 Kant, *The Critique of Pure Reason*, p. 341.
35 *Ibid.*, p. 342.
36 *Ibid.*
37 RZ, p. 61.
38 AQ, *A Procura da Verdade Oculta*, p. 82.
39 *Ibid.*, p. 74.
40 *Ibid.*, pp. 90–1.
41 RZ, p. 242.

42 AQ, *Poesias de A. de Campos*, p. 226.
43 EH, p. 118.
44 RZ, p. 194.
45 L. Wittgenstein, *Philosophical Investigations*, trans. G. E. M. Anscombe, Oxford: Basil Blackwell, 1963, section 116, p. 48.
46 EH, p. 20.
47 C. A. van Peursen, *Ludwig Wittgenstein, an Introduction to his Philosophy*, trans. Rex Ambler, London: Faber and Faber, 1969, pp. 86–8.
48 For this and subsequent references see Roman Jakobson and Morris Halle, *The Fundamentals of Language*, The Hague: Mouton & Co., 1956.
49 RZ, p. 196.
50 AQ, *Paginas Sobre Literatura e Estetica*, p. 101.
51 AQ, *Poesias de A. de Campos*, p. 206.
52 RZ, p. 245.
53 R. Jakobson, 'Two aspects of language and two types of aphasic disturbances', in *The Fundamentals of Language*, pp. 55–82.
54 Julia Kristeva in *The Kristeva Reader*, ed. Toril Moi, Oxford: Basil Blackwell, 1986, p. 111.
55 *Ibid.*, notes 12–14, pp. 125–7.
56 RZ, p. 246.
57 EH, p. 20.
58 RZ, p. 134.
59 Stéphane Mallarmé, *Selected Poems*, trans. C. F. M. MacIntyre, University of California Press, 1959.
60 AQ, *Obra Poetica de F. Pessoa, Poesia II, 1930–33* p. 92.

British, Muslim, writer

I

I hate winters.

The one in 1962 was particularly bad. Months of sub-zero temperatures, they skated on the frozen Thames that year – just as Dickens wrote. And the snow! It piled up everywhere and refused to budge, week after week. How on earth could one play *guli-danda* in weather like that? Try as I might it was impossible to shape a snowball into the pointed *guli*, the torpedo-shaped piece of wood, to launch it into orbit with a determined whack from the *danda*, a large, flat stick. The snowballs disintegrated on collision with any hard object. Anyway, how can anyone attempt to shape a decent *guli* through thick gloves with frostbitten fingers that refuse to respond? At home, when I was there, winters were cool respites from the heat. A child's life was spent outdoors marauding with friends, winter was just the addition of a sweater. Now this was home and life outdoors was a painful obstacle course. Not for the first time I ran indoors on the verge of tears.

She ran her fingers through my hair, melting the frozen coconut oil that had given a sculptured look to my hair. 'I know it's very cold, *baitay*', she said, 'and it could get colder. You will need something to protect yourself from the harsh European winters, something that warms you from the inside and keeps the cold at bay, something that anchors you to your being.' She pulled up a chair and I sat on her lap. 'Urdu poetry is our most cherished inheritance. It will warm you when everything around you turns into ice.' With one arm around me, she picked up the ageing, well-thumbed copy of *Diwan-e-Mir*. Flicking through the pages, her eyes came to rest on a particular poem. She began to hum, the humming turned into words, the words turned into fire, and I was engulfed:

> Look you: it is emerging from the soul of my heart!
> Where is this smoke coming from?

II British

My mother was distraught when she learned that my father was leaving for England 'He *had* to go', he said. But there was nothing to worry about as we would be joining him within a year or so – 'as soon as I find a job and a place to stay'. Within a week of his announcement my father was gone.

It took us a year to work out why my father had to go. The strike was broken. His fellow union leaders were arrested by the martial law administrators. The biscuit factory where he had worked as an engineer was closed down. We received regular letters from him, but none of them actually described what he had discovered in London. Then one day I received a parcel; it contained a number of books, none of which I could read, all of them bearing the legend, 'The Great Books of Mankind'. Also enclosed was a short note. 'Dear son,' it read, 'I know you will find it difficult to read these books, but do try your best. When you come to London, you will meet my friend Lady Birdwood.'

'Who is this Lady Birdwood?', I remember asking my mother. The answer was long and involved, just the kind of tale from family history that I most enjoyed. It appeared that my grandfather had served with the British Army against the Chinese during the Boxer rebellion under the command of a certain Lord Birdwood. The British were impressed by his courage and gave him the title 'Sardar' or 'Leader'. Eventually, Sardar became our surname. Originally we were Durranis, descendants of Nadir Shah Durrani, a Persian warlord whose most noted achievement was the ransack, and subsequent capture, of Delhi. Sardar seemed less bloodstained than Durrani.

I struggled with the books that my father kept sending me. Sometimes I was helped in this endeavour by my aunts and other regular visitors to our house. I started with *Black Beauty*. One of my aunties read *Treasure Island* and *Kidnapped* aloud to me. Ploughing through *Oliver Twist* and *David Copperfield* was a real chore. *Wuthering Heights* marked the outer limit beyond which I refused to immerse myself further in great literature. Much better to read the dreaded Biggles, old chap! Then I made the independent discovery of the much more approachable escapades of the *Famous Five* and the *Secret Seven*, ripping fun!

This eclectic introduction to the English language came with a whole set of associations. I came to think of England through the aura created by what I read. It seemed that England was indeed the centre, possibly the original home of what it claimed were all 'the great books of mankind'. In the pages I stumbled over were all the polite civilities, and the high-flown notions of justice, fairness, democracy, order. They were the objective of the high-minded, all-inclusive search for human betterment, the refinement of the mind through science and learning. All this was encoded in the hopefulness with which my father dispatched the books to me and the struggle that went into reading them.

We joined our father two years later. We left Karachi on a bright sunny day and arrived in Hackney on a dark, rainy night. My father had rented two rooms in a terraced house belonging to a West Indian couple in Randlesham Road. Mr La Verne was a quiet man who spent most of his evenings in the pub. Mrs La Verne was a big, gregarious woman; I found it strange that she called me 'Love'. 'Love,' she would call me, 'would you like to watch television?'

Then she would escort my sister and me to one of our neighbours who had television. I sat glued to a wobbly chair watching 'Gunsmoke', 'Rawhide' and 'Bonanza', interspersed with all our favourite advertisements: 'Murraymints, Murraymints, too good to hurry mints.' 'John Collier, John Collier, the window to watch.' 'BumBumBum, Esso Blue.' During the year that we spent at the La Verne house, Lady Birdwood was supposed to come and see us several times. But she always failed to materialize.

It was only when we moved in to bigger accommodation in nearby Hillsea Street, under the auspices of a white landlord, that the Dowager Lady Birdwood first came to see us. A tall, elegant, meticulously dressed woman, she was accompanied by a playful dog. No sooner had she arrived, than she complained of a smell. 'It's called curry', I told her in my broken English. She stayed only a short while and left without eating the dinner that my mother had spent half a day preparing in her honour. Before leaving, she placed a couple of pamphlets in my hands and issued a stern order. 'You must learn to speak pukka English,' she said, grinding her teeth, 'and do read these books'.

Right in front of our house on Hillsea Street was the Millfield Primary School. But I never saw the inside of the school. No sooner had we moved to our new address than I began to have strange pains throughout my body. I hated sweaters, pullovers, overcoats, scarves, gloves – all the paraphernalia that while protecting one from the cold also makes one indistinguishable and hence invisible to the outside world. Despite all my parents' efforts to cover me with layer upon layer of protection, I would go out in my *kurta pajama* or the cheese-cotton shirts that we brought with us from Pakistan. The pains increased, and I began to forget all that I had learned naturally – to run, to walk, to laugh. Eventually rheumatic fever was diagnosed and I was hospitalized for almost a year. In Hackney Hospital, the doctors kept me firmly attached to a bed: the only thing I could do was to lie horizontal and read. And I read. All the time. And everything. I read Lady Birdwood's pamphlets on immigration, on the 'Jewish conspiracy' and on the Holocaust. I read the copy of the *Protocols of the Elders of Zion* and a book called *The Longest Hatred* that she sent me through my father. I read the copy of the Bible that some visiting missionaries had left by my bedside. But most of all I read the Urdu books that my mother, fearing I would forget the language, kept discreetly leaving behind every time she came to visit. Many of them were historical novels: the magnificent *Akhri Chatan* and *Muhammad bin Qasim* by Nasim Hijazi, which deal with the early history of Islam; the novels of A. R. Khatun and Razia Bhatti, mostly about the pain of migration, racial and ethnic hatred and adjusting to change; and my all time favourite, Sadiq Siddiqui's *Andulus kay do Chand* ('Two Moons of Andalusia'), an epic saga of the rise and fall of Moorish culture in Spain. Occasionally my mother would treat me to what she called 'more serious books': texts on Indian history, eyewitness accounts of the 'Indian Mutiny', the Indian assessment of the Raj, classical works on Islamic thought, Sufi wisdom, translated anthologies of Islamic literature; and 'diwans' of Urdu poets: apart from Ghalib and Mir, I devoured *Diwan-e-Zafar*, the tragic poems of the last Mogul Emperor of India. Then there was an Urdu translation of the autobiography of ibn Sina: he had mastered Plato and Aristotle by the age of ten, he wrote. My age, I thought!

When I recovered, I was sent to a convalescent home for children in Broadstairs. Every day of the six months or so that I spent in Broadstairs was divided into four parts. In the morning, I would learn to walk again: with the aid of nurses, I would take short, gentle, wobbly steps up and down the hallway. After lunch, I would 'play' cricket. I would be totally uninvolved in the game till it was my turn to bat. Then I would be taken by the nurses and placed in front of the wicket where I stayed till the game concluded. Since I could hardly walk, a runner was assigned to do my running. Within a few days, I became one of the most hated boys in the home. After tea, I would sit with the staff nurse and talk about what I had read or was reading. Nurse Scott was, it seemed to me, the most beautiful woman in the world. She was slightly chubby but quite tall. She had 'classical features', just as Sadiq Siddiqui had described in the *Two Moons of Andalusia*. Indeed, she was one of the moons. She said she was a socialist; and she tried her best to answer my questions. Sometimes, when she could not answer my questions, she would go and look for a book and then read out appropriate passages to me. In the evening, I would sit in a rocking-chair and think. I could feel an inexplicable anger building up within me. I would conjure up pictures of Lady Birdwood as a *churail*, as one of those ferocious demonic women that try to entrance the hero in all Urdu fairy-tales. I was also seething with anger against my father.

When I rejoined my family, I discovered that Lady Birdwood had become a regular visitor to our house. She would come at least twice a month, always with her dog, and during each visit she would make it a point to correct and improve our English. Then she would start lecturing my father, who would occasionally nod in agreement, but would never utter a word. Before leaving, she would enquire about my 'progress' and ask whether I had read all the books she gave me.

The day after I returned from Broadstairs, I walked into Brooke House Secondary School at Clapton Pond and asked to be enrolled. The school secretary to whom I presented my request was astonished, but eventually allowed me to see the headmaster, Mr Harris. He was a very gentle and considerate man, who, I would later learn, loathed punishing his pupils, but the lack of discipline at the school often left him no choice. Mr Harris asked me to come back a couple of days later and take an 'intelligence test'. I failed the test – miserably – and consequently joined the bottom stream: 1.6. I had problems at the school right from the start. By far the worst of my problems was Mr Brilliant, our history teacher. He looked like Einstein, without the moustache, and thought himself pretty clever, too. First, I found it difficult to understand how Mr Brilliant could talk about Victorian England without talking about what Victorian England did to India and Africa. Then I found his account of the 'Indian Mutiny' too difficult to swallow. But most of all I resented the fact that he was not interested in *my* history at all; 'Not in the syllabus, lad. Can't talk about it.' I became so incensed with Mr Brilliant's inflexible approach to history that, one day, I stuffed all his textbooks in my desk and attempted to set fire to them. I was brought before Mr Harris who, reluctantly, administered 'six of the best'.

But it was not just at school that I had problems. It was clear to me that I was not accepted on the streets. The walk to and from school was the most painful part of my day. The gangs of youths I encountered on my daily journey had discovered a new game – 'Paki-bashing'. I was the perpetual *guli* to their *danda*. I made it a principle to fight back and frequently arrived home with cuts and bruises, and on notable occasions even with a broken nose and then a leg. I was learning that being British meant forgoing essential parts of one's anatomy. At school, they castrated chunks of your history. On the streets, they took lumps out of you. It is only over time that I have begun to understand the significance of the lumps considered appropriate for excision and why they could not be conceded. It was in response to this determined process of extraction that I began to learn about proactivity, the resistance that defines the nature of my Britishness.

Not all resistance is aggressive. When all my contemporaries seemed to be gladiators on some new battlefield I found that, as before, my friends were all old people. But there was something very different about the old I befriended around Hackney. I could not understand why society excluded them and left them lonely. All the old people I knew in Pakistan were the opposite, they were happy tyrants engaged in exercising great power over large families, which kept them endlessly busy and at the hub of all affairs. When we moved to Seaton Point, in the white heat of urban renewal, I could look down from the seventeenth floor at little old ladies standing mournfully at the entrance of adjacent blocks. Why don't they have anywhere to go? I wondered. Why do they come out of their flats, all dressed for an outing, and just stand there?

This was not the mystery I had begun to imagine. The enigma was resolved one day on walking home from school when I stopped to chat to one of the sentinels. Little old ladies found it difficult to battle against the hurricane-force winds that whistled between the tower blocks. They had to wait for a convoy to form before setting out across the windswept concrete oceans that separated them from the nearest shop. And that's how I became involved in Hackney Citizens' Rights: at my stall each Saturday in Dalton market, I got to listen to the complaints of old people that no one else seemed interested to hear.

There was more than an instincitve warmth for old people in these friendships. Or perhaps the instinct was not quite what I expected or thought at the time. These old people in Hackney were like me in ways I only now begin to rationalize: uprooted migrants, people stripped of the community and associations that sustained them, flotsam cast aside by the grand ideas of a society that knew it all and knew it knew best. With these old people and their rambling stories, tortuous complaints and vibrant memories you could see the underside of the utopia Britain proclaimed itself to be. The landscape these old people inhabited was one encrusted by hypercritical cynicism. I was becoming part of the old people's Britain, a marginal, excluded, unremarked Britain – but one that knew it was real, and that its reality gave the lie to the fictions the nation maintained about itself, to itself and to the rest of the world.

Lady Birdwood was trying, slowly but surely, to indoctrinate me with the ideology of exclusiveness, the rationale of exclusion. Here she was, the grand lady, straight out of some nineteenth-century novel, on her visits to the deserving. But her message had nothing, or seemingly nothing, in common with those works of the great tradition, the great books of mankind I had read. They had taught me of the need to be included. They were the umbrella of great ideas under which everyone should try to find a place safe from too much glare of the sun. The great books of mankind were the civilization to which all peoples had to aspire, because all else was darkness and silence.

On one particular visit, Lady Birdwood concentrated on a exegesis of the recent 'rivers of blood' speech by Enoch Powell. Powell is right, she said, 'Britain is in danger of being swamped by immigrants'. As most immigrants do not and cannot speak proper English, as their uncouth cultures are totally alien to the green pastures of England, as their eating and hygiene habits are so different from ours, there's bound to be strife. There will be running battles in the street. Then she suddenly turned round and spoke directly to me. 'Zia, would you help? Would you join us in our crusade?' I sat motionless. Lady Birdwood continued. 'Join the British National Movement. It would be such a coup to have a young Asian amongst us.' I sat motionless. 'We are about to start a new magazine. It will be called *New Times*. We are looking for people to help us with it. You can write for it. And help us distribute it.' I looked at my father, who was looking at me – there was no expression on his face. Lady Birdwood fidgeted: 'What do you say?' I looked at my father again: this time there was a smile on his face. Not a grin, but a suppressed, gentle smile. A smile that spoke directly to me. A smile that gave me permission. 'Erupt, volcano, erupt.' There was an explosion.

Lady Birdwood was stunned. Perhaps she had not expected an articulate and reasoned, but ferocious and loud, attack from this, this – a mere Asian teenager. Perhaps she thought she was getting through to me and was shocked at the extent of her failure. Her pale face turned white, and as I continued my denunciation, she became visibly more and more tense, rapidly becoming so rigid that the nerves of her face stuck out like the canals on Mars. I spoke without pause, without commas or full stops; and stopped only when I finished. Sensing that something was wrong with her mistress, the dog barked. Lady Birdwood patted the dog, turned away in visible disgust from me and looked at my father. There was a smile on his face. A smile of relief that slowly spread across his face and became a wide grin. Without saying a single word, Lady Birdwood put the leash on her dog, got up, corrected her composure, and glided towards the door. My sister ran out in front of her and opened the door for her. As Lady Birdwood walked out of the door, my sister shouted out, 'And I hate your dog, too.' We never saw Lady Birdwood again.

But Lady Birdwood has always stayed with me. In her contradictions there is something essential to the Britishness that has surrounded me since I came to this home. It is something this home has never allowed my Britishness to attain. Lady Birdwood is and was then a woman full of unresolved, unperceived, unanalysed incommensurables; as such she was not an aberration of Britishness, but its quintessence. I am reminded of this, having recently read that she has been fined for disseminating exactly the same literature she used to insist I read. Racism as overt as that preached by all her hate literature is merely the flip side of the Great Tradition, the underlying but unstated message of 'the great books of mankind' that I read in my childhood. It is the notion of civilization as a one-way street, an inexorable path of progress that must take all peoples towards the same pinnacle, by the same route. The definition of what it is to be civilized would have been no different for me had I never left Pakistan. It would always have been what it is: an extrapolation from the experience and history of Western civilization, the defining, over-writing civilization of domination that literally dominates not just the globe but the minds of all the world's peoples.

I have been part of a rapidly changing Britain. But my overall experience is of the changeless nature of Britain. During my adolescence in the heady sixties and seventies, it was conventional for the young revolution to pour scorn on the old ways. 'Let it Be, there will be an answer, Let it Be.' Today's answer to my Britishness is as quintessentially confused, unresolved and unaware as Lady Birdwood's. The politics of identity and its champions have ensured that my presence has rippled through the metropolis of erstwhile empire. Sadly, it has left the crumbling heart of that empire shaken, but hardly stirred. The identity I am alleged to have helped forge is an eclectic choice from among an infinite set of possible, potential identities. Personal choice, shifting allegiances, fragmentary, partial people are the order of the postmodern day. Who are these people, the British? Without self-analysis, and unaware of self as ever they were, they are still convinced they are the centre, the unwritten orthodoxy that measures and positions everyone else's identity.

That's what civilizing mission is all about: to give people identies, not to enable them to discover their own. Such labels as 'immigrants', 'Pakistanis', 'Asians', 'Blacks' are ways of retaining and managing control. Chunks of my being are declared appropriate and fit to be included in the Britishness that is imposed upon me. Now, as in my childhood, bits of my physical and historical being are extracted and discarded; artificially created, superficial identities are grafted on. You are thus supposed to behave according to the grotesque stereotype that has been created out of you.

Racism is an abstract term for an abstract, personless situation. In real, personal relationships, racism is an unease and a certain kind of fear about what the other person may do. It is the actual inheritance of stereotypes that are at large in the culture and its history and in the air we breath. It does not preclude people from interacting, but it surrounds their meetings and dealings with uncertainty. That's real racism: the package deal of identity British people see sitting on my shoulder whenever they talk to me, their certainty about what I must *really* be like, that I must at some point conform to the expectations they have created for me. It is a certainty that denies me the right to be sure of who I am, to know that I am not the person British society takes me for.

In the midst of all this fuddled, fudged thoughtlessness I am really British. I am British because I have had to become self-aware: consciously alive in my identity, which is not a shifting, infinitely alterable array of poses and positions, a collage of associations. Britain has made me the person I am because of the enduring human need to be whole. Like the old people I befriended during my youth, I live my reality, and like them, I will not allow others to dictate what my reality is. That is why I am such a problem, and pose such a threat, that I must be marginalized. Nobody else ever intended that I, or anyone like me, should be self-consciously British, and proud of it.

III Muslim

Of course it never occurred to anyone that I would consider myself British, because I am also self-consciously Muslim, and proud of it. The obligatory daily ordeal by news media gives one no option but to be conscious of one's Muslim identity. Part of a vast new diaspora, I read of and watch the turmoil within the Muslim world, the plight of Muslims everywhere from Palestine to Bosnia. Hardly a day passes without Islam being in the news, or the news throwing up some question that disturbs the complacency of the conventions of my Muslim inheritance. Where I live and how I live gives me no option except to be conscious of my Muslim identity. I don't take being a Muslim as a given; for me, being a Muslim is a challenge.

The challenge is to walk a tightrope. To fall in any direction is fraught with danger. On the one hand there is the slough of disaffection nourished deep in virtually every Briton on the potentially hazardous topic of 'the Muslims'; and on the other is the vast world of Muslims ready to be offended or hurt or maddened by omissions or commissions of which I am easily capable. To be a British Muslim means teetering on multiple broncos of identity, concentrating on holding myself upright, with head held high.

My Muslim consciousness lives with the fact that everyone else in Britain is blithely oblivious of what a Muslim is. There is an age-old stereotype that lies buried in the subconscious of most people in Britain, rather like the herpes virus – it is there, ever-present, and nothing seems able to cure it. Its presence becomes known only when it is triggered. Whenever Muslims make their presence felt in Britain (for example, by making a demand, say for Islamic schools), whenever an 'Islamic issue' emerges in a distant part of the world, whenever Islam is seen as a threat to (Western) civilization, the herpes virus is activated, the Muslims become an unbearable irritant that must be scratched, scraped, chafed. Muslims everywhere now acquire familiar contours: bearded Mullahs waving scimitars, irrational fanatics with a propensity for chauvinism and brutal violence, the lot of them. This conventional portrait of Muslims has a deep resonance in the British mind. Otherwise rational and respectable individuals of both the Left and the Right have not the slightest qualm in parading it as an objective, learned, universal representation. The invariance of this Pavlovian response makes me think that ultimately Britain is not comfortable with having a thriving Muslim community in its midst.

My Muslim consciousness is also a reactive, or proactive, product of the overt representation of Islam by contemporary Muslims. Muslims everywhere exist in a time warp; the interpretations of Islam that predominate pertain to the so-called 'Golden Age of Islam', and were first arrived at least a thousand years ago. Islam has been frozen in history, for centuries it has been denied the oxygen of new interpretation, its thought and traditions – from being dynamic and life-enhancing – have been fossilized and preserved in stone. To be a conscious and conscientious Muslim today requires constant struggle against obscurantism, against chauvinistic interpretations, against legal opinions that have served their purpose in history, against traditional notions direly in need of transformation, against blind imitation, against the tyranny of out-of-context quotations and anecdotes. The challenge of being a Muslim today is the responsibility to harness a controlled explosion, one that will clear the premises of all the detritus without damaging the foundations that would bring down the house of Islam.

Perhaps this is the common link between my British and Muslim identity, two volcanic imperatives, with me the molten and merged lava flow they generate. When I examine my Muslim identity, it is like excavating through a series of volcanic strata, burrowing through overlaid layers that form the ground on which I now stand. My early schooling in Islam was through my mother, who taught me to read the Qur'an as well as the basic tenets and rituals. There is nothing special in this, it is so conventional one might even neglect to mention the fact. It is an experience repeated in households the world over, the Muslim world, that is. The intimacy of one's Muslim identity is its domesticity. As I learned from my mother, so I have watched my wife teach my children. Through this most resilient tradition we are always closing the distance between Islamic identity and ourselves, hopefully so that we can take it deep inside ourselves.

I learnt to read the Qur'an and its sounds percolated deep. Yet like the majority of Muslims the world over, I read the Qur'an without knowing the meaning of the words; I was taught, and read, the Qur'an as a Pakistani struggling with Arabic as a second language. What is closest to home is a sphere of meaning that constantly challenges my understanding, that I must exert myself to know. Application of energy has never been my problem. From an early age I began joining in a wide diversity of activities. The Hackney Citizens' Rights group was counterbalanced by the London Islamic Circle. I was chairperson of both, even though I was the youngest member of both. Not just a joiner, it seems I am innately attuned to being an organizer.

The London Islamic Circle met at the Regent's Park Mosque, a kind of mini-United Nations where Muslims of every shade and variety from every possible source gathered. If Hackney gave me a distinct feeling of being British, Regent's Park gave me citizenship of a whole world and made me acutely aware of and involved with this world's problems. Unlike many a nascent activist of the sixties and seventies, for me the world and its problems had an intimate human face through the friends I acquired. To this day wherever I go in the world there is always an old friend I can look up, and an intriguing number of them have become powers to reckon with in their home countries. Back then we were all young, eager, concerned and committed; what we had to discuss endlessly every Saturday night was how to make a better world. The conundrum was how Islam would feature in and fashion the transformations we considered urgently needed. The threat that bound us together was the conviction that the status quo in the house of Islam was unsustainable.

To be agents of change it was not sufficient just to be a young and committed Muslim, one had to acquire an effective Islamic education. So in my late teens, I became a pupil of Jaafar Shaikh Idris, a Sudanese scholar. Jaafar is a gentle giant, a calm colossus with the most winning smile that crinkles around the tribal marks on his face. He was working for his doctorate in philosophy at Oxford, under no less a luminary than Popper, and was persuaded to teach me, and a few others, on a regular basis. We met every Thursday, for a period of seven years, in a *usra* group: according to tradition we would sit in a circle around the Shaikh while he systematically educated us in Islamic tradition. He took us through the classic texts: commentaries on the Qur'an, early biographies of the Beloved Prophet, books of authentic traditions, monumental works on Islamic jurisprudence and philosophy. Jaafar taught me all that – but he also taught me something else: the meaning and relevance of tradition in shaping a Muslim identity.

Tradition is the force to be reckoned with in the life of every Muslim and in the Muslim world at large. Tradition – the word evokes a solid object, an edifice of layers of old stone gone quite cold, and now being worn bare through over-use. Which is not to say that tradition does not have many pleasing aspects. A few years ago I was making a series of television programmes in Malaysia. One of the 'Faces of Islam' we had engaged to appear in the series was Jaafar Shaikh Idris. He was due to fly in from Pakistan to record his interview. When he arrived he was dressed in his traditional Sudanese garb, snow-white cotton *gelabeyah* topped with white turban, he had lost his luggage *en route*, including the suit he planned to wear for the interview. What is more, he had allowed himself to be persuaded to have his distinguished, greying hair hennaed while in Pakistan. This traditional specific, hennaing grey hair, had turned his hair a brilliant orange, as it sometimes does. He was the walking nightmare of a studio lighting man. What better metaphor for traditional innocence abroad? Calm, collected and compliant as ever, Jaafar allowed himself to be whisked to a shop to be rapidly outfitted in suit, shirt, tie and shoes and thence to the make-up department, where the only answer to his orange dilemma was to have his hair painstakingly mascaraed. As usual Jaafar smiled and laughed through it all, while everyone else was wilting from nervous exhaustion. At last he settled himself into his chair and was microphoned up for the interview. Then the hidden, underground explosive power took over. For there is nothing inert and lifeless about the understanding tradition evokes in his mind. A series of very sharp and pertinent expositions with the volcanic force to overturn the most determined complacency or sweep aside the most naked power ploys was set forth with the most gentle, humble, humorous and lucid clarity.

When I was sitting in the *usra* circle I liked the sense of timeless continuity of this simple tradition. But tradition itself became a monumentally oppressive force upon me. History is not just continuity; it is an increasing burden, for the most part unrelieved by the gentle intelligence of a Jaafar. Through his teaching and the discussions it provoked I came to realize that tradition is a complex and rich idea. But the wealth of connotations of our Islamic tradition have been buried under the overpowering edifice of an official tradition consciously fashioned out of its worst features. Where Jaafar gave us the spark for thought and discussion, most official Islamic education promotes *taqlid*, the blind following of received unwisdom. Official tradition has been crystallized into a power-ploy, a territory meticulously mapped out and signposted as a reserved enclosure for the exclusive use of the faithful. The boundaries and signposts are policed by the *ulema*, the ones supposedly learned in the traditional sources. Their vision is a straight and narrow path circumscribed by an endless list of do's and don'ts that obviates any need for thought or even personal reflection. When in doubt the Muslim should simply go to the leader and be told what is to be done. My problem was that the array of so-called leaders I encountered did not even understand the questions I asked, let alone how to find a prepackaged answer from the traditional storehouse.

By the time I got to university I was able to become an officially active member of FOSIS – the Federation of Students' Islamic Societies in UK and Eire; I had been unofficially involved for some time. In the late sixties and early seventies, the Federation boasted several thousand members from almost every Muslim country. Many of the members were also active in the world-wide Islamic movement. I was brought into direct contact with the two main strands of the 'Islamic movement': the Jammat-e-Islami of Pakistan and the Muslim Brotherhood of Egypt. With the help of elder 'brothers', I embarked on a detailed study of contemporary Muslim thought. I devoured the works of such leaders of the Islamic movement as Maulana Maududi and Syyed Qutb, their numerous followers as well as their critics. I was plunging ever deeper into a realm of ambiguities.

On the one hand I was a student, allegedly reading physics at the City University at the height of flower power and student empowerment through protest. On the other I was spending a great deal of my time with my Muslim brothers, whose preoccupation was the antithesis of letting it all hang out. I belonged to both, but was an enigma in both spheres. To fellow British students my Muslimness seemed out of place, while to the brothers my left-wing agenda and concerns seemed inimical to their approach. Not for the first time I found myself the only person not in the least perplexed by such a provocative and helpful juxtaposition of ideas and influences.

One other thing was clear: the modernist Islam of the brothers left me cold. In particular, I was disturbed by their instrumental piety – a piety that combined prayer and (self-)righteousness with efficacious technology and naked political ambitions. It seems to me that modernist Islam, like official traditional Islam, has imbibed the worst aspects of modernity. It is so gung-ho about the concept of modernizing to appropriate the power of the West it excoriates that it has never paused to analyse, let alone question, what makes the modern world tick. An Islamic A-bomb? 'Why, of course,' they say, 'let's have one', quoting a *hadith*, an isolated statement of the Prophet, to cover their paucity of intellectual or moral rigour. But where, I keep asking, is there a Muslim ethical debate on nuclear power and its uses and abuses? Where some wrestling with the concepts and ideas that generate the powerful instruments of modernity? Neither in the lexicon of modernists nor of traditionalists, comes the stark reply. Indeed, the modernists seem so set on getting to the point of power and dominance of the West that they effortlessly assume all the aspects of modernity I have consciously rejected: instrumentalism, progress (in the case of the Islamic movement, political progress) at all costs, expedient use of power, and fear and loathing of those with a different perspective. Worse: modernist Islam rests on a foundation of traditional thought from which all the life-enhancing juices have been filtered out.

Both traditional and modernist varieties of Islam leave me frigid, because they fail to engage with contemporary concerns. For me, being a Muslim means engaging with the world, understanding it, changing it, reforming it; not living in a distant past or some artificially brought-over, bussed-in 'modernity'. Both of these dominant brands of Islam look at the world with an atomised, black-and-white lens. They skim over the surface of what perplexes me in the modern world and assume that if they call a thing Islamic, all will be well. Why? The answer was provided at a seminar I attended in Chicago by a most convinced *alim*, a traditional scholar. While the rest of us had been passionately and vociferously debating hot issues of moral and ethical complexity for days, he had sat quietly. Maddened by his silent, contented expression, eventually I turned to him and demanded his views. 'Brothers', he said, surveying the room with a beatific gaze (and ignoring the female participants) 'we have no any problem – the *ulema* have answered all questions.' While some engaged in a pantomime exchange of 'Oh no they haven't' to his 'Oh yes they have', I made a mental refusal to shut up shop. Neither for the first nor last time I resolved that someone had to assume responsibility for the unasked questions this totally innocuous product of the Islamic reserve had made virtually unaskable.

Over the years the 'no any problem' syndrome has become a standing joke I share with a group of friends. It is black humour, laughing at our nightmares to keep us going through the endless crises. The worst thing is, the world belongs to the 'no any problem' brigade, those who offer the battered and bemused Muslim communities the ready-made, packaged, Islamic-state-on-a-plate scenario. This is why wherever traditional (for example, Iran) or modernist (for example, the Sudan) Islam has triumphed, the introduction of so-called Islamic injunctions has led to an increase in injustice and oppression. I tend to agree with ibn Tayymiah, the classical Muslim political scientist, who argued that it is better to have a just non-Islamic state than an unjust Islamic one!

Because they are seriously out of sync with the contemporary world, both traditional and modernist categories of Islam have generated a perpetual identity crisis amongst their adherents. Muslims of traditional and modernist persuasions have to wear their Islam like a banner around their necks and proclaim their identity as loudly as possible at every juncture. This is largely done by over-emphasizing what has come to be seen as the external manifestations of Islam – beards for men, *hijab* for women; rote prayer and formulaic pieties; biblical punishments; and unconditional obedience to the leader – shouting banal slogans such as 'Islam is the answer' and 'the Qur'an is our Law' and by hurling abuse and venom at the West.

Both traditional and modernist Islam seek to place a barrier between Muslims and their sacred texts. It is the interpretations of the classical scholars that have now become confused and infused with the *sharia*, or Islamic law, that is supposed to govern Muslim thought and practice. The problem with the 'no any problem' notion is that it is not the historically-bound answers of long-gone vigorous minds that are important. It is how these thinking Muslims of the past wrestled with the questions of their time and place that we should treasure. It is my questions that bind me to the glorious history of Islamic civilization, and its tradition of provocative, fearless and determined thinkers, not the stock answers that seek to make the history of Muslim thought a permanent full stop. *Sharia*, the dictionaries tell us, literally means 'the way to a watering-hole'; it is, therefore, a source of unchanging moral and ethical principles that must be regularly revisited, an absolute reference frame to which questions must be subjected for analysis time and time again. By arrogating the monopoly of interpretation largely to classical scholars and partly to contemporary obscurantist, traditional leaders, the Muslim community has been cut off from the basic source that shapes its identity. To be comfortable with my Muslim identity, I had to go back to the source: the Qur'an.

The Qur'an speaks to me in its totality, it is its spirit, its principles and conceptual framework that I imbibe; not the list of do's and don'ts that the scholars have gleaned from it. The challenge of my Islam is to keep making that walk to the watering-hole and constantly drink deep of its refreshment. Despite the several outer layers of Muslim identity that I carry with me – the Pakistani, the traditional, the modernist – it is the internalized Islam that is the essence of my true Muslim identity. And because I am quite comfortable with it, I am hardly aware of its existence. I do not have to parade it, underline it or wear it constantly about my person. It's just me. All of me. Including the bit that writes.

IV Writer

Like food, drink and sex, writing has become a biological necessity for me. It fountains forth, I wish . . ., most often it dribbles like a rusty tap, but by whatever means of inducement, cajoling or excruciating pressure of posterior on chair, I've just got to scribble. When the mechanism dams up it is as though bodily functions are on strike, nothing feels, tastes or looks quite right. I cannot remember when I first recognized the basic necessity of this fundamental bodily function, but the *Hackney Gazette*, Brook House Secondary School magazine, *Sixth Form Opinion*, *Zenith*, the monthly magazine of Muslim youth and *The Muslim*, the FOSIS journal, all received early outpourings before I had realized the importance of the stream they had tapped. The joiner and organizer soon found himself pressed into service as an editor, too.

In writing I am a majority of one, a totality, tackling problems head-to-head, and after all the angst, anguish and agony – in a single bound I am free, setting the words on the page, setting my ideas straight. There were other brothers in the London Islamic Circle and FOSIS who shared my analysis of the Muslim predicament and felt like me. Together we concluded that the havoc caused by suffocating tradition and murderous modernity to Muslim societies is so extensive that it may not be possible, or even desirable, to repair and restore their existing social orders. Our task, as we conceived it, was not to be patchers and potchers, but creative thinkers seeking fundamentally different, alternative social, economic, political and scientific systems for Muslim societies throughout the world. But how does one conceive new alternatives? We looked around for someone to guide us, channel our youthful energies and nascent ideas in a positive direction. And settled for Kalim Siddiqui.

Siddiqui, then a Marxist writer with Trotskyite leanings, worked for the *Guardian*. He had just published a typically pugnacious book, *Conflict, Crisis and War in Pakistan*, which had brought him to our notice. He received us enthusiastically, declaring: 'Yes! I would lead a new movement of ideas.' He insisted that the new, avant-garde Muslims, who were neither traditionalists nor modernists, should have an institutional base which would serve as a magnet, attracting like-minded thinkers and writers. Thus was born the Muslim Institute; its function, as the full title suggested, was to undertake 'research and planning', conceive new Islamic social, economic and political systems and develop alternative visions of future Muslim societies. Siddiqui appointed himself the Director and I became the Institute's first Research Fellow. But hardly had the Institute started functioning, from Siddiqui's house in Slough, than our brave new Muslim world started to look very old and familiar. The search for a potential leader was necessary because we had already been mauled over by so many of the self-appointed leaders who abound in the British Muslim community. Each one of these leaders is convinced he is the answer to the multiple dilemmas of the Muslims, who, if they would only listen to the words of the leader, could instantly solve all their problems. Every organization, whatever its impressive global title, turns out to be a one-man-band dedicated to expressing the views and ideas of a single leader, repeated to the echo by a dedicated band of acolytes. We wanted a tutor, a mentor, a galvanizer, someone above and beyond the Muslim organization syndrome. We got more of the same. Siddiqui, too, began to manifest his dictatorial tendencies. There was a mass exit of 'founder members' within a few months and I, having raised a vast sum of money for the Institute, was totally sidelined.

During my FOSIS days, I had became close to Abdullah Naseef, a Saudi from an influential Jeddah family, who was doing his doctorate in geology. A warm and gregarious person, Naseef not only represented all the Arab virtues of hospitality and generosity, he also seemed to have synthesized the best of tradition and modernity in his personality, along with a wicked glint of humour at the absurdity of so much in Muslim circles that would twinkle when you eyed him across a crowded room. Naseef returned home to become the General Secretary of the newly-formed King Abdul Aziz University in Jeddah, rising rapidly to become the Vice-President and then President. When in 1974 he invited me to join the University's Hajj Research Centre the offer seemed too good to be true. It was a way out of Siddiqui's tyranny, and, Naseef assured me with his usual generous smile, I would have ample time to write. He was right. I did.

Hajj, or the pilgrimage to Makkah (Mecca), is one of the fundamental pillars of Islam. Every Muslim is required, if he or she can afford it, to undertake the journey to Makkah at least once in his or her life. The word *hajj* literally means 'effort', and the actual performance of *hajj* requires considerable physical and spiritual effort on the part of the pilgrims. The *hajj* emphasizes the equality of all – men as well as women, black as well as white, Arab as well as non-Arab, before God; it is the global Muslim fraternity in action. The *hajj* is the ultimate exercise in humility and submission, a total denunciation of materialism and violence. It is the most sublime, most elevated, most cherished part of a Muslim's spiritual life. Research on *hajj* can only be done by those who have themselves performed the *hajj*. I performed my first *hajj* in 1975, and a further four in the subsequent years. The first time I simply went as myself; the second time I tried to assume the personality of a rural Pakistani to experience the *hajj* through the eyes of a poor villager; the third time, I travelled in comfort with a group of rich Saudis; the fourth time I joined a group of middle-class Egyptians. But my last *hajj* was perhaps the most ambitious. I walked from Jeddah all the way to Makkah, across the desert and over the mountains, with a donkey. The idea was to follow the ancient caravan route and try to perform the *hajj* as it was performed, say, a few hundred years ago. When I and my donkey, Ghengis, finally completed our *hajj*, I removed my pilgrim garb (two towels wrapped around the body) and in considerable pride indulged in my first bath after three weeks on the road. This, I told myself, was something worth writing about. I could almost feel the mantle of special effort wafting down on me as I began to compose a first draft of my exploits. Not only had I returnd to the remembrance of the past, I had put a special imprint on myself by avoiding the horrors of the *hajj* ordeal by motorcade. As I wandered around Makkah, still crowded with pilgrims, I almost expected everyone to notice the special aura I exuded. Just then I was stopped by a brother asking for directions, and in benign mood I engaged him in conversation. He was from Sudan, and had completed his first *hajj* – by walking all the way from his home village, as he would walk all the way back! The writer I have become was saved and reconstituted right there and then by someone whose name I do not even know.

Hajj research wrestles with the predicaments caused by the rapid rise in the number of pilgrims. Piety, with ill-distributed affluence and modern communications, brings over two million pilgrims each year to Makkah, all anxious to stand on the same spot at the same time. This not only creates formidable problems of accommodation, transportation, health and safety, it is also having a devastating effect on the geology, ecology and the sacred environment of the holy areas. The intervention of modern technology in the form of new and better multi-lane roads, overhead bridges and spaghetti junctions was only making matters worse. Every technological solution produced a host of new problems. The most sacred territory of Islam was stubbornly defying all the logic of conventional, modernist solutions. And the conclusions one had to draw from research and experience were not things the authorities wanted to hear.

As the President of the University, Abdullah Naseef tried his best to shield me from its vast, Byzantine bureaucracy. An unenviable task. Diplomacy has never been in my repertoire, to me spades are shovels, and I am without a scintilla of patience – easy meat for career bureaucrats who know a million ways to get their own back while keeping a sympathetic smile on their face. Without Naseef's protection I would not have been able to realize my plan to travel systematically around the Muslim world. Starting from Morocco, I travelled methodically through every Muslim country right down to Indonesia. I spent as long as I could in each country, looking at its academic and research institutions and talking to scientists and administrators. In February 1976, at the age of 25, I sat down to write my first book.

I had gathered a truly awesome amount of material and I knew what I wanted to say, but had little idea of how to organize it, sift through it, analyse it, turn it into a coherent book. After several months of agony, I turned in desperation to Kalim Siddiqui. His response was short and sharp. 'I am too busy to help young upstarts with their books', he said dismissively. 'Anyhow,' he continued, 'the Muslim Institute is not big enough for two writers. I don't want you undermining my authority. Take your book and yourself elsewhere: you are not welcome here any more.' He paused to reflect on what he had said. Then, looking away from me, he uttered his final sentence from the side of his mouth: 'If you come back here again, you will leave with broken legs.' The Muslim Institute was on its way to becoming a mouthpiece for the terror unleashed by the Iranian revolution.

In the classical Golden Age nurturing writers had been the strength of Islamic education and leadership. Now, there was nowhere and no one in the Muslim world I could think of to turn to. So I reached out to my Maimonides. I 'phoned Jerry Ravetz in Leeds. 'Get on the train, lad,' he said, 'and we'll sort it out.' I met Jerry when he was the Secretary of the Council for Science and Society, a high-powered body that studied and published reports on the social and cultural problems of science. He had rung out of nowhere to invite me to join the Council's working group on 'the information explosion'. He was a reader in the History and Philosophy of Science at Leeds Univesity. When I arrived we sat closeted for a few days while I poured out my problem and Jerry bobbled, bounced and flapped his hands, in characteristic fashion, as he engaged with my ideas. His advice was invaluable, but his enthusiasm was even more precious. Over the next year, in occasional meetings and by long-distance Jerry simply talked me through the process of writing the book.

Eventually, the bureaucracy at the King Abdul Aziz University caught up with me. They simply refused to grant me an exit visa for any purpose whatsoever. Unable to leave Jeddah, I turned to the desert. Every weekend – that is, Thursdays and Fridays – I would leave the city and spend the time in the desert with an assortment of Bedouin friends. Smoking my *sheesha* (hubble-bubble) amongst the sand dunes, discoursing on the nature of time with my nomad friends, I dreamt of an oasis: I developed a vision of a future civilization of Islam that fused life-enhancing tradition with the irrigating qualities of modernity. I wrote *The Future of Muslim Civilization* surrounded by the stillness of the desert, inventing new words as I went along to describe the movement of Muslim societies towards a desirable future. The book sealed my fate; it also expressed something very important about my relationship to the future. My Muslim civilization is an oasis at a crossroads, an open civilization inviting to everyone and closed to no one; after all the vision it records could not have been conceived without my Maimonides, and probably not without Hackney.

On leaving my job at the King Abdul Aziz University in 1979, I decided to become a full-time writer. I had no other option. It was my way of declaring my difference from other Muslims; my way of affirming my unique and distinct identity. I paid my bills by freelancing first for *Nature* and then for *New Scientist*, but spent most of my time writing, travelling around the Muslim world, and published another eight books in rapid succession. It began to dawn on me that while my work found much appreciation and praise in the West, most Muslims, for whom it was largely written, found it indigestible. I craved for criticism, yet none was forthcoming. Slowly I began to notice my intellectual loneliness ... My friends from the London Islamic Circle and FOSIS had dispersed to the four corners of the earth, going by different routes to involvement with contemporary problems. I was on my own again, an enigma voyaging through a sea of ambiguities.

As in the worst romances, at my lowest ebb serendipity took over. I began receiving letters and phone calls from places such as Stockholm, Houston and Ottawa bringing invitations to address Muslim gatherings. Invariably I would arrive at an airport to be studiously ignored by a welcoming committee who would shoo me aside with 'Yes, brother, we'll deal with your problem later, but we're waiting for an important writer, he must have got lost.' I would pester them persistently until I convinced them that I was indeed the author for whom they were waiting. They would eye me suspiciously and cautiously and ask why I did not have a long grey beard and arched back. It seems I have always been too young for the things I've had to say. But after the initial awkwardness in each of these fortuitous trips, I found myself blessed with a new friend, a kindred spirit who knew my aloneness because it was the same as his or hers.

After a few dry years, this slow meeting of streams achieved critical mass. The channel that brought us together was the formation of a new monthly magazine, *Inquiry*. I persuaded, browbeat and generally insisted that all my new friends become regular contributors – no was not a possible answer. Together we all began wrestling with words to find expression for our ideas. In *Inquiry* we were tempered in a common fire and eventually found ourselves in riotous assembly on the same flight to Chicago. Aloft over the Atlantic Ocean we made a pledge to become a group; it took the rest of the flight to determine what the group should be called – one of our members is a linguist with a penchant for etymology. We never discussed the function of the group – that was self-evident: mutual support as the antidote to the isolation we had all endured. Ijmal, as we call ourselves, which means the beauty of synthesis, has been in existence for a decade. It is the most formally informal of groups, though it does have ground rules: every member must write. *Inquiry*, which brought us together, is long gone, but the Ijmalis have kept going, they refer to me rather deprecatingly as the Tunku (the Malay word for prince) and I sometimes wonder whether they really appreciate what Ijmal means to me and has enabled me to achieve. For the pooling of our isolation has subtly changed my outlook. Together we have argued and discoursed, often sitting through the night in a noisy circle sprawled over the cushions in the living-room of my house, and my ideas, aspirations and creative vision have matured exponentially in consequence. Books and articles have been forthcoming from all the Ijmalis, and because there is Ijmal, we all have an image of an audience ready to receive our outpourings. The faceless, amorphous, personless void that initially made it so hard for me to write has acquired a character that makes a sense of communication possible. We have collectively forged a body of ideas on a broad range of topics concerning the future possibilities of the Muslim societies and the present potentialities of Islam in this rapidly changing, battered world.

Thanks to Ijmal I have indeed trekked out of the desert and reached a well-watered oasis. What is refreshed and sustained by this intellectual home is a new sense of my own identity, not just as a writer, but the identity of myself as a whole person, an integral part of an array of communities. It is a beautiful synthesis: this composite self who belongs to many homes with passionate, tough love. But for a world ruled by a linear, binary dialectic, dominated by sequential techniques of quantification and negation, and shaped by the perception and perpetual presence of the demonic Other, complex and composite identities are a constant source of irritation. I am not a problem for *me*; the process I have been forced to undergo has not been a self-transformation, but a clarification and deepening understanding of the potential possibilities and unsuspected commensurabilities of all the heritages I am heir to. It is other people who have the problem. By profession other people are dedicated to the ideas that such composite self is impossible, or permissible only when fashioned in differently proportioned chemical recombinations, according to their recipe. There are fundamentalists and totalitarians on all sides whose definition of identity, nationality, culture, society, the nature and purpose of being deny ijmal, the infusion that sustains my *joie de vivre*. Whether it be right-wing Britain or left-wing British activism and the race relations industry; traditionalist or modernist Muslims; secularist or libertarian ideologists or squads of postmodern intelligentsia – it is they who cannot deal with my ease with myself. From their variety and diversity of directions and approaches they all seek to delimit, to define strictly who I am and what I can, should or ought to be. Yet the oasis and synthesis of my self unfolds beyond arbitrary limits of other peoples' horizons. They would have me permanently sprawled on pin-heads of their own tangled misconceptions, hidebound by answering the question of identity as they define the issue. But I have a life to live, a living to make, a contribution to offer, that cannot passively await other people's readiness to allow my existence. So I say to all comers, the world is richer and more varied than you imagine; now let us begin to tackle its problems from the place where we now stand. I can neither reconstruct nor deconstruct myself because I really am a British, Muslim, writer.

V

It is autumn.

Outside my house in north London the trees are disconsolately shedding their leaves in a gathering gloom. I sit in my eyrie, my study perched at the top of the house, planning things I will write. There is the book on rethinking Islam, an essay on Urdu poetry, another on postmodern religion and that review for the *Independent*. Then there will be a third book to complete my trilogy on the future of Muslim civilization, to be dedicated to my youngest son, as the previous ones have been dedicated to my older daughter and son. In the warm pool of light inside my study I have the confidence to write as an expression of my identity, that peculiar amalgam that has been forged, merged and nurtured by Britain, the whole gamut of the Muslim world, and essentially by my friends. I have found my voice.

I turn and reflect on the gathering dark outside the window. In terms of multicultural expression it seems to me that Britain has arrived at autumn without ever having had a summer. I think of Pakistan. In that climate autumn without a summer, where plants flourish, is impossible. In Britain a cold summer of stunted growth is a likely occurrence. The arrival of so many cultures within Britain in the years since the ending of World War II was a potential spring of new growth, but these seedlings have arrived in autumn, the autumn of neo-Nazi revival across Europe, of racism, of perpetual prejudice, of the lack of forbearance without ever experiencing a summer, or only such a summer in which winter-wear remains a necessity. It is as if everyone has kept hats and scarves and ear-muffs on, so that they cannot hear, or can hear only muffled sounds they shape into old, received patterns, missing the nuances of a new language, a new kind of conversation. Thus Britain today is creatively stunted.

Out of rememberance of all that I am, I write; you can hear what I have to say only if you will. From the stereo the sounds of Muni Begum drift into my consciousness. She is singing a *ghazal*, an Urdu poem, by Quateel Shafai:

> On damp autumn nights, elusive tales enfold me. I remember.
> Glimpses of past experience, memories of her youth. I remember.
>
> As buds trembling to unfold, those blossoming lips
> In an idle reverie, their words come back to me. I remember.
>
> I had forgotten who left me alone in this world –
> When I recall my past, one face emerges. I remember.
> Road-wearied feet, a few tears, loneliness, the dust of travel
> Of my lost companion, every single feature I remember.
>
> I, Quateel, the destitute, what have I to say to the world?
> Yet in another's strange story, my youth finds its voice,
> I remember.

Severed tales; or, Stories of art and excess in Nietzsche and Géricault

In a passage from his book *The Gay Science*, Nietzsche poses an important question to contemporary scholars, asking whether they are fully committed to the artistic enterprise of overcoming humanist rationale and thought. Through the example of philology he implies that they are in danger of becoming overly dutiful in their studies and preventive of the creative process.

> That some books are so valuable and so 'royal' that whole generations of scholars are well employed in their labours to preserve these books in a state that is pure and intelligible – philology exists in order to fortify this faith again and again. This presupposes that there is no lack of those rare human beings (even if one does not see them) who really know how to use such valuable books – presumably those who write, or could write books of the same type ... all of it is work *in usum Delphinorum.*[1]

On one level, Nietzsche is respectful of the philologist's 'labours'. But on another level, a critical reading emerges. In Nietzsche's opinion the spirit of conservation taken to an extreme, whilst valuing learning, severs the links between art and power. These become displaced into an imagined scenario where 'true' creators exist to revivify tradition. As a consequence, power devolves on to a representation of authority – signified by the Crown Prince (*in usum Delphinorum*)[2] – and the philologist is made subject to his rule.

Part of the reason for the philologist's reluctance to assume power is the fear of the sacrifices involved, although this fear only arises as a consequence of the assumed purpose and value that lies in the 'labours' of philology. By reproducing the tautologies upon which the mentality of the philologist is based, Nietzsche not only reveals the insidious repression of art but also affirms that creative power is inextricably linked with the sacrifice of conventional notions of identity. This is underlined by Nietzsche in a further passage from *The Gay Science* in which he analyses the creative force of Roman poets who, in translating Greek literature, displayed none of the philologists' reverence: 'As poets, they had no sympathy for the antiquarian inquisitiveness that precedes the historical sense ... They seem to ask us: "Should we not have the right to breathe our own soul into this dead body? For it is dead after all ...".'[3] Nietzsche acknowledges that for the Roman poets, 'translation was a form of conquest',[4] but this was done in the spirit of creating anew. In this instance, the Romans sacrificed the desire to ascribe to the Greeks pre-existing values and significations. As a result, they sacrificed themselves – to a universe without an a priori meaning or identity: 'How deliberately and recklessly they brushed the dust off the wings of the butterfly called moment!'[5]

Nietzsche's interrogation of philosophy and its refusal of sacrifice remains of relevance for contemporary scholarship, reaffirming the need to reflect on methodological assumptions governing the production and signification of knowledge. This relates both to the idea of knowledge as an object of production and to the notion of the subject as producer. Nietzsche's 'remark for philologists' suggests that there is a threat of the former concept taking priority over the latter, whereby the subject is supplanted from the site of production into a network of representations and images *of* power. The section entitled 'Translations' demonstrates that the answer to this predicament does not lie in a humanist project of renewal or regeneration, but in revaluing the object and subject through their relationship to violence and death.

The purpose of this chapter is to analyse these issues further by outlining Nietzsche's account of metaphysics and its construction of identity. The starting-point for this analysis lies in a passage from *Twilight of the Idols*, entitled 'How the "true world" finally became a fable: the history of an error'.[6] In this section Nietzsche brings to bear a critical yet rigorous logic to the metaphysical opposition between truth and appearance, which not only exposes the inherent contradiction of such an opposition, but also indicates the means for its overcoming. The subsequent loss of presence – which Nietzsche refers to as 'the death of God'[7] – does not leave a sense of lack. Instead it opens the possibility of a freedom from repression which leads to the formulation of representation as a power 'beyond good and evil'.[8]

What are the consequences of Nietzsche's ideas for art, and for interpreting art? How might they affect ideas of history and tradition and their relationship to the present; above all, what are their implications for rewriting previous discourses of art in ways which affirm the integral link between creativity and power? Answers to these questions are developed in this chapter through an analysis of the work and 'genius' of the French Romantic artist J. L. -A. T. Géricault. The analysis includes a discussion of the Romantic myth of the artist as a means of considering the implications of Nietzsche's ideas for biographical studies and histories of the subject. Thereafter, these issues are developed in relation to two of Géricault's paintings, the *Charging Chasseur (Equestrian Portrait of M.D. ...)*[9] and the *Wounded Cuirassier Leaving the Field of Battle.*[10]

In the passage 'How the "true world" finally became a fable: the history of an error', Nietzsche recounts the history of metaphysics and the conceptual error upon which it is based. This history is told in six short parts, beginning with Plato, then proceeding through Kantian philosophy and Positivism, concluding with a revaluation of the 'error' of these philosophies. Owing to the brevity of this account of metaphysics by Nietzsche, a great deal of the detail and complexity of the philosophies involved is left out. However, despite these shortcomings, this piece of writing contains important insights into the assumptions sustaining metaphysics and the means by which they can be revalued. For the purposes of this enquiry it is appropriate to begin with the second section: 'The true world – unattainable for now, but promised for the sage, the pious, the virtuous man ("for the sinner who repents"). (Progress of the idea ... it becomes Christian.)'[11] In this section Nietzsche refers to the 'origins' of metaphysics, within which Platonism and Christianity are implicated. According to Nietzsche, both ideologies are indistinguishable from each other in so far as they commit the same conceptual error upon which metaphysics is based. How is this the case? And what are Nietzsche's reasons for identifying Platonism with Christian ideology?

The answer lies in the way in which both Platonism and Christianity are organized around a hierarchical opposition between the notion of a divine, transcendent realm and a corporeal world. For both, the transcendent realm is equated with Truth ('the true world'), whilst the corporeal world is a site of (relative) falsity ('the apparent world'). Mankind inhabits the corporeal world, and therefore is divided from the state of absolute unity and perfection associated with the divine. Formerly Man's soul was in harmony with the divine; whilst this is no longer the case, it is advocated that the soul can become whole once more. In Platonism, this is supposedly achieved by leading a wise life, as one who loves divine knowledge: the dutiful philosopher or 'sage'. For Christianity this is attained through the practice of 'faith, hope and charity'; hence, it is 'promised ... for the pious, the virtuous man ("for the sinner who repents").' Thus, despite certain differences over the means by which transcendence can be sought, both Platonism and Christianity rely upon the same fundamental precept whereby Truth is 'unattainable for now', yet ultimately achievable.

According to Nietzsche, this remains the implicit agenda of Kantian and Positivist philosophy:

> 3 The true world – unattainable, undemonstrable, unpromisable; but the very thought of it – a consolation, an obligation, an imperative.
>
> (At bottom, the old sun, but seen through mist and scepticism. The idea has become elusive, pale, Nordic, Königsbergian.)
>
> 4 The true world – unattainable? At any rate, unattained. And being unattained, also *unknown*. Consequently, not consoling, redeeming, or obligating: how could something unknown obligate us?
>
> (Grey morning. The first yawn of reason. The cockcrow of Positivism).[12]

Although Kant (referred to in section three) attempted to delimit the concept of the transcendental, which he referred to as 'noumenon', by arguing that it was beyond representation, he nevertheless maintained its existence. Positivism, by concentrating upon an empirical enquiry into phenomena, also diverted attention from transcendental immanence. At its most extreme, it became sceptical about the existence of God, and, therefore, doubted the idea of an absolute, objective truth, substituting a sense of relativity in all values. For Nietzsche this marks 'the first yawn of reason'; however, his regard for Positivism is qualified, since the idea of the transcendental still haunts Positivism, if only through its absence.

Nietzsche recognizes that metaphysics revolves around a central paradox which, once exposed, renders the whole system invalid: that an absolute concept prohibits the possibility of both oppositional and conditional values. Yet both Platonism and Christianity attempt to deny this by maintaining 'the apparent world' in a state of disconnection from 'the true world', even though 'the true world' is conceived of as an absolute. Kant makes the same mistake by assuming that the transcendental 'noumenon' is other than 'phenomenon', hence, as Nietzsche writes, 'The true world' in Kant remains 'a consolation, an obligation, an imperative'. Positivism also failed to escape the paradox of metaphysics; all that it can do is invert the structure of Platonic and Christian ideology by positing the lack of an absolute. Positivism's refusal to recognize the full consequences of conceiving an absolute lack is taken up by Nietzsche in the last sections of 'How the "true world" ...', where he stresses that all oppositional and relational values are abolished in the wake of abandoning 'the true world'. By this he means that there can be no representation of, or for, an absolute; this is true just as much for a concept of absolute presence as for a concept of an absolute lack:

> 5   The 'true' world – an idea which is no longer good for anything, not even obligating – an idea which has become useless and superfluous – *consequently*, a refuted idea: let us abolish it!
>
> (Bright day; breakfast; return of *bon sens* and cheerfulness; Plato's embarrassed blush; pandemonium of all free spirits.)
>
> 6   The true world – we have abolished. What world has remained? The apparent one perhaps? But no! *With the true world we have also abolished the apparent one.*
>
> (Noon; moment of the briefest shadow; end of the longest error; high point of humanity; INCIPIT ZARATHUSTRA).[13]

The last two parts of 'How the "true world" ...' reassess the opposition in metaphysics of truth and appearance to discover that the underlying opposition is really that of presence and absence, in which the implicit agenda has been to continually repress or mis-recognize absence. In this respect, Kant and Positivism are little different from Platonism or Christianity, since like these latter ideologies they hold absence in a dialectical relation to presence. Nietzsche's philosophy breaks down this relationship and overcomes dialectics. As there is no concept of presence – abandoned with Nietzsche's declaration of 'the death of God' – absence loses its connotation of (pure) negation, as metaphysics had formerly fantasized. With this 'end of the longest error' comes 'the high point of humanity' and the (re-)birth of 'the Overman', signified by Zarathustra, a Nietzschean figure of unleashed creativity. This figure is no longer a subject in a metaphysical sense, as there is no dependency upon an object for definition. For Nietzsche both representation and the identity of the subject are subsumed by absence; in fact, they *are* absence, since there is nothing else. Yet, because absence is non-categorizable, and beyond any point of comparison or contrast, it must also be irreducible. Thus, the metaphysical concept of representation as a signification of the (absent) object disappears, replaced by the idea that absence *is* re-presentation. Within this revaluation the (post)modernist conception of 'the death of the subject' is exceeded: there is no a priori subject of death. Death, like absence, is the subject and vice versa; in these two reversible formulations lies the irreducibility of death/absence, as a 'process' that is always other than itself, yet the same. In metaphysics this was fetishized as life.

According to Nietzsche, the foregoing ideas can only be incorporated by metaphysics into its web of paradoxical thought, with a failure of the necessary imagination to realize that absence, and not presence, is perfection. Re-presentation as absence is both model and (false) copy, both a fragment of the original and the original itself. Wherein also lies the perfection of the violence of re-presentation, as a perpetual process of severance and destruction without limit. Yet infinity is also utterly finite, since it only exists as death. Imagination, too, can only thrive in and as absence, otherwise it is harnessed to the dialectic of trying to conceive of the impossible. Nietzsche's project is to re-conjoin the imagination with 'the impossible', such that representation and identity exist a priori as extinction. Thus, they are consumed by absence, and extinguished even before they are conceived: this is Nietzsche's sense of the absolute perfection of Creation: a 'process' of perpetual loss that is necessarily formative and productive (of loss). Nietzsche uses various strategies and devices to describe and refigure this process of loss. The principal character of re-presentation is that of the artist or 'the Overman' (Zarathustra). This is because the artist gives rather than receives,[14] and is both creator and creation, although the creative process is purely destructive (of the artist). In other words, the artist is both source and effect of the artwork/gift which is given. However, this process of giving in which the artist is involved is without origin, so both creator and creation are entirely fictitious and illusory. This is what enables the creative process to be so various and multiple in its effects; it is also what gives art its sense of intoxication, which Nietzsche says is 'the feeling of enhanced power; the inner need to make of things a reflex of one's own fullness and perfection'.[15] Thus, the artistic process, in Nietzsche's terms, is that which metaphysics never dared imagine, although metaphysics always suspected that it was constitutive (of madness). This process does not conform to the mentality of double-entry bookkeeping which has sustained and conserved identity since Platonism, since it requires no reciprocal income to balance its outflow and expenditure. Metaphysics has always maintained that such an economy of squandering and wastage

would quickly dissipate its resources and soon lead into exhaustion and impotence. However, Nietzsche's revaluation of absence demonstrates that there is no
finality to 'expenditure'. Thus, the opposite principle to that which metaphysics
envisaged applies, though with certain differences: instead of 'expenditure' leading to a decrease in energy or resources it results in a continual increase of
stimulation, the more the process continues; however, this 'stimulation' cannot
be dependent upon a source (of energy) for its force, nor does it lead to an
accumulation (of energy), since it is always created from dissipation as death:

> the extreme sharpness of certain senses, so they understand a quite different
> sign-language – and create one – the condition that seems to be part of many
> nervous disorders – extreme mobility that turns into an extreme urge to com-
> municate; the desire to speak on the part of everything that knows how to make
> signs – a need to get rid of oneself, as it were, through signs and gestures; ability
> to speak of oneself through a hundred speech media – an explosive condition.
> One must first think of this condition as a compulsion and urge to get rid of
> the exuberance of inner tension through muscular activity and movements of
> all kinds; then as an involuntary co-ordination between this movement and the
> processes within (images, thoughts, desires) – as a kind of automatism of the
> whole muscular system impelled by strong stimuli within – inability to prevent
> reaction; the system of inhibitions suspended, as it were ... A kind of deafness
> and blindness towards the external world.[16]

Nietzsche describes the process of re-presentation, as it applies to the 'exceptional
states that condition the artist',[17] in terms of a contagion or nervous illness, in
which a sense of interiority is continually short-circuited through the collapse
of boundaries between interior and exterior. This elimination of identity, however, is taken up by the ceaseless discharge of signs and images. These, in their
turn, create blockages between inside and outside, which result in a profound
disconnection between the subject and the outside world: hence the madness of
the subject. Yet the resultant (absence of) interiority is constitutive of the identity
of the artist (as sign), even though this identity is lost or trashed before it is
formed. It is often claimed that Nietzsche's description of the artistic condition
in terms of an intense expenditure of forces, and as a sickness or contagion, is
close to that of the Romantic myth of the artist in which the subject is consumed
by a sense of inspiration bordering upon madness or illness. However, this
proposed link between the Nietzschean and Romantic artist frequently depends
upon a mis-recognition of Nietzsche's notion of 'expenditure'. This is harnessed
into a dialectic of creation and destruction that reconfirms a fantasy of presence.

These ideas can be examined further in relation to the Romantic myth of
Géricault, whose personality and work has often been represented in terms of
genius and excess. This is particularly true of the biographies and accounts of
the artist written in the nineteenth and early twentieth centuries, but it is also
applicable to more recent studies. However, in this analysis it will be unnecessary
to cite particular sources or variations in opinion, since it is offered both as an

outline of the biographical material that is referred to in every account of
Géricault, and as a discussion of the unconscious motivations through which it
is organized and repeated.[18]

The story of the development of Géricault's personality is always fraught
with tension and melancholy. This begins with the death of his mother in 1808,
when he was 16 years of age. Thereafter, Géricault's life is a catalogue of disasters.
A reckless love-affair with his aunt whilst in his mid-twenties produces a child;
the family intervenes and imposes a permanent separation between Géricault,
his lover and their child. A few years later, Géricault suffers a nervous breakdown;
a year after this the artist attempts to commit suicide. In the last few years of
his life, Géricault dissipates his private fortune through gambling and ruinous
investments. He contracts tuberculosis, which is exacerbated by a series of riding
accidents, and dies two years later after much suffering at the age of 33.

Letters written by Géricault to family and friends seem to confirm a personality that was emotionally disturbed, subject to severe bouts of depression
and paranoia; 'how you will pity me when I talk with you calmly about the
terrible troubles into which I have recklessly thrown myself ...'.[19] 'Why have
you left me, my friend ... I try in vain to find support; nothing seems solid,
everything escapes me, deceives me. Our earthly hopes and desires are only vain
fancies, our successes mere mirages that we try to grasp. If there is one thing
certain in this world, it is our pains. Suffering is real, pleasure only imaginary.'[20]
Contemporary descriptions of Géricault, such as those of the English architect
C. R. Cockerell, portray a man of extremes, prone to lengthy bouts of depression
periodically interrupted by outbursts of maniacal energy, 'lying torpid days &
weeks then rising to violent exertions. Riding, tearing, driving, exposing himself
to heat, cold, violence of all sorts'.[21]

In the prevailing accounts and representations of Géricault which have been
written since his death, the artist's experience of pain and suffering, and his
degeneration into madness and ill-health are seen as the preconditions for his
exceptional artistic talent. The intensity with which Géricault suffers, and the
loneliness he feels, is transferred for certain periods of time into an intensive
and singular commitment to making art that verges upon the masochistic. Thus
as a youth he studied composition and the old masters 'without going out and
always alone'.[22] Whilst working on The Raft of the Medusa he confined himself
to his studio and shut himself off from the outside world for almost eight months,
shaving his head as a sign of difference from the society life.

Although Géricault eventually died of natural causes, the suspicion arises
that his lifestyle may have precipitated his illness, or at least made him more
vulnerable to disease. As it cannot be proven otherwise, Géricault's life is
represented at the very least as imprudent or negligent, if not actually careless
and irresponsible. In this representation the subject finds confirmation, and
simultaneously gains control over Géricault's life, such that it is made into both
a source of, and an obstacle or a site of resistance to, creativity. This repeats a

metaphysical structure of presence and absence: the unobtainable fantasy of purity (in this case, that of unadulterated creativity) to which representation (Géricault's creative/destructive life of emotional intensity) refers, but fails to achieve. In this way Géricault's 'madness' – as a signifier of passion and excess – is returned to him as a subject: it creates and destroys Géricault, just as he creates and is destroyed.

The story of Géricault's life is always represented in terms of an inevitable decline (that begins at least as early as 1808) and of an untimely death. This story only comes into being with Géricault's death, which, at the age of 33, confirms the fact that his life was one of tragic loss – for himself and his acquaintances as well as for humanity. Although the legacy that Géricault left is that of a genius, the potential that his life contained is understood to be unfulfilled. This sense of a life which always verges upon another, equally or even more fruitful life (that never exists) becomes particularly acute in the descriptions and accounts of Géricault's last years, when the artist is bedridden and racked with pain. Although Géricault continues to produce numerous sketches and paintings, as well as lithographs, an overriding sense of unrealized ambition haunts the representation of these years. This centres upon the uncompleted plans for a Salon work, of which there were three (preliminary sketches exist for the *Reddition of Parga*, the *Opening of the Doors of the Inquisition* and the *African Slave Trade*). Géricault's own statements from this time are full of regret and yearning: 'If only I had painted five pictures! But I have done nothing, absolutely nothing!'; he called *The Raft of the Medusa* 'a vignette', and dreamt of working on enormous surfaces 'with buckets of paint and brooms for brushes'.[23] In this way Géricault's own words anticipate the dialectical strategies of later representations. His illness and death become the means for circumscribing his life with a qualification, such that it can be described as either relatively successful or relatively unsuccessful – it matters little which, since in either case a sense of inadequacy or lack predominates. A fantasy is, therefore, established of a better, perhaps more perfect, life – the one that was cut short and/or the one that could have continued, if degeneracy and death had not intervened.

In the metaphysical representations of Géricault's genius there is little or no difference in status between those offered by contemporary sources – whether they are written by the artist himself, or by acquaintances – and those of the biographers and historians of the artist. In effect, all reinforce metaphysical assumptions about the subject who is produced through repeating humanist misconceptions about absence and death. In Géricault's own texts the notion of the subject is maintained partly through the convention of writing in the first person (as one who formulates ideas and represents experiences), as well as through the idea of a person struggling with external conditions and circumstances, trying to make sense of their significance by communicating them to others. (This is a characteristic of most autobiographical texts.) In contemporary documentary sources written by friends and intimates as well as in later biographies and historical accounts of the artist, the concept of the subject is sustained through discussion of the struggle between creation and (self-)destruction that apparently overdetermines Géricault's personal life and his desire to make art. (To a large extent, this dynamic also informs Géricault's own writings.) As forms of narrative, both autobiographical and biographical texts continually oscillate between a series of polar oppositions that encompass aspiration/desolation, ebullience/depression, health/illness, rise/decline, potency/impotency and success/failure. In turn, they are framed by the oppositions of creation/destruction, birth/death and life/absence. These last series of oppositions govern the others, such that all aspects of Géricault's life are seen not only as a conflict with (self-)destruction, but more fundamentally as forces that are dialectically opposed to death/absence. Thus, 'death' is displaced as the death of the artist/subject and absence is trivialized as the absence of life (of the subject/artist). Metaphysical forms of representation and history rely upon these displacements; from them arises the idea of an individual subject such as 'Géricault', the producer of a particular, specifiable *œuvre* who was born in 1791 and died, after a life of creative struggle, in 1824.

As Nietzsche's philosophy stresses, 'death' is not subject to representation, although death is re-presentation (of absence). The Romantic and metaphysical myth of the artist repeatedly mis-represents this. Yet there are ways in which the documentary and historical accounts of an artist such as Géricault can be read in affirmative terms, so that death is freed of dialectical constraints. To this end it is important to recognize the vitalistic sense of exuberance in Géricault's character as the re-presentation of an energy or force that is continually outflowing without limit. That which is fantasized by metaphysics as an obstacle or a form of resistance to (in)finite production, such as alienation or madness or sickness, is revaluated as the effluence of death that binds the subject into the inexorable flow of death. This force of production is not attached to an individual, since the 'individual' is simply the product of the force, although s/he also re-presents it. Within this process of 'expenditure', that is, Géricault, everything is dissipated and integrated as 'loss'. There is, therefore, no need to interpret Géricault's actions and motivations from a psychological or psychoanalytic perspective, and certainly no need to dwell upon the 'melancholy' and alienated side of his personality. His 'alienation' is simply confirmation that the 'individual' lies beyond representation: 'the terrible troubles' into which he is recklessly thrown are unknowable, the 'days and weeks' of lying torpid are blank (they were for Cockerell in 1820, and they will remain so for us, today; such is the 'truth' of Géricault's personality). Similarly, the only importance that lies in the documented activities and exploits of 'Géricault' is that they, too, are void: they are the acts of a madman, without sense or purpose – this is as much true of his acts of recklessness or indulgence as of his acts of creativity. To try to describe or contextualize them in terms of motivations or influences is to miss their point, as no purpose lies behind them (which is not to say they are without purpose). Yet Géricault was never overcome by madness, just as he was never overwhelmed by sickness and disease: there never was a subject to be overcome or killed. The (insane) mind and the (dying) body are already death, in the same way as the subject is dead even in the moment of birth.

Once the metaphysical opposition between the (life of) the subject and (its) absence is overcome, then the issue of 'biography', as well as of 'historical' documentation and representation is revalued in its wake. The historical persona 'Géricault' thereby becomes interchangeable, for instance, with a certain Claude Petit who signed a contract to serve as his substitute in the army in 1811.[24] Petit died the following year in an army hospital in Germany. Some historians may see in this episode a further dialectical relation between the subject and (its) absence, describing Géricault's subsequent life and work as a form 'of substitution and compensation'[25] (of death). However, a Nietzschean reading of history suggests that Géricault *is* the dead soldier Petit, although 'Géricault' is also discontinuous with 'Petit', since 'they' are not united, even in death. Therefore, Géricault and Petit are subjects, but only in so far as they are conceived of as both loss and re-presentation.

What, then, are the implications of interpreting Géricault's art in Nietzschean terms, and how might the histories and narratives of its production be affected or revalued by this interpretation? Two paintings may serve to highlight some of the issues at stake in these matters, whilst also drawing out further Nietzschean ideas about the subject, through his conception of the tragic hero as 'will to power'.

The *Charging Chasseur (Equestrian Portrait of M.D. ...)* (Figure 1) was exhibited in the Salon of 1812, and alongside the *Wounded Cuirassier Leaving the Field of Battle* (Figure 2) in 1814. The two paintings have frequently been analysed in terms of a set of contrastive differences. Thus in his article on Géricault, 'Roman Virtue', Tom Crow divides the paintings into the oppositions of 'light versus heavy, active versus passive, mounted versus earthbound, vigorous versus debilitated'.[26] An earlier study, by Géricault's first biographer, Charles Clément, extends these oppositions into a story in which the *Charging Chasseur* and the *Wounded Cuirassier* are seen to symbolize France's rise and decline in the Napoleonic wars:

> In 1812 success was still in the air, whilst in 1814 everyone knew they were facing defeat ... The echo of the cries of distress from our suffering armies on the plains of Russia resounded through the lands. Hearts were full of fear and terror. It is this universal feeling which Géricault expressed in his painting and explored in the *Wounded Cuirassier* ... He painted two pictures, the first about glory and the other about faded glory.[27]

On one level, these analyses seem to respect the differences between the paintings. However, on another level, a metaphysical error is sustained, especially in Clément's text, in which a dialectical opposition is constructed between power

FIGURE 1. Théodore Géricault, *Charging Chasseur (Equestrian Portrait of M.D.)*. Oil on canvas, 1812

and loss. Clément suggests that the story of the Napoleonic wars is one of power's decline. Therefore, the concept of power emblematized by Géricault's paintings is made the subject of (its) lack. Inevitably, this idea is circumscribed by the fantasy of absolute power or presence – although it is in the nature of this fantasy that it can never be realized or fully acknowledged.

Within a Nietzschean schema of thought, there is no originary notion of

FIGURE 2. Théodore Géricault, *Wounded Cuirassier Leaving the Field of Battle*.
Oil on canvas, 1814

power which can be put into decline, as loss is the a priori condition of the subject
as re-presentation. 'Power' resides in the 'intoxication' of the re-presentation of
loss, and not in the control or suppression of a pre-existing identity. To try to
deny this is tantamount to waging war on death; an impossible task, but one
which has obsessed the history of metaphysics and ensnared the subject in a futile
attempt to assume responsibility for (his or her) destruction. From this arises the
'modern' concept and practice of warfare (and, indeed, of science) as violent
struggle or combat with death.

The absurdity of these ideas is put to the sword in Géricault's paintings: the violence of metaphysics is pitted against violence as excess. In both paintings battle, and the landscape of battle, are elemental forces filling the agitated atmosphere with turbulence and violence. Since the cuirassier is situated at the edge of a cliff or ravine where dark clouds loom overhead, it is unclear whether the atmosphere is natural or produced. In effect, Nature and war are conjoined: the fire of the sun is the glow of battle in the *Charging Chasseur*, and this turns (back) into blackness in the *Wounded Cuirassier*. Darkness enshrouds the figures and landscape of the *Wounded Cuirassier*, drawing the clouds into a veil where they meet the light in the distance; a veil of haziness also hangs over the scene of the *Charging Chasseur*. As a consequence, it seems as if there is no source of light for the battles' saturated atmosphere: the sun's disappearance is replaced by a volatile, destructive pall which burns the sky. This becomes the illusion of the sun's presence at the edges of the pictures, a raw image emitted in pervasive density. These are the conditions of the battle and the light by which it is fought; the gleam of explosions from the cannons and the fires of the burning wreckage have their own separate intensity, but in another sense they are inseparable from the surrounding incandescence. In the background of the *Charging Chasseur* artillerymen advance into battle; in immediate proximity other soldiers and horses ride the flames of war. They are already burnt by its ferocity, dark spectres which only exist by virtue of the immense destruction in which they are embroiled. Further waves of soldiers and cavalrymen follow in their trail, of whom 'M.D.' is one. His grey stallion expresses the intoxication of battle, rearing upwards with flying mane and foaming mouth. Clément suggested that this stallion is 'the horse of War',[28] thus maximizing the violence of the horse's emotions: it is not simply fear that fills his wide, staring eye, but a sublime sense of destruction already in excess of Austerlitz.[29] As a consequence, the specific, historical battle of Austerlitz is also transformed into (the image of) excess.

Although the chasseur is also inflamed by the heat of battle, and his sword is drawn, ready for combat, his head is turned away from the soldiers ahead. The studied artifice of the pose seems to draw on the vanity of a cavalryman who was a member of Napoleon's elite corps, and, on another level, arises as a consequence of the convention of portraiture. A sense of artifice, even theatricality, is also evident in the *Wounded Cuirassier*. This is produced by the unusual combination of a single figure and monumental history painting; in addition, it is created by the soldier's awkward stance and the severity in the foreshortening of the horse. Crow suggests that the contrived nature of both paintings is a result of Géricault's limited experience in tackling monumental work.[30] But this implies an opposition between Géricault's paintings and an ideal or standard of history painting. However, Crow's criticism is helpful in so far as it demonstrates the impossibility of situating Géricault's painting, like all representation, in relation to a fantasy of prescribed rules and taste. In this way the mannered poses of the cavalrymen are thrown into another register, wherein they merge with an image world that arises as the counterpart to the absence of metaphysics. Nietzsche calls this world the 'Apollinian', one of two 'artistic energies which burst forth from nature herself, *without the mediation of the artist*'.[31] That images arise naturally and spontaneously is affirmed, according to Nietzsche, by Dionysian 'will', the correlative of the 'Apollinian' tendency, whose essence is illuminated by the legend of Dionysus: 'wonderful myths tell that as a boy he was torn to pieces by the Titans and now is worshipped in this state as Zagreus. Thus it is intimated that this dismemberment, the properly Dionysian *suffering*, is like a transformation into air, water, earth and fire'.[32]

In Nietzsche, dismemberment is another term for (the irreducibility of) death, so that the mutilation performed by the Titans is not specific (only) to a moment in the god's life, but rather is executed perpetually. Suffering, or the agonies of mutilation, precedes the god's existence and this 'excess' of violence simultaneously creates the subject – both the god and the 'individual' hero. Yet both are also representation (the four elements of Phenomemon).

Dionysian myth highlights the nature and extent of the cuirassier's wound. Metaphysics conceives of a wound as a laceration upon the body bearing a dialectical relation to death; hence, it is interpreted in terms of debility and as a potential source of impotence. The cuirassier's wound is not a partial infliction upon a historicized body. 'He' is anonymous; a personification of 'the unknown soldier' killed in episodes of war beyond memory. Similarly, the chasseur whose identity lies in the absent 'M.D. ...'. The wound of the cuirassier, therefore, is totalizing. It cannot be envisaged in metaphysical terms: this is why it does not appear upon the soldier's body; instead, wounding is perpetrated upon the elemental landscape, where it pours through the blackness, consuming horse and rider. Nature's disjection creates emptiness: the cuirassier's ghostly pallor, the horses's severed body, the ravine below. Emptiness is also constitutive of the chasseur's implacability, as he sits atop his horse, an Apollinian image born of destruction, absorbed and glamorous. The soldier turns in on himself, only to be discharged as a vortex of fire. The cuirassier, too, is implacable, in the thrall of infliction. As both soldiers turn away with viduous eyes, they look towards an undecidable spot, within the space of the picture yet beyond it. The viewer is transfigured within the discontinuity of the gaze, becoming both sign and witness. Like the soldiers, we are conscripted into apocalyptic service, for which no funereal rites remain.

Notes

1 F. Nietzsche, *The Gay Science*, New York: Vintage Books, 1974, book II, section 102, 'A remark for philologists', pp. 157–8.

2 W. Kaufmann explains, '*In* (or *ad*) *usum Delphini*: originlly, an edition of Greek or Roman classics, prepared especially for the Dauphin, i.e. the crown prince of France. Nietzsche uses the plural to refer, figuratively speaking, to future royalty', *ibid.*, p. 158, n. 50.

3 *Ibid.*, book II, section 83, 'Translations', p. 137.

4 *Ibid.*

5 *Ibid.*

6 F. Nietzsche, *Twilight of the Idols*, in *The Portable Nietzsche*, ed. W. Kaufmann, New York: Penguin, 1976, pp. 485–6.

7 W. Kaufmann includes an extended list of references to this infamous idea of Nietzsche's in a footnote: *The Gay Science*, p. 167, n. 1.

8 The title of a book by Nietzsche, first published in 1886.

9 Oil, Paris, Louvre (292 × 194 cm).

10 Oil, Paris, Louvre (358 × 294 cm).

11 Nietzsche, *Twilight of the Idols*, p. 485. For an account of the first section of 'How the "true world" finally became a fable; the history of an error' and how it may compare to the following sections, cf. M. Heidegger, *Nietzsche*, vols I and II, San Francisco: Harper & Row, 1991, pp. 203–4. The last part of this quotation reads in full, '*it becomes female*, it becomes Christian'.

12 Nietzsche, *Twilight of the Idols*, p. 485.

13 *Ibid.*, pp. 485–6.

14 cf. F. Nietzsche, *The Will to Power*, New York: Vintage Books, 1976, p. 428.

15 *Ibid.*, p. 428.

16 *Ibid.*, pp. 428–9.

17 *Ibid.*, p. 428.

18 For a selected bibliography on Géricault, cf. L. Eitner, *Géricault, His Life and Work*, London: Orbis, 1983, pp. 364–6.

19 *Ibid.*, p. 134.

20 *Ibid.*, p. 135.

21 *Ibid.*, p. 220.

22 *Ibid.*, p. 77.

23 *Ibid.*, p. 273.

24 *Ibid.*, p. 19.

25 T. Crow, 'Roman Virtue', *Artscribe*, 90 (February/March, 1992), p. 52.

26 *Ibid.*

27 C. Clément, *Géricault, étude biographique et critique*, Paris, 1867 reprint, with preface and catalogue supplement by L. Eitner, New York, 1974, p. 65 (my translation).

28 cf. L. Eitner, *Géricault, His Life and Work*, p. 28.

29 *Ibid.*

30 T. Crow, 'Roman Virtue', p. 52.

31 F. Nietzsche, *The Birth of Tragedy*, New York: Vintage Books, 1967, p. 38.

32 *Ibid.*, p. 73.

PART 2

Refiguring identity
in politics

The ecstatic solace of culture: self, not-self and other; a psychoanalytic view

With hindsight it seems evident that, at its best, feminism inaugurated a complete revolution in the developmental spiral of human understanding. To extend Althusser's metaphor[1] of every advance in human understanding taking place at the cost of a blow to human narcissism, and extending it probably well beyond what he would have approved, the Copernican, Darwinian, Marxist and Freudian revolutions were followed by a revolution which, unlike its antecedents, will never bear the name of a paternal leader. The truth, and perhaps beauty, of feminism is that it can never be owned by any of its makers. The anonymous may have contributed more than those whose career depends on establishing a name for themselves, and without romanticizing the intellectual, political and daily practice of feminism by casting it as an anarchist heroine, its meaning and its transmission never resides in the self-advancement of individuals.

A further blow to the narcissism of philosophy followed the decentring of geocentric, anthropocentric, egocentric, middle-class and patrilineal traditions when it became evident that further, and even more unacceptable, distortions issued from the Eurocentrism that had become hegemonic within imperial and colonial histories. Post-colonial theory offers another revolution in the evolution of the humanities, and has effects in the theory and practice of sciences too. The white narcissism that defends the fragile European ego from becoming conscious of its capacity for destructiveness and sadism has become a liability within European culture. And it is the challenge to this narcissism that has fully developed the use of the concept of projection, as an explanation of the mechanism through which 'otherness' is constructed and deployed.[2] The concept of projection is used in its psychoanalytic sense as well as its common sense, to account for the way in which aspects of the self which are disowned and repudiated may be attributed to a concept of 'not-self' or 'other' which is then experienced as belonging to someone or something in the outside world. An extremely powerful mechanism, which can affect objectivity, projection has a logic which is far from the logic of rational scientific thinking, but yet has the power to affect perceptions of reality. To distinguish its technical definition from its common-sense usage we shall relate it to its kindred concepts of identification and projective identification.

The redefinition of the concept of self lies at the heart of feminist practice, and so leads us to find a competent and adequate understanding of the constitution of the self in its relation to, and responsibility for, others. Well beyond a Romantic problem, it is a task for science and not only for moral philosophy, ethics, religion or poetry, and so feminism has turned to anthropology and psychoanalysis to provide descriptions and explanations of what constitutes the 'self' for any given society. If anthropology emphasizes the variations of how societies and cultures place an individual in relation to others and self within their social and cultural structures, psychoanalysis has emphasized the immutability of certain Oedipal and pre-Oedipal structures that constitute the self, whatever social form of recognition these are given in the representations and culture of a society.

In the Classical tradition of European culture the form of recognition given to wisdom is that of self-knowledge. 'Know thyself' is the Sphinx's admonition to Oedipus, enabling the audience of the Greek myth to use the surface of the narrative to reflect on the enigma of self, not-self, and other. This unholy trinity is echoed in the narrative enigma of time, with the three intersecting axes of origin, destiny and choice. For the self to solve the riddle of the Sphinx, origins must be disinterred and known; if the Sphinx, half wild animal and half woman but all id, represents the riddle of human ageing and the unconsciousness of the Oedipus complex, it is a riddle that every listener must fathom for him or herself. For Oedipus to reach the crossroads of choice without being compelled to commit parricide and to flee from conflict, time and its future, destiny must be actively grasped and not passively endured as a fate foretold by the oracle. Narratives can play the part of the oracle in the Oedipus myth, foretelling comic or tragic narrative closures against which we may measure the significance of our lives. They take us outside ourselves, transporting us through identification to the time and place of another; the predicaments of our own lives are temporarily suspended, supplanted by the actions and passions of protagonists such as Oedipus. In his narrative, as in other aspects of culture, we are offered access to the sublime, a transcendence of the prison of the limitations of the self, the limitations of our time, space and knowledge of the effort and work required to change these. Both terrifying and uplifting, access to the sublime depends on our acceptance of a certain kind of death, a death of the self within its immediate needs, and a rebirth of the self within the sphere of representation, a release, simultaneously losing and refinding.

This is one use of identification. It is when part of the ego is temporarily suspended, as in the 'suspension of disbelief' required to turn the proscenium into a world, inky marks into words and coloured moving lights into a diegesis, and in its place the ego is able to cathect, or invest with meaning, the imaginary characters inhabiting the world of representation. The absence and presence of the ego's first ontogenetic object, the mother, is transformed into awareness of the flux of feeling good or bad; the world 'being there' or things falling apart.[3] The psychoanalytic definition of identification covers a range of linked experiences such as those of empathy, imitation, assimilation and projection, and can be used to describe intrapsychic relations as well as relationships between people. In order to distinguish between these relationships it has been suggested that identification should be differentiated from 'incorporation', 'introjection' and 'internalization':

> Incorporation and introjection are the prototypes of identification – or at any rate of certain modes of identification where the mental process is experienced and symbolized as a bodily one (ingesting, devouring, keeping something inside oneself, etc.). The distinction between identification and internalization is a more complex one, since it brings into play theoretical assumptions concerning the nature of what it is that the subject assimilates himself to.[4]

The bodily nature of incorporation and introjection refers the subject back to the infantile prototypes of adult relationships, and above all the the development of a very gradual emergence of self from the illusion of infantile omnipotence, the primary form being the infant at the breast, and child care in general, during which the infant is unaware of dependence. If food is incorporated, a corporeal and emotional experience is introjected, one which could be put into words as the gradual mastery of frustration and satisfaction of need. To return to Yeats's metaphor, there is a centre once again, whch can 'hold'.

Internalization refers to a more sophisticated reworking of these two, more primary processes; it is a third turn of the spiral of development. The metaphor of an 'inner' world has been suggested as a description of psychic reality, and is a term which has the advantage of implying a clear opposition between the supposedly physical, material nature of external reality and whatever it is that is conceived as 'mental', psychological, emotional. Unfortunately this convenient opposition is oversimplistic and therefore tends to be distorting. Joseph Sandler[5] has proposed the term 'representational world', which has the advantage of recognizing the relational function of representation, and does not oppose inner to outer. If psychic reality is understood as representational, this does not prescribe the nature of the signifying material, which may be an aspect of material reality, of actions and institutions as well as dreams, emotions and fantasy. 'The theory of identification presupposes that the world of 'external reality', in so far as it is significant, is rendered so by virtue of being cathected with psychic meaning. Or, more accurately, that meaning depends on the relationship between a subject and his or her objects.

In Lacanian terms this definition includes a recognition of the role of the Symbolic, along with the Imaginary and Real, but unlike the structuralist thought of Lacan's theory, the Symbolic, for Sandler, is not seen as a greater determinant of subjectivity than is the body. In theoretical terms, linguistics is juxtaposed with biology, and both are recognized as component sciences of psychoanalysis. A brief discussion of Freud's metapsychology may help to clarify the theoretical basis of contemporary uses of these concepts.

The general theory of the mind that Freud developed from his clinical work he called the metapsychology, and it is possible to trace the development of this general theory as an autonomous process, as the history of science, as well as to understand it in terms of the development of therapeutic practice, or in terms of the development of Freud's own life. There is a subtle and complicated relationship between the clinical practice in which psychoanalysis was being used to attenuate or cure the suffering of those who recognized their illnesses as psychogenic, and the hope that psychoanalysis could become a science with the ability to describe the structure of the mind, as well as to identify and cure its illnesses. From the outset, with his early *Project For a Scientific Psychology*, Freud attempted to set out a general theory of the mind; and by 1900 with the theoretical chapters of *The Intepretation of Dreams* the construction of the metapsychology as we know it today was under way. By 1925, Freud could retrospectively define his metapsychology as being composed of three axes of co-ordination; 'the *topographical*, the *dynamic*, and the *economic*, respectively'.[6] Although there are references to each of these axes of theory throughout his work, Freud reserved the term for describing work which attempts to describe mental phenomena in relation to all three co-ordinates simultaneously. The topographic aspect describes the mind in terms of its agencies or component 'parts'.

The first topography, dating from the *Studies in Hysteria*, describes the mind in terms of an archaeological layering of surfaces and depths, the uppermost system of consciousness overlying a system of preconsciousness, and these two underpinned by a radically different mental system of the unconscious. Not only could this account for the 'absences' of hysteria, by understanding these as successive alterations in the subjects' layers of consciousness, but this first topography was adequate to theorize the functioning of dreams. The dream images that remain in memory on waking are representations that operate in the system of the preconscious or consciousness (so-called secondary process thinking), and are the manifest content of a dream, a disguised version of the latent dream thoughts which emanate from the unconscious (and its primary process thinking). To intepret from the manifest content to the latent content, the four mechanisms of the dreamwork: condensation, displacement, symbolization and secondary revision are used. For example, just as dreaming may involve the condensation of the images of wife and queen to represent the memory of mother, or the image of a room filling with water to represent the ego being 'flooded' with emotion, so the interpretation of dreams involves conceptually inverting these mechanisms to deduce the significance of the latent dream thoughts. As a further complication, dreaming makes use of the experiences of the previous day, the 'day's residues', as material for significant images and memories for the unconscious to express itself.

The second topography, sometimes called the structural topography, was developed alongside the use of the first when clinical material could no longer be satisfactorily explained in terms of consciousness and unconsciousness, and it was finally conceptualized in 1923 in *The Ego and the Id*, where Freud describes the mind as comprising id, ego and super-ego. The fact that both topographies contain a tripartite structure is not irrelevant, but it is wrong to simply map the first on to the second. Both topographies continue to be used separately and sometimes simultaneously in comtemporary practice. Lacan's tripartite topography is occasionally added to Freud's two versions. What the metapsychology's topographical axis makes very clear is that the process of identification involves a range of different kinds of communication. Some may be from unconscious to preconscious, from super-ego to ego or from super-ego to id, and this may take place as communication between people as well as between intra-subjective agencies. An entire psychological school has been built up on classifying relationships through the 'transactions' of the parent, adult and child components of one subject addressing and responding to the similar components of another subject.

The economic axis of the metapsychology describes the way in which energy, emanating from the instincts and drives, is active in a psychological sense. It describes a drive in terms of its pressure, source, aim and object. The dynamic axis describes the way that the topographic interacts with the economic, how drives animate and motivate the agencies of id, ego, and super-ego, for example, and how drives are modulated and transformed by psychic processes such as neutralization and sublimation. Dynamic processes such as cathexis, transference and anxiety arising from intrapsychic conflict are central to the process of identification. Identification is a process that is characteristic of the 'normal' mind, as well as playing an important part in psychic illnesses. Hysteria may involve the unconscious identification of a subject with a number of significant individuals or predicaments from the subject's infancy. Perversion, with its regressive qualities, entails an idealization of infantile identifications. Melancholia, or depression, includes identification with a lost or hated object which binds ambivalence within a subject's psyche. In order to understand identification it has to be considered from the perspective of all three axes of the metapsychology, which then enables identification to be discussed as a component part of culture: the ability to inhabit a 'representational world'.

One of the most useful of Freud's essays, from the point of view of gaining a metapsychological understanding of identification, is his description of how absence of a love object changes the ego of a subject, and how ambivalence is awakened by the absence of constancy of love. This he describes and theorizes in *Mourning and Melancholia* (1915), where he compares the spontaneous reorganization of the ego in bereavement and mourning a loss, with the equivalent changes in depression or melancholia, where the ego behaves as if it has suffered a traumatic loss. Freud notes that melancholia has three preconditions: 'loss of object, ambivalence and regression of libido into the ego'; depression involves the regression of 'narcissistic object choice to narcissism'.[7] A central comparison is how the work of mourning enables a lost object to be re-created within the ego and invested with a love equivalent to the object, enriching the ego and its relation to the external world, whereas melancholia, when it is a pathological form of mourning, cannot 'lose' the object, nor find another, and thus retains the ambivalent relationship to it, thereby impoverishing the ego and its relation to the external world. Freud's essay, focusing on the part played by aggression in the form of ambivalence, opens up the exploration of other manifestations of aggression, from sadism and masochism as perversions, to the internalization of aggression turned against the self, or the compulsion to destroy hope, as in unconscious guilt.[8] In *Beyond the Pleasure Principle* (1920) Freud explores forms of repetition based on trauma, and proposes a concept of the death instincts, in which aggression is conceived as primarily directed against the self and only secondarily directed outward in the form of aggression or destructiveness.

We discussed above how entering into the game of culture and narrative involves a play of losing and refinding within the structure of identification, where myth can temporarily hold the subject's representational world by being internalized and thereby enriching the subject's ego. Melancholia prevents a subject from risking such a loss, and from entering the world where, to quote Robert Frost: 'Only when love and need are one / and work is play for mortal stakes.' Culture can enable a subject successfully to mourn certain inevitable losses, and can provide the ecstatic solace of communication, the shared community of representational worlds. It does so through identification. If it is evident that culture gives form to a range of drives and their dynamic and topographic vicissitudes, there is still the question of the part played by the death instincts in culture. Do they find a particular form of expression, such as their sexualization in perversion as it exists particularly in forms of sensuous and visual imagery? Are there expressions of the death instincts in the repetitions and fragmentations of modernism? Is it narrative closure and the disillusion of the identificatory bond that holds the subject within the text that is the expression of death within culture?[9]

Cultural theory, of course, defines many different types of identification. Literary analysis has explored authorship studies, which imply that writers find a special kind of personal significance in the texts they produce, even where such studies do not use terms such as 'transference' or 'catharsis'. Textual analysis explores the structures internal to the text, describing the complex economy of characters, narrative, diegetic spaces, setting, dialogue and narration which comprise some of the structures that hold the reading subject in identification. Structural anthropology, with Levi-Strauss's analysis of myth, and Russian formalists such as Vladimir Propp, provided prototypes of this kind of analysis. More recently, novels have included references to the act of reading in the structure of the novel itself; intertextuality, formalism and references to the libidinal economy of literature as seduction are common tropes in modern writing.

In film theory there has been a similar development, with auteurism implying a psychological biography of director or producer. The industrial nature of film made literary analysis largely irrelevant except in art cinema, where film was seen to be striving towards acceptance as 'the seventh art'. Structural analysis of narrative proved immensely successful as anonymous industrial production resembles the collective nature of myth in pre-industrial societies. Christian Metz differentiates a number of approaches to the psychoanalysis of cinema, and sets aside the auteurist, the analysis of film scripts, and the psychobiography as diversions from the real task confronting film theory, which is to understand the nature of the spectator's cinematic experience with what Metz calls the 'imaginary signifier', which differentiates film from literature, painting, drama and opera. Psychoanalysis enables Laura Mulvey, for example, to differentiate between primary and secondary identification in the three gazes comprising the hierarchy of looks in classical film narrative, where primary identification revolves around the spectator's look at the screen and the camera's look at the pro-filmic event, and secondary identification revolves around the intra-diegetic looks of the characters within the film. On a dynamic level, Mulvey suggests that primary identification depends on the activation of sexual instincts within fetishistic defences, and that secondary identification depends on the activation of ego instincts within narcissism. Her description of the visual pleasure in narrative film uses both Freudian and Lacanian concepts and is a fully metapsychological description of identification in this cultural form.[10]

There is a range of approaches to interpreting the structure of identification in arts such as painting and sculpture. Psychoanalysts such as Chasseguet-Smirgel have emphasized the regressive aspects of visual art, which is based so much in corporeal reality, and she has explored the relationship between creativity and perversion.[11] Kleinians such as Hanna Segal have modified Freud's critique of art as being a withdrawal from the reality principle and a turning towards pleasure, and in its place she has suggested that art has the power to release reparative wishes, and therefore enables the (creating or viewing) subject to broach experiences of death-like depression that are not usually encountered in daily life. Segal suggests that the artist has a particular sensitivity to certain forms of reality, to the materials with which he or she works such as colour, line, texture, substance etc., and towards 'inner reality', which is the Kleinian designation for the psychic reality of states of mind, emotions, thoughts, moods etc.[12]

Lacan's concept of the mirror phase is very useful here, as it offers the insight that the structure of the image is inherently connected to the subject's desperate quest for imaginary unity, to counteract the feeling of fragmentation and powerlessness that precedes the mastery of the ego. The satisfaction felt by achieving imaginary unity through the construction of a merged ego and ego-ideal in visual representation is at the cost of the structured alienation of self into divided identities of observer and observed. Lacan notes that the fusion and fission of this psychic process generate enormous amounts of aggression, which are then bound within the subjectivity of spectatorship. This theory offers a valuable insight into the origins of the philosophical need for a 'unitary' subject, and why, within the humanities, it has recently become possible and necessary to think of a 'divided' subject.

The forms of identification at work in music are, I think, very difficult to put into words. It is said that music is the art form which most closely conveys emotional states, and words are already a more abstract form of equivalence of emotions. It is well known that strong emotional states make it difficult to speak or use words in a coherent and rational form.

Projection is a mechanism that plays a part in identification. It, too, is both normal and potentially pathological. Normal uses include the ability to empathize and the ability to attribute to others aspects of one's own experiences. Idealized projections may be at work in religious phenomena such as the belief in God as a benevolent and supreme power. Like identification, projection is often found in strong emotional states such as falling in love, falling out of love and in transference (a term usually reserved for qualifying the relationship of analyst and analysand in treatment, but according to Freud, this is not necessarily its only manifestation). More typically, projection is used as a concept in clinical theory to describe the way in which 'negative' attributes of the self that are in some way unacceptable to the ego are denied, 'expelled from the self and located in another person or thing. Projection so understood is a defence of very primitive origin which may be seen at work in paranoia, but also in "normal" modes of thought such as superstition.'[13] More normal aspects of projection would include the subjects' ability to project themselves on to a character in a narrative text or to allow such a character to be projected on to themselves; and these are really aspects of identification.

When it is an aspect of paranoia it can be a defence of psychotic intensity and chronic immutability. The original analysis of paranoia, Freud's 'Psychoanalytic notes on an autobiographical account of a case of paranoia' (1911), better known as the Schreber case study, shows how the paranoid delusions that Schreber felt to be persecuting him were systematic projections of unacceptable desire, particularly homosexuality.[14] For Freud the regressive aspect of paranoia was manifest in the delusions of grandeur that are characteristic of this psychosis, and the projection of sexual desire manifest in the form of delusional jealousy.

Melanie Klein sought to establish the 'psychotic core' at the centre of normal adult subjectivity by connecting it to early infantile emotional development. She proposed that early infancy is characterized by what will later be a 'paranoid-schizoid position', and that this can be transformed into the possibility of growth through entering the 'depressive position', where the latter is not descriptive of the depressive illness theorized by Freud, but refers to the capacity to accept object loss and to symbolize. For Melane Klein the 'PS and D positions' remain as psychic structures within adult subjectivity and can be found in many forms of neurotic and psychotic illness, as well as in 'normal' behaviour. The former is characterized by its relation to part objects (fragments rather than entirely human phenomena), and these part objects are split into good and bad, reflecting the subject's projection of the affects of love and hate on to satisfying or frustrating aspects of the relationship. The defence of splitting results in the subject's weak and unintegrated ego relating to idealized or terrifying, good or bad objects; if the bad object is internalized, the fear is that it will cause death. Whereas a healthy, stronger ego (one in Klein's D position) is capable of using symbols to represent objects, and thus to think about and tolerate or control anxiety, the subject in the PS position employs especially the defences of splitting, denial and projection, and is therefore in a constant state of action.[15]

Of particular interest to us here is the Kleinian concept of *projective identification*, which is one defence mechanism closely associated with the PS position described above. The prototype of this defence mechanism is, according to Klein, to be found in the infant's predicament when reaching the height of the development of sadistic impulses, at an age when the ego is too immature to employ other means of control. The infant has a phantasy (unconscious fantasy) of forcefully entering the mother's body, so as to control and destroy it from within; this is a phantasy of projecting part of, or its whole self into a container, the mother. Whereas this may be an actual experience of threat and relief for an infant, it continues to operate in adults as a phantasy. A curious fact is that this psychotic mechanism can be employed quite commonly in daily life, and a subject can make someone else have an emotional experience that the subject is incapable of experiencing for him or herself. As projective identification usually entails the expulsion of denied aggression, the intolerable emotional experiences associated with it, those that tend to be activated in the recipient, are those of guilt, pain and despair. As a form of communication that goes from unconscious to unconscious, it can create feelings of unreality and nightmare or dream qualities in the bond between projecting subject and recipient subject. Sometimes the recipient is aware of the fact of being caught up in a representational world; sometimes, if it cannot be understood as communication, it is just 'meaningless' suffering inflicted by one person on another.

Betty Joseph describes the use of such a concept in analytic practice, when a patient was able repeatedly to create feelings of failure and despair in the analyst, which she then interpreted as part of a sado-masochistic intrapsychic relationship being played out within the transference, with the analyst cast in the role of the helpless victim. Was this an attempt to create a masochistic relationship, or was it a communication of despair?[16] The difficulty of this question is one with many implications beyond therapeutic practice. Although projective identification is most easily recognized within the clinical setting, where transference phenomena are especially activated, it is by no means limited to being manifested within clinical work alone. For those who believe that there is an active psychotic core in all subjectivity, its presence is ubiquitous. For those who understand projection as a particularly primitive defence, it is manifest in a range of situations which create regression.

In a political context we find projective identification active in the forms of persecution that are characteristic of sexism and racism. In situations where women are subjected to control through abusive or violent behaviour, there is obviously a relationship of a regressed subject to his or her 'bad object', who takes the place of a real or integral person. Equally obvious is the way in which a group distinguished by its ethnic difference may come to function as the 'bad object' of a regressed society; the persecution and near extermination of European Jews fifty years ago is an example of how an entire continent can actively participate in a psychotic action which thereby becomes historically 'normal'.[17] These two examples are from political areas that are sometimes considered secondary, marginal or diversionary in relation to the 'real' politics of class exploitation. Over the last decade a new category of politics has emerged. Variously described as postmodern, post-Marxist, or identity politics, it is characterized by its recognition of the necessarily heterogeneous, if not fragmented, basis of alliances or interests. This is in contrast to assuming that there is a unified mass of shared interest or need, which would automatically lead people to identify their political interests. If historical materialism provided a unified and rational theory of the politics of class, there seems to be no equivalent unification of the history or theory of identity politics. In fact the limitations of historical materialism could be seen as the starting-point of identity politics. Classical Marxism omits any sustained understanding of gender identity, race or ethnicity, childhood and ageing, as countless critiques have pointed out.

Identity politics is often contrasted as the weaker half in opposition to policy politics, the former implying transience, which contrasts with the latter's permanence; imaginary predicaments to the other's reality; fragmented and irrational thinking to the other's unified and rational theory. It is likened to a hysterical woman who, by making adjustments to her image, believes herself to be restructuring her position in the world, or to an actor who can speak any lines, but cannot tell whether his own words are 'lines' or not. These are contrasted to the solidity and masculinity of strongly-felt socialist conviction. For many, the question of 'identity' is simply classified as so much irritating and irrelevant 'nonsense' which threatens to deflect meaning from the gravity of the real issues which should be our responsibility.

The long courtship and 'unhappy marriage' of feminism and Marxism has offered many explanations of why either gender or class should be understood as the 'primary contradiction' of society. In Britain the debates around domestic labour sought to establish whether or not the unpaid labour of women within the home contributes to the accumulation of surplus value within capitalism, and thus whether women's political loyalty was allied to class politics or not. This complex issue was never resolved, but it did lead to an exploration of the multiple dimensions of women's experiences and to a radical questioning of how the 'public' and 'private' worlds should be demarcated. New thoughts on the effect of subjectivity on external, objective reality began to be possible. What had previously been designated the province of mysticism, moral philosophy, religion, romantic love, or even mind-'expanding' ventures with chemical, psychological or emotional intoxication began to become the subject of sustained rational thinking. The concept of projective identification, if considered in its psychoanalytic sense, can provide a materialist way of understanding this kind of communication and this level of interaction. Although it is often thought of as an uncanny, or supernatural, phenomenon it is a well-known and understood occurrence in psychoanalysis.

There is more to the recipient's response than an ethical question of assuming, say, Christian charity in forgiving those who 'do not know what they do', as it becomes the responsibility of the 'victims' to think for themselves through the unthinking psychosis, which is the ignorance and power of their persecutors. The experience of being rendered powerless, often through being subject to such strong emotions that thinking becomes very difficult, is one that is a paradoxical privilege when it is understood as a message about what the powerful find intolerable about themselves. It enables the powerless to understand the dynamics of envy and to continue with their project of self-realization without being thwarted by the weakness and limitations of the powerful. This, it seems to me, is the dimension of a politics of identity. However, as we have described above, if the concept of a politics of identity is taken seriously, which means that identity becomes the focus of a sustained exploration and understanding, we have the opportunity of extending the responsibility and integrity which is a possibility for human destiny.

Notes

1 Louis Althusser, 'Freud and Lacan,' in *Lenin and Philosophy*, London: New Left Books, 1971.
2 Sander Gilman's *Difference and Pathology*, Ithaca and London: Cornell University Press, 1985, *Freud, Race and Gender*, Princeton, NJ: Princeton University Press, 1993, *Inscribing the Other*, Lincoln, Neb.: University of Nebraska Press, 1991, provide the most explicit and sustained use of this concept of projection.
3 This memorable line from W. B. Yeats's poem 'Sailing to Byzantium' has been much used; African writer Achebe uses it as a title for his novel *Things Fall Apart*; British psychoanalyst Nina Coltart uses it in her exploration of states of mind that could be called prelinguistic in her essay 'Slouching towards Bethlehem', in *The Independent Tradition*, ed. G. Kohon, London: Free Association Books, 1987.
4 Jean Laplanche and Jean-Baptiste Pontalis, *The Language of Psychoanalysis*, London: Hogarth Press, 1973, p. 207.
5 Joseph Sandler, 'From safety to superego' in *Selected Papers of Joseph Sandler*, London: Karnak Books, 1978.
6 Sigmund Freud, 'An autobiographical study', Standard Edition, 20, p. 58.
7 Sigmund Freud, 'Mourning and melancholia', Standard Edition, 14, p. 250.
8 In a recent essay 'Assimilation, identity and entertainment, the Hollywood solution', Barry Curtis and I explore the use of what Anna Freud named 'identification with

the aggressor' in assimilation, particularly in the lives of eastern European immigrants to the USA earlier this century.

9 Ivan Ward suggests this in an unpublished paper.

10 See Laura Mulvey, *Visual and Other Pleasures*, London: Macmillan, 1986; see also D. Rodowick, *The Difficulty of Difference*, London: Routledge, 1991.

11 Janine Chasseguet-Smirgel, *Creativity and Perversion*, London: Free Association Books, 1985.

12 Hanna Segal, 'A psycho-analytical approach to aesthetics', in *New Directions in Psycho-Analysis*, ed. M. Klein *et al.*, London: Maresfield, 1977.

13 Laplanche and Pontalis, *The Language of Psychoanalysis*, p. 349.

14 Sigmund Freud, Standard Edition, 12.

15 Melanie Klein, 'Some theoretical conclusions regarding the emotional life of the infant', in *Developments in Psycho-Analysis*, ed. M. Klein *et al.*, London: Hogarth Press, 1952.

16 Betty Joseph, 'Addiction to near death', *International Journal of Psychoanalysis*, 1982, 63(4).

17 Martin Wangh, 'National Socialism and the genocide of the Jews: a psychoanalytic account of a historical event', *International Journal of Psychoanalysis*, 1967, 45, pp. 386–95.

Nine, out of many

Xenophobia, fantasy and the nation: the logic of ethnic violence in former Yugoslavia

The violent ethnic nationalisms which replaced Yugoslavia's communalist ethos of *bratstvo i jedinstvo* ('brotherhood and unity') when, in 1991, the Socialist Federated Republic of Yugoslavia fragmented into its constitutive republics, took observers by surprise, and the bloody ethnic warfare that has continued to rage in the territories of former Yugoslavia since that time has substituted trepidation for the enthusiasm with which most Europeans greeted the collapse of communist hegemony in eastern Europe. The character of the nationalism's of former Yugoslavia, furthermore, challenges the optimism with which theorists of nationalism such as Eric Hobsbawm heralded the demise of a phenomenon they believed – in the light of the developing global economy – could only be seen as atavistic. Hobsbawm's elegiac *Nations and Nationalism since 1780* closes with an assertion which, after Vukovar and Mostar, resonates with modernism's tragic hubris:

> [T]he world history of the late twentieth and early twenty-first centuries ... will see 'nation states' and 'nations' or ethnic/linguistic groups primarily as retreating before, resisting, adapting to, being absorbed or dislocated by, the new supranational restructuring of the globe ... [T]he very fact that historians are at least beginning to make some progress in the study and analysis of nations and nationalism suggests that, as so often, the phenomenon is past its peak. The owl of Minerva which brings wisdom, said Hegel, flies out at dusk. It is a good sign that it is now circling round nations and nationalism (Hobsbawm 1990: 182–3).

Contemporary nationalisms and the ethnic identities they mobilize may seem, when considered from a global perspective, to be irrational in so far as from that point of view the national states they strive to realize seem inappropriate to the economic structure of today's world. I will argue, however, that such a viewpoint is incapable of comprehending the powerful appeal ethno-nationalist rhetorics can have for people caught up in the day-to-day struggle to sustain, and improve, the ways in which they live. In the local domains in which people live and emote, exclusivist identities and strategies seem to be as powerful and goal-oriented as they were in earlier periods – if not more so. In this chapter I will analyse the logic of ethnic antagonism as it is manifested in the new nations which have sprung up in the territories of what was Yugoslavia in order to suggest that ethnic nationalism cannot be understood in the terms of the modernist rationalism of its analysts. Instead, I will argue, it is often constituted within political discourses which link passion and rationality in a manner which modernism – with its image of humankind as intellectively rational – is incapable of explaining or undermining. Former Yugoslavia may be a harbinger of a long period of ethnic wars engulfing not only the territories which were, until very recently, stabilized by communist rule, but also other regions which had been politically fixed by the global antagonism between communism and capitalism. An understanding of the processes which led to the bloody collapse of the Yugoslav federation may thus enable social scientists to devise new models for the analysis of identity which may allow comprehension of the 'irrational' resurgence of impassioned exclusivist communalisms and the inter-communal wars they promote.

The collapse of the communist federal system's legitimacy, which began in 1988–9 when the Serbian nationalist leader Slobodan Miloševic abrogated the autonomy of Kosova and the Vojvodina and deposed the government of Montenegro, inaugurated throughout the republics of what was then Yugoslavia a search for new ways of legitimating power structures which, in all instances, were already in place (the state apparatuses of the respective republics remained operative during the transition from republican to national statuses). The discourse in which this new mode of legitimation took place was, without exception, democratic; Yugoslavs, caught up in the pro-Western ecstasy that swept through eastern Europe after the fall of the Berlin Wall, accepted the Western panacea of democratic elections as the cure for all ills that had afflicted them under communism. Elections took place in the republics of Slovenia and Croatia in April 1990, and in Macedonia, Bosnia-Herçegovina, Montenegro, and Serbia in December. The results of these elections differed considerably: Slovenia and Croatia voted in centre-right anti-communist coalitions; the Macedonian elections produced a hung parliament, and a coalition government encompassing old Communist Party *nomenclatura* as well as reformist communists and nationalists was subsequently negotiated; Bosnia-Herçegovina set up a coalition of Croats, Muslims and Serbs which excluded the communists; and Montenegro and Serbia reinstalled their communist leaderships.

The politicians who took power in these elections did so in contests in which they claimed that the programmes they wished to enact were the programmes 'the people' really desired. In a situation in which the people had previously had little, if any, say in what was enacted by the state, there were no elaborated 'popular platforms' which could be appropriated by political candidates (Gaber 1993); the prevalent sense among the populations of the various republics was simply that the previous system had not worked and had, particularly through the previous decade of unequal economic development and massive foreign debt,

led to a substantial decline in their standards of living. Thus the only popular
will to evoke was one of gross dissatisfaction, and the most convincing programmes to develop out of that were ones which promised to find, and abolish,
the reasons because of which the system had failed. The sudden collapse of
socialist hegemony in Yugoslavia and throughout eastern Europe, which was
for the most part brought about by economic bankruptcy and not by organized
internal resistance, gave rise to popular fantasies of transformation which were
virtually millenarian; people felt that if they took the magical draught of democracy proffered them by the West they would instantly move into a new, and
far better, world. Political platforms were thus not organized around plans for
serious and rigorous structural changes in the political and economic domains,
but around talismanic pronouncements that if the parties running were elected,
they would transform the state into something that expressed the real will of
the real people, and would expunge from the nation all those agents and agencies
which had in the past perverted that will. What the elections all had in common,
then, was the assumption that legitimacy devolved from 'the people', rather than
from the self-ordained mission of the previous communist leadership, which was
that of realizing what the 'people's state' communist ideology saw as the inherent
goal of the historical process. The central question, then, which was fore-
grounded in all the elections, was, 'who are the (real) people?'

   The answer provided by those politicians who won the elections – which
was evidently the answer the majority of the voters wished to hear – was that
the real people were the members of the dominant ethnic groupings of the
respective republics. In Slovenia, for example, the victorious centre-right DEMOS
coalition argued on a nationalist ticket that Slovenians were inherently industri-
ous and productive, and that if they could destroy the influence of the communists
and the other ('southern') non-Slovene national groupings which interfered with
their work, Slovenes would become as wealthy as the capitalists of neighbouring
Austria, who they emulated. The ticket was effectively 'Slovenia for Slovenians',
and this 'programme' was far more attractive to the electorate than the platform
of the left reformist coalition which demanded full civil rights for all persons
resident in Slovenia, as well as radical, and arduous, changes in social and
economic organization. At the other end of the political spectrum, the winning
argument in the Serbian elections, in which Miloševic's national socialist party
was returned to power, was that Serbs were true communists who would, were
they not impeded by anti-Serbian foreign conspirators (people like the 'Croat'
Tito, who Miloševic claimed had orchestrated a 'Vatican-Comintern' conspiracy
against Serbia), re-establish a 'Greater Serbia' as wealthy and as powerful as the
(imagined) one which had ruled over vast areas of Balkans in the period before
the Ottoman conquest. The only 'Yugoslav' ticket present in all the republican
elections was that of the League of Reform Forces led by Ante Markovic, who,
as federal prime minister, had instituted radical economic reforms throughout
Yugoslavia in 1989 and 1990. Markovic's platform called for 'an undivided

Yugoslavia with a market economy, political pluralism, democratic rights and freedoms for all citizens' (quoted in Thompson 1992: 104). He was soundly thrashed in all the elections, carrying only Tusla, an industrial town in Bosnia-Herçegovina.

Two specific elements operated within the political discourses of the victorious parties, whether anti-communist or communist. The first was an evocation of the essential character and desire of the 'people' being appealed to; the second was a scapegoating of 'the other', who denied the people their true realization and the rewards it would bring about. Each of these elements appealed to a nationalist definition of identity elaborated in ethnic terms. The Yugoslav elections were won by parties which called upon people in terms of their ethnic identities and attributed the problems which afflicted them to persons and groups which had in the past been their neighbours (neighbours not only in the sense of the residents of contiguous republics but also, in many cases, in the sense of literal neighbours in ethnically mixed communities) The appeal of these platforms served to drive wedges between peoples who had previously lived together or in close proximity (see the *Disappearing World* documentary, 'We are all neighbours', directed by Debbie Christie and based on the work of Tone Bringa). Thus 'ethnic cleansing' was already set out as a political agenda in the 1990 republican elections, in so far as what the victorious political programmes sketched out in theory would subsequently be given body on the ground in Croatia, Bosnia-Herçegovina, and areas within Serbia such as the Sanjak and Kosovo. It is important, however, to stress that this project was choreographed by the political leadership. Generating ethnic antagonisms provided a facile means for people in power to hold on to it and for persons seeking power to achieve it, at a time when previously effective means of grasping and holding power were being undermined and overturned.

It is not, however, sufficient to say simply that this was 'done' to the people by an opportunist and unethical political leadership. We must investigate the enthusiasm with which elements of the Yugoslav populace responded to being 'hailed' (Althusser 1971: 162–3) as ethnic nationalists who had to destroy their neighbours in order to affirm their selves. The brutalities which have characterized ethnic interaction in the succeeding three years could not, I contend, have been foreseen by an observer of the patterns of coexistence which had characterized the post-war years; after the eruption of nationalist fervour, intermarriage, co-residence and economic co-operation were replaced by mutilations such as the gouging out of eyes and hacking off of genitals, as well as by the rape of women and children, the wholesale massacre of ethnic groups within towns and villages, the desecration and destruction of the properties and houses of those viewed by the perpetrators as ethnic 'others', and the collection of men, women and children in concentration camps where torture, murder and genocidal deprivations of food and water were commonplace. Such activities have been carried out by Serbs, Croats and Bosnians and, although Slovenia has not seen ethnic warfare, because of the relative homogeneity of its population, I have observed brutal harassment by Slovene police of persons who were ethnically non-Slovene, whose only 'crimes' were being within the borders of Slovenia. The ethnic hatred which has erupted throughout the territories of former Yugoslavia may have been instigated from above, but the popular response to that fomentation has been enthusiastic. Tomaz Mastnak, a Slovene social philosopher, points out that the volunteer militias, which have carried out the larger part of the atrocities, are not anti-social anomalies but are expressions of precisely the sort of society which has developed in ex Yugoslavia: 'The militias are exactly the people in arms – civil society at its most uncivil' (Mastnak 1992: 7). Analysis of the current situation must not only ascertain why ethnic divisiveness has served as a suc-cessful means of grasping power, but also determine why the call to arms against former neighbours has been responded to with such passion.

When new states separate themselves off from an old state in which their peoples had been consolidated, the problem of how to determine which people belong to which new nation is problematic. In the case of the new states which have sprung up on the territory which was Yugoslavia, the clear-cut boundaries of 'inside' and 'outside' are poorly defined territorially. The modernization proc-esses which affected Yugoslavia and its peoples in the twentieth century further mixed ethnic populations already intermingled by earlier experiences of living under the Ottoman and the Austro-Hungarian empires (see Hammel 1993). Bosnia-Herçegovina, which was 40 per cent Muslim, 33 per cent Serbian, 18 per cent Croatian and 9 per cent 'others' (a census category which designates other national and ethnic groups as well as persons who refuse to define themselves in national or ethnic terms) is not a demographic anomaly: Croatia is 75 per cent Croat, 12 per cent Serbian, and 13 per cent 'others'; Serbia, not counting its allegedly autonomous regions of Kosova (10 per cent Serbian and 90 per cent Albanian) and the Vojvodina (56 per cent Serbian, 21 per cent Hungarian, and 23 per cent 'others'), is 65 per cent Serbian, 20 per cent Albanian, 2 per cent Croat and 13 per cent 'others'; and even Slovenia, which considers itself ethnically homogeneous, is 90 per cent Slovene, 3 per cent Croat, 2 per cent Serbian and 5 per cent 'others' (van den Heuvel and Siccama 1992: frontispiece). When substantial populations of persons who do not share the ethnicity of the hegemonizing group reside on the territory of the state that group is attempting to create, the process of legitimating statehood in ethnic terms foregrounds the question of what to do with inhabitants who have no ethnic rights to membership in that political collectivity. When the boundaries between 'us' and 'them' do not run along defensible territorial borders, but through the middle of towns and villages and, all too often, through the middle of families, the desired 'national entity' can be discursively presented as penetrated and occupied by 'enemies' who must – at least – be disarmed by disenfranchisement (Dimitrijevic 1993) and – at 'best' – be neutralized by exile or extermination.

This discursive project of transforming neighbours into enemies opposes the dominant state discourse of the previous forty-seven years of 'Yugoslav nationality', which naturalized co-operation and consanguinity. The traditions which had constituted identities since the Second World War were designed to efface inter-communal antagonisms and to establish Yugoslav *bratstvo i jedinstvo* as the only viable means of ensuring the survival and well-being of individuals. Yugoslav federation had been posited on the drawing of different borders between the 'inside' and the 'outside'. The partisan war against the Nazi occupation had forged solidarity between individuals from all of Yugoslavia's ethnic groups in defence of the 'homeland', and had simultaneously brought Tito and the Communist Party to power. It had been followed by a brutal purging of the 'enemy within', which resulted in the deaths of tens of thousands of Yugoslav 'collaborators' and the driving into exile of many more. Subsequently the *Ustaše*, Croats who – with Nazi encouragement – had waged ethnic war against non-Croats during the period of wartime occupation, were defined in state rhetoric as 'Nazis' (i.e. quislings of a foreign power), rather than as Croats: 'Communist rule entailed ideological control over the representation of the past, [and] those horrible events that would disrupt the new inter-ethnic co-operation were not to be mentioned, except in the collective categories "victims of fascism", on the one side, and "foreign occupiers and domestic traitors", on the other side' (Denich 1991: 2). A later boost to Yugoslav solidarity was provided by Tito's break with the Soviet Union in 1948, when 'the greater part of the nation rallied behind Tito in the face of the Soviet threat' (Auty 1966: 247). Subsequent developments in state policies kept Yugoslavia 'balanced' between 'East' and 'West', and the interests of the nation – and of the various peoples who constituted it – could thus always be drawn up in opposition to the conspiracies of a labile set of enemies threatening Yugoslavia from beyond its territorial, and ideological, borders.

Thus discourses of ethnic antagonism could not easily call upon hegemonic tradition to justify the division of communities, in so far as the hegemonic tradition of the communist state argued to the contrary that the survival of the Yugoslav peoples depended on defensive co-operation. Agencies wishing to establish exclusively ethnic identities had, therefore, to 'invent' traditions (Hobsbawm 1983) of ineluctable antagonisms which could validate radical redefinitions of the field of sociality and co-operation. Such invention did not, however, involve the conjuring-up of grounds for antagonism *ex nihilo*; the successive Yugoslav constitutions (there were four, with the latest written in 1974) had kept markers of national identity alive within the federation, and many incidents and episodes in recent and not-so-recent Yugoslav history could be re-remembered and interpreted to provide the basis for arguments that putative neighbours were in fact, because of their different ethnic identities, blood enemies in disguise. It was not so much, therefore, that traditions of inter-communal antagonism were 'invented', but that a discursive shift was effected which allowed peripheralized and muted 'memories' to become the central points of new definitions of identities.

Demographically Yugoslavia is made up of six major national groupings (Slovenes, Croats, Serbs, Montenegrins, Macedonians and Muslims) and twelve minority nationalities (Albanians, Hungarians, Turks, Slovaks, Gypsies, Bulgarians, Romanians, Ruthenians, Czechs, Italians, Vlachs and Ukrainians) scattered throughout an area characterized by diverse regional histories and considerable variations of wealth. Under Tito six republics were recognized, five corresponding to the dominance of national groups within them, and one (Bosnia-Herçegovina) peopled by three major national communities (Croatian, Serbian and Muslim). Two autonomous regions (Kosovo and Vojvodina) were furthermore created in acknowledgement of the majority population of Albanians in Kosovo and the large proportion of Hungarians in the Vojvodina. The major nationalities can – for the most part – be differentiated in terms of religion and/or language: thus Slovenes are Catholic and speak Slovenian, Croats are Catholics who speak Serbo-Croatian (the 'Croatian' language is mainly distinguishable from the 'Serbian' by the fact that the former is written in Latin script and the latter in Cyrillic), Serbs speak Serbo-Croatian and are members of the Serbian Orthodox Church. Not only, however, do persons of one 'national' identity live within the territorial bounds of another 'nation's' republic, but there are also categorical anomalies, such as Serbs who are Catholic. Furthermore, some of the other nationalities appear to be products of communist state policy rather than of 'natural' cultural distinctions. Thus, for instance, Montenegrins are recognized as a national community, but speak Serbo-Croatian and share Orthodox affiliation with neighbouring Serbs. Macedonians, who have a distinct language, only took on a religion nominally distinct from that of the Serbs and Montenegrins in 1967 through the machinations of the Yugoslav state (see Pavlowitch 1988: 105–6). The Muslims, a Serbo-Croatian speaking 'nationality' without a territorial base, were only given national status in 1968 in order 'to remove them from the competition to demonstrate their "real" identity as either Serbs or Croats ... [so as to] neutralize the territorial aspirations of either with respect to Bosnia' (Allcock 1992: 283).

As is demonstrated by the anomalous Muslim 'nation' – a national group without a national territory – the granting of national status was a discursive ploy which functioned in certain instances (as when Serbs and Croats wished to lay ethnic claim to Bosnia-Herçegovina through asserting that Muslims were Serbs or Croats who had converted to Islam during Ottoman rule, or when Serbs wished to assert that Macedonia or Montenegro was 'really' Serbian) to disenfranchise ethnic claims, and in others to provide a strategic sop to ethnic groups being consolidated within a multi-ethnic state. In the second instance the communist state provided a rhetoric within which people wishing to assert identities which were not fully assimilated within and dominated by the communist state were able to declare ethno-nationalities. State patronage of such supplementary identities, which served as a means of dispersing potential federation-wide anti-statist solidarities, encouraged the subsumption of national identities within the encompassing identity provided by the Yugoslavian state. In so doing it maintained those identities as what Edwin Ardener has referred to as 'blank banners' (Ardener 1971: xliv) — signs of identities which are not linked to specific programmes but which can, when appropriate situations arise, be mobilized as icons and given contents appropriate to those situations. Thus national identities served during the period of state hegemony as means of expressing regional conflicts (mostly economic) which could not be expressed in the rhetoric of a unified communist federation (Allcock 1992: 281–7). When, however, statist ideology lost both its legitimacy and its power to control regional disputes in the late 1980s and issues of unequal economic development among the republics became grounds for the expression of opposition to the old order, these national identities provided discursive foundations on which to base political activity. Dissatisfaction with the central government, provoked by perceived injustices affecting all the inhabitants of a region, regardless of their ethnic affiliation, could thus most easily be articulated in 'national' terms, and this ensured that it would be the nationalist road, rather than any other, which would be seen as leading beyond the impasse of communist politics. With the effective self-destruction of communism, the source of the disasters of the past and the deprivations of the present had to be sought in terms of national or ethnic antagonism.

The process of redefining official discourses on identity and developing the political implications of those transformations began in the early eighties when Milošević fuelled his ascent to power in Serbia by stirring up popular animosity towards Kosovan Albanians by promulgating the belief that 'Muslims' were, as they had in the fourteenth century, threatening to drive Serbs from their historical homeland of Kosovo. The official Serbian press began to run stories telling of instances in Kosovo of Albanian 'Muslims' raping Serbian women and desecrating Orthodox monasteries, as well as recounting the allegedly frequent expulsions – authorized by Albanian officials empowered by Kosovo's autonomous status – of Serbian families from their houses and lands, so that those properties could be taken over either by illegal immigrants from neighbouring Albania or by the children of the profligately breeding Kosovans (Ramet 1992: 200). There was, simultaneously, an official blessing and promotion of old traditions (frowned upon as 'folkloric' during Tito's regime) recounting the heroic struggle of the Serbian nation against the invading Ottoman armies. *Vidovdan*, the annual celebration of the defeat of the armies of Prince Lazar Hrebeljanovic by the Ottoman armies on the 'Field of Blackbirds' on 15 June 1389, became an official ceremony in the period leading up to the abrogation of Kosovan autonomy. Prominent members of the Serbian government, including Milošević, would listen to village minstrels lament the melancholy fate of the Christian heroes who died 600 years earlier defending Serbia against foreign invasion, before presenting rousing speeches on the theme of 'never again'. On *Vidovdan* 1989, with Kosovan autonomy crushed and a state of siege in effect in the towns and villages of

Kosovo, the bones of Prince Lazar, which had rested in Serbia since his defeat six centuries before, were ceremonially paraded through the towns and monasteries of Serbia before being 'returned' with great fanfare to the Orthodox monastery of Gračanica at the heart of Kosovo.

The articulation of a Serbian discourse, which was grounded on antagonism to Albanians, served to reconstitute 'Serbia' as a locus of identity and 'Serbian interests' as a focus of concern. At the same time as this was occurring in Serbia, Croatia too was moving into a nationalist phase in which the definition of the community and its appropriate concerns were central issues and devices. Partly in response to the perceived threat of Serbian nationalism and partly as a means of gaining power, nationalist politicans called for the separation of Croatia from the Yugoslav federation on the grounds that, under communism, the Croatian people as a whole had been punished for the activities of the Ustaše (Dukić 1993: 251) and had, consequently, had their rights as Croats and Yugoslavs suppressed by the 'Serb-dominated' state. Croat nationalists invoked memories of the Titoist government's crushing of the 1971 'Croatian Spring' movement (a large-scale political agitation which had demanded a degree of political decentralization and greater financial autonomy for the republic of Croatia) in order to illustrate this thesis, and argued that, as long as the central government was in control, the Serbs would continue to deny Croats their historic rights as a people. In 1989 Franjo Tudjman – once a communist partisan, at that time president of the newly-established 'Croatian Democratic Union' (HDZ), and now president of Croatia – cleansed the Croat national image (sullied by years of an equation being drawn between Ustaše fascism and Croatian nationalism) by announcing at Jasenovac (site of the most notorious Ustaše extermination camp) that the Ustaše depredations were nowhere near as extensive as state propoganda had claimed and, furthermore, that they were no different than any of the other brutalities which had been effected in that period (Tudjman 1990). Subsequently, the press in both Croatia and Slovenia provided apparent validation of the latter point by publishing pictures of the bodies of thousands of victims (those of Slovene and Croat collaborators as well as of Serbian anti-partisan Četnici (Chetniks) – and members of their respective families – who had fled from Yugoslavia in front of the victorious partisan forces only to be handed over to the partisans by British troops) of massacres carried out by the partisans after the close of the war. Photographs of caves full of stacked bones flooded the newspapers of both republics, giving rise to campaign rhetorics in which these persons, previously referred to in non-national terms as 'Nazis' or 'quislings', became 'Croatian victims' or 'Slovene victims' of communist brutality.

The Slovene nationalist ticket was, at base, simply an anti-communist ticket, and the positivity of a Slovene identity had to be invented. In the period leading up to the vote for independence a number of icons of Slovene identity were mustered, including – most successfully – the kozolec, a device for drying hay particular to certain regions of Slovenia, and a day before independence was announced heated discussions were still going on in parliament about what the new-born country would use for a flag (nearly every suggested pattern was refused by the parliament because members could discern traces of the old Yugoslavia flag in it). It is the absence in the Slovene instance of a mobilizable history of specific ethnic antagonism towards a neighbouring group which enabled Slovenia to escape the inter-communal warfare that has desolated the rest of former Yugoslavia. This lack contributed to the downfall of the nationalist Right in the period following independence. A central programme of the elected DEMOS coalition was opposition to abortion, on the grounds that 'Slovenia is a small country surrounded by large enemies, and women should not have the right to abort future defenders of the nation'. A substantial number of women felt, however, less threatened by an external antagonist than they did by this attempt to abrogate their powers over their bodies, and this new antagonism engendered numerous pro-abortion groups which joined with other oppositional parties in a coalition which overturned DEMOS's parliamentary majority and returned a liberal coalition in large part concerned with local issues (Salecl 1993). Thus while in Slovenia the drive for independence was fuelled by antipathy towards communism and the federation which imposed it on Slovenia, once the old order had disintegrated Slovenians were left without the convenient distraction of external enemies and with the difficult task of envisaging and creating a viable national identity for themselves.

In Croatia, on the other hand, the 'blank banners' which the anti-Yugoslav parties raised in opposition to the Yugoslav state soon became inscribed with the emblems of earlier collective struggles. Despite Tudjman's partisan past and his attempts to exorcize the ghosts of the *Ustaše* from Croatian nationalism, he adopted many of the programmes and symbols of the *Ustaše* Independent State of Croatia as soon as he was called upon to articulate a programme for the HDZ. Campaigning for the presidency in the election campaigns of spring 1990, Tudjman and the HDZ called for an independent Croatia which would expand to Croatia's 'historical borders' (thus encompassing most of Bosnia Herçegovina), would fly a national flag on which the red star of the Yugoslav state would be replaced by the 'chessboard' pattern (*šahovnica*) which had graced the national flag of the 'Independent State of Croatia', and would purify the Croatian language of all 'Serbian' words. He also, according to Denich, announced that the 'World War II Independent State of Croatia was not ... a "quisling" formation, but an "expression of the historical aspirations of the Croatian people (nation) for its own independent state"' (Denich 1991: 6). 'Positivity' was achieved for Croatian identity through the taking on of a previous anti-Yugoslav Croatian identity, and this assumption of the trappings of the 'real' Croatia not surprisingly terrified the Serbs who lived within the borders of Croatia. They saw before them – realized once again – the same nightmare order under which they, or their relatives, had suffered between 1941 and 1945.

Bones once again played a substantive role in the constitution of identity (Salecl 1993: 81 and Bloch 1982 and 1989: 170) as Serbs of the Krjina region of Croatia invited local and Serbian journalists and photographers into caves where the skeletons of Krjina Serbs massacred by *Ustaše* had been cached. Not only did these monuments to the fate of Croatian Serbs under the *Ustaše* serve locally to legitimate Croatian Serb resistance to the new Croatian order (a resistance which led to the Krjina establishing itself, by force of arms and ethnic cleansing, as an independent – albeit internationally unrecognized – Serbian state), but they also provided a focal point for the articulation of ethnic hatred towards the Croats in Serbia proper. Denich points out that while

> the rebellions of Serbian communities in Croatia were motivated by their own memories of the Ustasha regime, now eerily recincarnated in the declarations and symbols of the new nationalist government ... the inhabitants of Serbia itself had not experienced the Ustasha terror, and their wartime suffering had come at the hands of the Germans and other foreign occupiers, rather than Croats. Accordingly, there was little history of overt anti-Croat feeling throughout Serbia (Denich 1991: 11).

None the less, the Miloševic regime ensured that Serbs in Serbia would recognize their own potential fate at the hands of 'Croats' in that of the Croatian Serbs who had died forty-five years earlier. The state-controlled Serbian media repeatedly presented television and newspaper images of the bodies and, as I witnessed when I was in Belgrade during the opening days of the war, the official publishing houses filled the bookshops with multiple-volumed, profusely illustrated texts recounting the until-then suppressed history of the 'Croatian' attempt to exterminate the 'Serbs'. Serbs in Serbia proper, who had already been convinced by the regime-orchestrated hate campaign against the Kosovans that they – as Serbs – stood to lose their ancestral homeland (not, note, their own homes, but the home of the Serbian people), were now being told that they – as Serbs – stood to lose their lives (see the Ministry of Information pamphlets by M. Bulajic 1991 and S. Kljakic 1991). With the successful promulgation of Miloševic's brand of national socialism, which involved the putting into circulation of previously discredited traditions and previously silenced atrocity stories, the Serbs gained the promise of a 'Greater Serbia' – invoked by the threat of its theft – and the brotherhood of a 'Serbian people' – conjured up by images of its extermination. Like those who followed the pan-pipes of ethnic nationalism in other regions of former Yugoslavia, the Serbian people were promised a utopian future in exchange for a commitment to the protracted struggle to destroy the enemies of that future.

What Miloševic, Tudjman and other nationalist politicians have gained by playing the ethnic card in their quest for power seems clear. By transforming the discursive field of the social from one based on cohabitation and co-operation ('unity and brotherhood') to one based on exclusivity and ethnic warfare ('blood and land'), they have been able, first of all, to displace people's self-interest on to a plane where self-interest is defined in essentialist terms as the interest of oneself as a 'Serb', a 'Croat', a 'Slovene', or whatever. When a person is induced to imagine his or her self primarily as a representative of an ethnic collectivity, a threat to that collectivity – like a threat to its power or to the life or property of any of its members who are presented as such – is simultaneously a threat to that person. He or she not only sees the threatened co-national as 'the same as' his or her self but also imagines that co-national's enemy as simultaneously an enemy to all those (including his or her self) who share identity with the threatened one (cf. Bowman 1993: 446–8). The enemy does not attack people as such; it attacks 'Serbs', 'Croats', or 'Slovenes'.

The second advantage gained by playing the ethnic card is that, while the social problems which had generated the initial dissatisfaction with the communist regime have remained in place and – in most cases – actually worsened, the conjuring up of an enemy (or a multitude of enemies) enables the politicians to fix the blame for those problems on that visible antagonist. It has not proven necessary, therefore, to take on the difficult task of restructuring society in either Croatia or Serbia; all that needed to be done to convince the majority of people that positive steps were being taken was to wage war against the enemy or enemies. One might argue that it is, in fact, the war which keeps the nationalist regimes in power. If the war were to stop, it would be more and more difficult to attribute the radical and increasing impoverishment of the people of Croatia and Serbia to the actions of their enemies, and the corruption and inefficiency of the ruling cliques would become apparent.

The final advantage gained by the nationalist leadership through the evocation of a world structured around an absolute, well-nigh 'ontological' (Kapferer 1988), antagonism between a 'them' and an 'us' follows from this Manichaeism. In former Yugoslavia, nationalist leaders lay claim to the need to abrogate the rights of the people they lead on the grounds that absolute power is necessary to destroy the absolute enemy of the people. If the enemy is the source of all evil, and the 'we' that would exist were that evil to be eradicated is inherently good, then the leadership which, in these sullied days, directs the struggle to destroy the evil is itself the personification of the principle of good. The elevation of the nationalist leadership, and particularly of the 'Leader' *per se*, to the status of 'agency of redemption' is evident in the impassioned waving of posters of Milošević in Serbian nationalist demonstrations and, even more saliently, in the placing of statues of Tudjman alongside those of the Virgin Mary in souvenir booths at the Croatian pilgrimage centre, Medjugorje (see Bax 1991 and Bax 1995 on the development of the shrine). The leader stands in as the charismatic representation of the 'will of the nation' and, as long as it is believed that he represents that will, any activity that he initiates will be seen as 'necessary' for the redemption of the whole. Such legitimation of power can be undermined in two ways. One occurs when people lose faith in the existence of the evil which serves to justify the state's violence and repression, as happened in Slovenia. Another occurs when people lose faith in the leader as charismatic representative of the principle of the nation, and the challenge offered Milošević by Vojislav Seselj of the extreme right-wing Serbian Radical Party in the 19 December (1993) parliamentary elections in Serbia was grounded on such a reassessment. Here the leader can be exposed as a 'false messiah', and his place can be usurped by another whose even greater violence and extremism seems better to manifest the violence the nation needs to destroy the violence that would destroy the nation.

The nationalist leaderships' discourses on the enemy, which are widely and powerfully promulgated by the media of communication they control, create, in effect, a world divided between two camps in which there is no neutral place to stand. Thus anyone who does not support the national leadership is necessarily a supporter of the enemy (this logic has justified the extreme repression of anti-nationalists in Serbia and Croatia as well as the brutal murders by Bosnian Serbs and Croats of co-nationals who refuse to take up arms in support of the national cause), and all elements of the social field have to be interpreted in terms of the side on which one stands. A widely-circulated story in Bosnia tells of an exchange of graffiti on the contested border between Serbian and Bosnian sectors of Sarajevo. Someone wrote on a wall of the Central Post Office, which stands on that boundary line, 'THIS IS SERBIA', and someone else soon after painted that message out and replaced it with 'THIS IS BOSNIA'. A third interlocutor crossed out the second message and wrote in its place 'THIS IS A POST OFFICE!'. Less humorous are other attempts to lay claim to places and cleanse them of the sullying marks of other presences; I refer here not only to ethnic cleansing *per se* but also to its landscaping correlate in which volunteer squads from Serbia come into areas of Bosnia which have been taken and purged of Muslims by the Serb militias in order not only to tear down mosques, but also to turf the ground on which they stood, plant trees, and install playground equipment. A pragmatic interpretation of this activity – based on the perpetrators' subsequent denials to visitors that a mosque had ever stood in the place of the park – would be that the landscapers are attempting to mask the ethnic cleansing that occurred there. I suspect, however, that in so far as the visitors are known to know that Muslims had lived there, the remaking of the landscape serves to create, for the Serbs themselves, an image of a new world, bearing no signs of the history out of which it was violently born. This elision of the historic process is a necessary element of a discursive legitimation of the violence involved in creating those 'cleansed' communities; the institution of the 'real' Serbia is a 'return' to a state of ontological purity, and such a state must be devoid of markers of the polluted and 'unreal' condition 'Serbia' was in before its redemption. The violence on which this new and pure order is founded is not part of the order itself; what is real is the world to come, in which evil will have no place and all that is in place will be good. This fantasy structure is evident in a story told me by a UN worker who recounted an exchange in which, after he berated a Serbian militiaman for having taken part in the destruction of the 'beautiful and ancient Old City' of one of the Bosnian towns, the man replied, 'but we will build a new and more beautiful ancient Old City in its place'.

In the preceding pages I have proffered an interpretation of the genealogy of this logic. Fantasies of the well-being to be experienced once the old destructive order is overcome are put into circulation by nationalist demagogues. However, once the communist regime is replaced by the new nationalist orders, the promised wealth and fulfilment fail to materialize and already-designated scapegoats – members of other national groups seen both to obstruct the national interests from outside and to sabotage their realization from inside – are shown not only to carry the blame for the inequities of the old system but also to bear responsibility for the failures of the new one. As the new nationalist leaderships attempt to gain firmer grips on state apparatuses, they demonize the nations' others by providing 'proofs' that these antagonists are not only opposed to the well-being of the people, but are also dedicated to their absolute destruction. Newspapers and radio stations, controlled by the national governments, circulate fear-inducing stories of murders and mutilations carried out against members of the national community by persons of other nationalities. By promoting widespread fear and distrust, the new leadership validates its call for the mobilization of the nation to wage war against internal and external enemies, thereby securing its hold on repressive state apparatuses. Milos Vasić, writing of the militarization of the Bosnian Serbs, demonstrates that 'first, warmongering chauvinist propoganda is spread by the Serbian-controlled media. Fear takes hold and the idea that "we can't live with *them* any more" becomes dominant' (Vasić 1993: 8). Popular acceptance of such stories of persecution itself engenders murders and mutilations directed against the 'other' which defensively returns like for like, thus giving rise to new rumours and stories of atrocities committed by the antagonist. As Christie and Bringa's 'We are all neighbours' shows, a spiral of reciprocal distrust and reciprocated violence is initiated by acceptance of these rumours, and this destroys patterns of sociality, replacing them with antagonisms based on fear and manifested in violent moves to destroy the enemy before it can destroy oneself (cf. Riches 1986 and Loizos 1988). Moves to destroy that enemy follow the logic of what Riches calls 'tactical pre-emption' (Riches 1986: 6–7); murdering children, women and the elderly in order to prevent them from becoming, procreating, or aiding those who will murder you makes good sense once the enemy is recognized as such.

That recognition, however, cannot be explained solely in empirical terms, especially when, as in the village portrayed in the documentary, the evidence of antagonism runs counter to the testimony of daily life. Although it is undoubtedly true that political forces play a significant role in giving shape to and disseminating rumours which generate fear and give rise to inter-communal violence, it is not clear why such rumours should be accepted as true and – perhaps more saliently – why they should be seen as pertinent to situations in which no signs of inter-communal antagonism have previously been evinced. The amount of violence now raging between the communities of former Yugoslavia was not manifest before nationalist mobilization; as Cornelia Sorabji demonstrates in the Bosnian instance, 'for the most part tolerance, good will, and a conscious desire for co-operative and civil relationships filled the joints between the three populations' (Sorabji 1993: 33–4; see also Bringa 1995). If we explain the extreme levels of brutality evident in former Yugoslavia today as something endemic to 'the Balkans', we not only deny such ethnographic evidence and ignore the recent history of modernization in Yugoslavia, but also effectively cast Yugoslavs out beyond the pale of what we term 'human society' (to act in that manner 'they' must be essentially different from 'us'). If, on the other hand, we accept that the political discourses of the contending leaderships of the former republics have somehow transformed Yugoslavs into something different than they were before, we are still left with the question, 'where has this penchant for extreme violence come from?' Peter Loizos, faced with analogous instances of genocidal violence in the Cypriot context (Loizos 1988: 651), argued that ethnic violence is focused on a specific set of subjects by antagonistic political rhetorics. He left in abeyance, however, the question of what in the people such rhetorics were addressed to called them to answer to its call and adopt an image of the other as enemy with such passion that the will to efface the presence of that other from the earth overcame the moral scruples which had regulated social interaction before the other came to be recognized as such.

While the 'Balkan mentality' argument manifests intellectual sloth in so far as it mobilizes commonsensical and racialist stereotypes in order to ignore the challenge of understanding other cultures, the political rhetoric argument in turn ignores the challenge offered to modernist conceptions of human nature by situations in which communities which have lived together in peace and co-operation suddenly fragment into warring factions. If, as enlightenment theories of human nature contend, human beings will act rationally and co-operatively when given the choice, then there is no reason why – when the options proffered are between a proven model of cohabitation and a radical paradigm of violent confrontation – the choice should be made for inter-communal antagonism and war. Although I have demonstrated in the preceding pages that the latter option was offered up to the peoples of Yugoslavia by opportunistic political factions, I have not been able to demonstrate any 'rational' reason why the people accepted the logic of inter-communal hatred as more real than their own experiences of cohabitation and co-operation. If, as Mastnak argues, the current situation is an expression of the will of the people, then it is important to try to discern what in people resonates to a call to rise up with a seemingly primal rage to destroy an enemy before that enemy is able to destroy them. I suggest – and in so doing follow the lead of Jacques Lacan – that we must look beyond the

rhetoric of social discourses to those primal fantasies mobilized by those rhetorics. These fantasies, generated by the first encounter of the human infant with
the symbolic order, resonate with and impel the subject to answer to the call to
inflict absolute violence against an absolute enemy.

The infant's entry into the symbolic order, initiated when the child learns that
it must call to another for what it desires, is simultaneously an expulsion from a
world in which it subsequently 'remembers' it had had everything it wanted.
Freud, in the opening section of *Civilization and its Discontents*, posits that 'the
infant at the breast does not as yet distinguish his ego from the external world as
the source of the sensations flowing in upon him', and that this experience may
give rise to inchoate memories of 'an oceanic feeling' like a 'limitless narcissism'
(Freud 1963: 3–4, 9). In this pre-linguistic state the child has no conceptual
apparatus with which to distinguish 'inside' from 'outside', and thus perceives
itself as both locus and source of sensation and what gives rise to sensation. The
child's entry into language expunges that sense of narcissistic omnipotence by
reordering the world in terms of a dualism; in separating from the mother, the
child goes from sensing that the world and itself are coterminous to knowing not
only that it is only part of a world, but, furthermore, that it is a small and helpless
part, which must call upon others who have the power to give it – and deprive it
of – what it wants. After the moment in which the world is taken up by language,
primal 'enjoyment' (which Lacan terms *jouissance*) remains only as the trace of an
absence (Lacan writes 'we must insist that *jouissance* is forbidden to him who
speaks as such' (Lacan 1977: 319)). That absence or lack serves as a screen on to
which we project fantasies of fulfilment – of full enjoyment – in the form of objects
or scenarios of desire. These 'part objects', which fetishistically stand in for the
jouissance which has been irrecuperably lost, seem to promise access to the
fulfilment from which language has banished us. As such, they cover the abyss of
that primal lack and enable us to fantasize that 'if we had this thing we would have
our happiness (*jouissance*)'. Thus, although that lack can never be anything more
this side of language than the wound of an amputation, it none the less remains
the field on which we inscribe the desires which drive our self-motivated activities.
The idea of amputation – of something brutal that has been done to sever us from
that part of ourselves which gave us our pleasure – brings up, of course, the
question, 'who has done this thing to us?' In Lacanian terms this violator is that
being which makes us know the foundations of language, by introducing us as
infants to presence and absence (self and not-self) through its demand that the
mother leave the child and come to it. Although Freud calls this figure 'the Father',
it need neither be personified nor gendered – it is something/someone outside the
union of the infant's body with that which feeds, comforts and sustains it, which
the infant, in its initial incursion into signification, recognizes as breaking that
union through the assertion of its presence – its 'voice'.

However, once the child comes to recognize the necessity of operating within
the symbolic order, it channels its desires into certain patterns of behaviour by

learning that certain activities will provide fulfilment (and others, punishment). Through its experience of parental reward and deprivation it comes to constitute for itself an image ('the ego ideal') of what it must be to earn the love of those it desires and the things with which those others can provide it. This image of the 'good self' serves, through an internalization of what the child perceives the parents desire it to be, to establish the child's identity within normative patterns of motivation and expectation. This apparently rational process of enculturation functions, none the less, through a process of temporary displacement, whereby the child imagines that it will still be able to fulfil all of its desires, despite having to modify its tactics to accommodate the demands of its parents. The narcissistic will to power still underlies the child's relationship with the symbolic order. It is only through negotiating the Oedipus Complex that the child learns that there are limits to its desire which cannot be evaded. The Oedipus Complex is resolved when the child, which until that time continues to demand the body of the mother (the first fetish substitute for *jouissance*) as the object of its desire, is 'convinced' that it must – in its own self-interest – abandon that demand. This occurs, in ways that differ according to the gender of the child, when the child is brought to realize that, if it continues to demand that which neither society nor the parental voice which 'speaks' for society will allow it, it will be deprived of the possibility of any future pleasure through what Freud asserts the child recognizes as 'castration' (Mitchell 1974: 74–100). The threat of castration is consequently internalized in the 'super-ego', which effectively serves to remind the child, and the adult it becomes, that if it is to have pleasure at all, certain objects of desire must be abandoned and replaced by objects which society acknowledges to be appropriate. The properly socialized person is, in other words, one who recognizes that full satiation – the return to *jouissance* that the Oedipal fantasy evokes before the threat of castration drives it back into the unconscious – is rendered impossible by 'reality'.

None the less, traces of this difficult construction of individual identity remain inscribed in the unconscious. People will always encounter – dispersed through the wide field of their activities – frustrations of their strategies of fulfilment, and such moments frequently evoke the pre-linguistic scenario wherein a generalized antagonist is set in opposition to a fantasy of pleasure and fulfilment. In such instances failures to achieve fulfilment are experienced as a consequence of the activities of the 'demonic' antagonist the infant first encountered when its primal omnipotence was shattered by the 'voice of the Father'. When frustration of desire evokes the fantasy presence of this antagonist – perceived in infantile terms as a being which exists only to steal from the child all it has in order to pleasure itself – persons are likely to respond by directing primal rage and violence against what they perceive as the source of that frustration. In most instances, however, such eruptions of unconscious materials into conscious life are subsequently interpreted (by both the actor and the recipient of his or her violence) as irrational behaviour (i.e. a 'temper tantrum'), and are forced back into quiescence by the individual's super-ego. However, certain individuals who have failed to internalize the requirements of 'reality' dictated by the super-ego impose the logic of a psychic structure polarized between desire and antagonism on to the full field of their relations with society. They thus interpret the world in terms of a dualism dividing all the elements of the social field into friend and foe (self and Other). In most instances such persons are perceived as paranoic and, if their violence proves endemically disruptive, are institutionalized. Certain discursive structures, however, draw upon the psychic opposition of antagonist and ego by establishing as real and normative a world polarized between obdurate enemies and a community threatened by them (Adorno and Horkheimer 1972: 187). The forms of nationalism which have been mobilized in Serbia and Croatia (and which were stripped of verisimilitude in Slovenia because of difficulties in arguing convincingly for the presence of a demonic antagonist) draw upon this unconscious structure and mobilize the passions caught up in it by setting up the 'real' nation as the part object which covers lack. In these nationalist rhetorics all real fulfilment follows from the realization of the Nation, and the 'other' (whether Jew, Croat, Muslim, Serb, Albanian or whatever) is inscribed in that rhetoric as precisely that which has as its only reason for being the desire to deny, steal and destroy the national identity that gives one what one wants and makes one what one really is; it steals land, rapes women, desecrates holy objects and, finally, annihilates the community in which one finds one's identity. These rhetorics not only define the Nation as the 'Thing' which recuperates *jouissance*, but also set up the Nation's 'others' as incarnations of the demonic antagonist threatening pleasure at the very root of its being (cf. Žižek 1990).

It is important, however, to recognize that people's identification with the structure set out in nationalist discourse is dynamic, and it is the processual character of this interpellation which enables nationalist rhetoric to evoke unconscious psychic structures. Liberation from what it defines as antagonistic repression and the legitimation of desires it posits as both essential and realizable set up projects for the subjects of nationalist appellation which promise not only to restore the true nation but also to realize their authentic identities for them. During the period of communist hegemony (a hegemony established by Tito and celebrated, until the fall of communism, under the omnipresent gaze of his portraits), the 'pleasures' of national identification were explicitly proscribed by the ideology of *bratstvo i jedinstvo*; Yugoslavs were told – and convinced – that they had to give up the fantasy of ethnic nationhood in order to guarantee survival and the construction of a social system which could provide them with well-being. Socialist ideology served, in other words, as a form of social super-ego, in so far as it asserted that if people were to continue to demand the fulfilment of nationalist aspirations they would be destroyed by the activities of external antagonists. The collapse of communist ideology occurred when the supra-national identity promulgated by the Yugoslav state came to be interpreted not as something which functioned for the self-interest of Yugoslavs but as something imposed upon them by 'external enemies' (the 'Croat' Tito, or 'Serbian hegemonists'). The Yugoslav state's proscription of ethnic nationalism came to be seen not as a rule one had to follow to survive and prosper in the real world, but as a manifestation of antagonism, and at that moment Tito and the order he represented became 'enemies of the people', and the nationalist fantasy became not something impossible and self-destructive, but something which could be – and should be – realized. The discursive field was transformed into what Adorno and Horkheimer term a 'paranoic' structure (Adorno and Horkheimer 1972: 179–200) by the popularization of the belief that possession of peoples' 'real' object of desire (the nation) was possible, and only prevented by the presence of others whose sole reason for being was denying that object to the people.

This structure was set in place by propaganda which simultaneously evoked the future 'restored' nation as a fantastic object promising the utopian recuperation of pleasures lost when, in some hazy past, the people were exiled from their 'homeland', and a demonic antagonist standing as the corporeal antithesis of all configurations of will and desire. However, while the promised 'motherland' is sketched in these nationalist rhetorics in edenic yet imprecise terms, the evil of the antagonist and the heroic devotion of the national leader to its extirpation are portrayed with graphic realism. In the nationalist fantasy it is the leader and the enemy which are the crucial, and operative, elements. One fights against the enemy under the guidance of the leader in order to 'recover' the nation, but since access to the pure enjoyment of being which the nationalistic rhetoric claims will be afforded by the defeat of the enemy is always already blocked by the limitations of both social and psychic realities, the destruction of the enemy will always prove inadequate. Implicit in the psychic structure on which nationlist rhetoric draws is a spiral of violence which leads the members of the national community to always, at the moment of victory, seek yet another enemy who can be blamed for the 'real' nation not being in the place they have just recovered from the enemy they have defeated (Žižek 1991: 6). If the Nazis had had the opportunity to exterminate every leftist, Jew, cripple, homosexual, and gypsy that could be blamed for blocking the advent of the 'Thousand Year Reich' they saw as their true heritage, they would have had to begin exterminating those Germans who, despite fitting all the criteria of 'pure Germans', were none the less the causes of the failure of the Milennium to materialize. Vesna Pesić suggests that the same logic operates in the Serbian instance, when she writes that 'after ethnic cleansing we will soon have traitor cleansing' (Pesić 1992: 7).

The nationalist rhetorics which have led to war in former Yugoslavia function, I contend, by prompting persons of a widely diverse range of social and historical backgrounds to recognize their essential identities as national, rather than as based on gender, occupation, class, or place of residence. They succeed in doing so through the discursive construction of enemies of the nation, which not only serve as scapegoats to be blamed for everything which goes wrong both in society and the lives of its members, but also function to evoke – through their negativity – a national positivity which people can fantasize would suddenly and paradisiacally emerge if the enemy were to be destroyed. I have suggested, following Freud and Lacan, that this process of creating nationalist fervour succeeds because it echoes – in the social domain – processes of identity-formation that individuals negotiate in their earliest encounters with social reality. The violence of the infant's entry into the symbolic order is mirrored in the violent scenarios through which nationalist propaganda presents the antagonism of the nation's other to the ways of life of the national community, and it is – I argue – the resonance between these two 'scenes' which impels individuals – regardless of their adult experiences – to recognize themselves as addressed by calls to join the national struggle.

Psychoanalytic interpretations of social action are perceived by most social anthropologists as profoundly antagonistic to the way of life of the academic community to which they owe allegiance. This is because it appears as though psychoanalysis challenges the axiomatic assumption upon which that community is founded – the a priori truth that social reality is a social construct. The interjection I have here attempted to make does not, however, oppose that axiom; instead it suggests that in so far as humans act within society because they recognize the identities with which society provides them as their own, so we must seek to understand the processes by which persons 'recognize' themselves in the subject positions provided by social discourses. The domain of the 'irrational', which analytic discourses based on Descartian assumptions of rationality and identity disclaim, is, I contend, what impels persons to desire to take up, and defend, the cultural identities offered in social discourses. The ex-Yugoslav instance is, in some ways, an extreme case, but, as I have argued, there is both a social logic operating in those political discourses which construct blood enemies out of previous neighbours, and a logic of identification – which draws upon moments inscribed in the human unconscious by the first encounter of the infant with the social order – which impels ex-Yugoslavs passionately to take up the bellicose ethnic identities proffered by those political discourses. Neither that social logic, nor the structure of the unconscious it mobilizes could, I suggest, independently create the uncivil societies we see active in former Yugoslavia, but brought together they engender logical, self-affirming social realities capable of both sustaining and reproducing themselves. Other articulations of the social and the unconscious create other, less 'extreme', social orders, where antagonisms are variously dissipated through the numerous social encounters persons have in the course of their daily lives; ex-Yugoslavia is an extreme instance only in so far as its politicians have succeeded in transposing fantasies of ethnic nationalism so effectively on to unconscious structures of antagonism. Such a juxtapositioning is not, however, anomalous, and other ethnic nationalisms active today throughout eastern Europe and beyond engage in analogous constructions of idealized essential identities and demonic others. The appeal of such discursive articulations is profound, and provides the nationalists who recognize themselves in the identities proffered with powerful and logical models of interpretation and motives for action. To understand such persons, and the communities they constitute, we, as anthropologists, must attend both to the discourses through which their real is constituted, and to the processes of identification through which they recognize those social realities as places in which to dwell and act.

References

This chapter is reprinted by kind permission of Berg publishers.

Adorno, T. and M. Horkheimer (1972) *Dialectic of Enlightenment*, London: Verso.

Allcock, J. (1992) 'Rhetorics of nationalism in Yugoslav politics', in *Yugoslavia in Transition; Choices and Constraints*, ed. J. Allcock, J. Horton and M. Milivojević, Oxford: Berg Press, pp. 276–96.

Althusser, L. (1971) 'Ideology and ideological state apparatuses (notes towards an investigation)', in *Lenin and Philosophy and Other Essays*, London: Verso, pp. 121–73.

Ardener, E. (1971) 'Introductory essay: social anthropology and language', in *Social Anthropology and Language: ASA Monograph 10*, ed. E. Ardener, London: Tavistock, pp. ix–cii.

Auty, P. (1966) ' "The post-war period" ', in *A Short History of Yugoslavia from Early Times to 1966*, ed. S. Clissold, Cambridge: Cambridge University Press, pp. 236–66.

Bax, M. (1991) 'Marian apparations in Medjugorje: rivalling religious regimes and state formation in Yugoslavia', in *Religious Regimes and State-Formation: Perspectives from European Ethnology*, ed. E. Wolf, Albany: State University of New York Press, pp. 29–54.

Bax, M. (1995) *Medjugorje: Religion, Politics and Violence in Rural Bosnia*, Amsterdam: VU Uitgeverij.

Bloch, M. (1982) 'Death, women and power', in *Death and the Regeneration of Life*, ed. M. Bloch and J. Parry, Cambridge: Cambridge University Press, pp. 211–30.

Bloch, M. (1989) 'Almost eating the ancestors', in *Ritual, History and Power: Selected Papers in Anthropology*, London: Athlone Press, pp. 166–86.

Bowman, G. (1993) 'Nationalizing the sacred: shrines and shifting identities in the Israeli-occupied territories', in *Man: The Journal of the Royal Anthropological Institute*, 28(3), pp. 431–60.

Bringa, T. (1995) '*Being Muslim the Bosnian Way: Identity and Community in a Central Bosnian Village*, Princeton, NJ: Princeton University Press.

M Bulajic, M. (1991) *Never Again: Genocide of the Serbs, Jews and Gypsies in the Ustashi Independent State of Croatia*, Belgrade: Ministry of Information of the Republic of Serbia.

Denich, B. (1991) 'Unbury the victims: rival exhumations and nationalist revivals in Yugoslavia', *American Anthropological Association Annual Meeting*, Chicago, pp. 1–14.

Dimitrijević, V. (1993) 'Ethnonationalism and the constitutions: the apotheosis of the nation state', in *Journal of Area Studies*, 3, pp. 50–6.

Dukić, D. (1993) 'An overview of important events in Croatian history', in *Fear, Death and Resistance: An Ethnography of War, 1991–1992*, ed. L. Feldman, I. Prica and R. Senjković, Zagreb: Matrix Croatica, pp. 241–54.

Freud, S. (1963) *Civilization and its Discontents*, London: The Hogarth Press.

Gaber, S. (1993) 'The limits of democracy: the case of Slovenia', in *Journal of Area Studies*, 3, pp. 57–64.

Hammel, E. A. (1993) 'Demography and the origins of the Yugoslav civil war', in *Anthropology Today*, 9(1), pp. 4–9.

Hobsbawm, E (1983) 'Introduction', in *The Invention of Tradition*, eds E. Hobsbawm and T. Ranger, Cambridge: Cambridge University Press, pp. 1–14.

Hobsbawm, E (1990) *Nations and Nationalism since 1780: Programme, Myth, Reality*, Cambridge: Cambridge University Press.

Kapferer, B. (1988) *Legends of People/Myths of State: Violence, Intolerance and Political Culture in Sri Lanka and Australia*, Washington, DC: Smithsonian Institution Press.

Kljakic, S. (1991) *A Conspiracy of Silence: Genocide in the Independent State of Croatia and Concentration Camp Jasenovac*, Belgrade: Ministry of Information of the Republic of Serbia.

Lacan, J. (1977) *Écrits: A Selection*, London: Tavistock Publications.

Loizos, P. (1988) 'Intercommunal killing in Cyprus', in *Man: The Journal of the Royal Anthropological Institute*, 23(4), pp. 639–53.

Mastnak, T. (1992) 'Civil society at war', in *Yugofax*, 16, p. 7.

Mitchell, J. (1974) *Psychoanalysis and Feminism*, Harmondsworth: Penguin Books.

Pavlowitch, S. (1988) *The Improbable Survivor: Yugoslavia and its Problems – 1918–1988*, London: C. Hurst and Co.

Pesić, V. (1992) 'The problems of minority rights in new nation states', in *Yugofax*, 16, p. 7.

Ramet, S. (1992) *Nationalism and Federalism in Yugoslavia: 1962–1991*, second edition, Bloomington: Indiana University Press, 1992.

Riches, D. (1986) 'The phenomenon of violence', in *The Anthropology of Violence*, ed. D. Riches, Oxford: Basil Blackwell, pp. 1–27.

Salecl, R. (1993) 'Nationalism, anti-semitism and anti-feminism in eastern Europe', in *Journal of Area Studies*, 3, pp. 78–90.

Sorabji, C. (1993) 'Ethnic war in Bosnia?', in *Radical Philosophy*, 63, pp. 33–5.

Thompson, M. (1992) *A Paper House: the Ending of Yugoslavia*, London: Hutchinson Radius.

Tudjman, F. (1990) *Bespuca Provijesne Zbilnosti*, Zagreb: Matrix Croatica.

van den Heuvel, M. and J. G. Siccama, eds (1992) *The Disintegration of Yugoslavia*, Amsterdam: Rodopi.

Vasić, M. (1993) 'The pattern of aggression: two against one in Bosnia', in *Balkan War Report*, 18, pp. 8–9.

Žižek, S. (1990) 'Eastern Europe's republics of Gilead', *New Left Review*, 183, pp. 50–62.

Žižek, S. (1991) *Looking Awry: an Introduction to Jacques Lacan through Popular Culture*, Cambridge, Mass.: MIT Press.

The German handshake

Die Mauern stehn
Sprachlos und kalt, im Winde
Klirren die Fahnen.

(The walls stand
Speechless and cold,
The flags clatter in the wind.)
         (Hölderlin, *Hälfte des Lebens* ('Half-way through life'))

The creative destruction of the 1989 Revolution in the former East Germany figured itself in the images of the crowds at the Brandenburg Gate on the night of 9 November reaching out their hands to each other, and the mutilated flag of the German Democratic Republic (GDR), with the emblem of the socialist constitution burnt out of it. The enthusiastic solidarity of the festive revolutionaries seemed to signal, however momentarily, an opening of cultural and political invention, while the charred hole in the flag bore witness to the destruction of the socialist constitution. Yet this revolutionary opening left an equivocal legacy: it quickly became apparent that the moment of creative destruction was unsustainable, that it was impossible to keep the empty space open for long enough to permit the emergence of new forms of cultural and political identity. Perhaps it was inevitable that the hole in the flag would be darned over with the national colours, especially in Germany, Hölderlin's land of speechless and cold walls.

Yet the legacy of the winter revolution in the GDR remains equivocal, and not only in the so-called New Federal *Länder*. For the revolution was marked by an explosion of cultural and political invention whose final effects are still incalculable. In many respects the revolution was a repetition of 1848, especially in its questioning of existing models of national identity and its exercise of constitutional imagination. While many of the projects generated by this revolution were rendered obsolete by the course of events, they continue, like the earlier *Paulskirchenverfassung* of 1849, to haunt the new German republic.[1]

The period of constitutional debate, ranging from the first calls for unification at the Leipzig demonstrations in November 1989[2] to the publication of the doomed Draft Constitution of the GDR 'Round Table' in the spring of 1990, was accompanied by a correspondingly complex and contested political iconography. Central to this iconography was the image of the handshake, which replaced the charred flags and enthusiastic crowds as an emblem of what Habermas described as the 'rectifying revolution'.[3]

The German Revolution was both a return and a new start, a settlement with the past and promise for the future captured in the image of a handshake extended across the ruins of the Berlin wall. Among many other things, this image managed to evoke the revolutionary enthusiasm of the night of 9 November while also marking its end in a new deal or post-revolutionary settlement. The significance of the handshake, indeed, is almost inexhaustible. It is charged with considerable formal ambiguity: whose hands are shaking, are they greeting or bidding farewell? Does this handshake clinch a deal, seal a promise, offer help, or is one of the parties in the implacable grip of the other? Does the handshake mark a recognition of difference, a unity which respects the borders between the parties, or is it the violation of these borders in the subjugation of one party to the grip of the other?

In the case of the German handshake, the formal complexity of the image is further complicated by the historical legacy inherited from its dominant position within the political iconography of the GDR. There, too, it served as the emblem of unity, but more specifically the unity claimed by the ruling Sozialistische Einheitspartei Deutschland (SED), the 'German Socialist Unity Party'. The party badge consisted of two hands clasped against a fluttering red flag – for this was the party with the wind of history behind it – ringed by an oval blue frame containing its name. The first two words – 'Sozialistische' and 'Einheit' – break at the top of the oval while 'Deutschland' curves around the bottom. This handshake signified the real power behind the hammer and the dividers which, inscribed upon the German national flag, served as the emblem for the socialist constitution.

The hands wielding the tools, signifying the unity of workers with hand and mind, were those of the German Socialist Unity Party, whose dominance was expressed in the 'leading role' clause in the 1968 Constitution (promulgated in 1974). In Article 1 of the constitution, the Republic is defined as 'a socialist state of *workers and peasants*' under the 'leadership of the working class and their Marxist-Leninist Party'.[4] In common with other East European socialist regimes, this clause legitimated the subordination of the functions and institutions of the state to those of the party. The duplication of state and party emblems expressed the duplication of state and party institutions, with the latter firmly in the grip of the SED.

Under the socialist constitution, the SED was ubiquitous in state and civil society; its members dominated the state bureaucracy, the factories, the armed forces and the crucial Ministry of State Security (the Stasi). Corresponding to the party's *de facto* domination of the institutions of the GDR was the ubiquity of its emblem of rule. Within the GDR the party handshake was far more conspicuous than the state emblem of the hammer and dividers. It was impossible to avoid the massive handshake attached to the front of the party's headquarters in Berlin, opposite the Friedrichwerdsche Kirche, but exquisite miniatures were also to be seen on the lapels of bureaucrats taking *Kaffee und Kuchen* in the Hotel bars on Unter den Linden, under the gaze of the Ministry of State Security's cameras. In shops, on trams, walking down the street – everywhere the disembodied handshake. The emblem was a sign of affiliation which established thresholds between the citizens of the 'first socialist state on German soil' and the 'class-enemy' across the wall. It was used, for example, as the seal to the 'ghost' underground stations in East Berlin through which ran the West Berlin *U-Bahn*. Omnipresent as the emblem of the SED's grip on power – a rebus of red magic – it distinguished them from us, and predictably provoked ambivalent feelings of fear, pride and hatred.

The (East) German handshake served as a visual shibboleth, an emblem of separation and inclusion whose meaning depended on who and where you were. The unity evoked by the emblem was complex, with a number of potentially conflicting and overlapping referents waiting up its invisible sleeves. At its most deceptively concrete, the emblem commemorated the agreement reached in the Admiralpalast[5] opposite Friedrichstrasse station in Berlin on 21–2 April 1946 to unify the Sozialdemokratische Partei Deutschlands (German Social Democratic Party – SPD) in the Soviet Occupied Zone with the Kommunistische Partei Deutschlands (German Communist Party – KPD). The recently refounded parties[6] had been negotiating the formation of a united party since the previous year. Early SPD enthusiasm for unification had waned following their growing electoral popularity, although in December 1945 agreement in principle had been reached on unification into an anti-fascist, progressive socialist party dedicated to a democratic Germany.

In spite of a referendum of party members in the Western Occupation Zone on unification during the spring of 1946 (members voting decisively against), the central committee of the SPD held a meeting to approve the unification on 19 April in the Theater am Schiffbaudamm (later the home of the Brecht Ensemble). Two days later, in a move of questionable legitimacy, the leader of the SPD in the Soviet Occupation Zone (SBZ/SPD) crossed Friedrichstrasse for the historic meeting with his opposite number in the KPD in the Admiralpalast.

Witnessed by 3,000 cadres and accompanied by the strains of Beethoven, Offenbach, Strauss and Albert Lortzing,[7] SBZ/SPD leader Otto Grotewohl and KPD leader Wilhelm Pieck shook hands on the unification of their parties in the German Socialist Unity Party. It is the historic handshake between Grotewohl and Pieck which was commemorated in the SED's emblem, yet there is more to it, since this pressing of flesh was itself pre-ordained and carefully staged. The handshake logo (derived from Austrian Social Democracy with remoter antecedents in Freemasonry) had already been used prior to the meeting of Grotewohl and Pieck in posters supporting the unification of the parties during the March 1946 referendum of party members in the Western Occupation Zone.[8] In these posters the sleeves were identified as KPD on the left and SPD on the right. The referendum posters called for those who supported the 'reconstruction and welfare of the nation' to vote for the unity of the two 'workers' parties': the only people who would not support this aim were presumably unreconstructed fascists.

The handshake was evoked to repair the breach between the social democratic and communist wings of the workers' movement and unite the two anti-Fascist parties for the benefit of German unity. It was both retrospective and prospective, serving as the seal of belated anti-Fascist unity and the promise of a German democratic republic. The shaking hands were, variously, those of the German workers of the SPD and KPD, and, finally, of Grotewohl and Pieck, who stepped forward on 21 April to occupy and embody the handshake.

There is an extraordinary photograph of the historic meeting which shows Pieck (on the left, of course) and Grotewohl in dark suits and loud ties shaking hands against a background of tiered party members (Figure 3). The ranked cadres, dressed, with the exception of the comrade in the sweater, as if for a funeral, in dark suits and black ties, seem incapable of controlling their hands. One delegate on the right of the first row seems to imitate the historic moment by shaking, or perhaps wringing, his own hands. His neighbour looks tense and seems to be holding something between his thumbs and foregingers, while in front of him a delegate seems to be steadying the table with his fingertips. At the back a comrade adjusts his tie for the photographer, seated beside what looks like his mirror-image, whose arms are folded and whose tie is almost concealed by its collar.

In the ritual foreground Pieck looks away from Grotewohl who, in turn, with his eyes closed, looks as if he is being pulled towards Pieck.[9] In the lower

FIGURE 3. Handshake between Wilhelm Pieck and Otto Grotewohl, 21 April 1946. Photographer unknown.

right-hand corner, the face of the GDR's strong man of the future – Walter Ulbricht (no hands) – looks shrewdly at the audience. Even the detail of the photographic handshake replicates the poster, revealing the back of Pieck's hand and his first two fingers, and Grotewohl's sinuous thumb with accentuated thumb-joint, three half-fingers and the tip of the fourth: this detail would be reproduced on millions of occasions during the following forty years.

The handshake of the unity of the anti-Fascist forces agreeing to rebuild Germany gradually assumed a different meaning. The agreement to bury differences between the workers' parties became the burial of the SPD. Furthermore, the symbol which the SED used to legitimate their rule came to represent for many East Germans not so much an agreement between equal parties as the people in the grip of the party. The handshake remained the same, but its meaning changed from promised agreement to coercion. And when the party's grip faltered in the autumn of 1989 the people took the meaning of the symbol into their own hands. In the Leipzig demonstrations the handshake was 'unfunktioniert' on the banners, with 'Tschüss' ('cheerio') written above it, as the people ('Wir sind das Volk') took their hand back from the party.[10]

Yet this was not the only metamorphosis undergone by the German handshake during the revolution. The image was also adopted as the emblem of German unification: the owners of the hands became the East and the West German peoples. This is dramatically illustrated by a 40 mm, 20 gram silver commemorative medal costing DM 69 (including VAT) issued by the Berliner Bank on behalf of AKTION GEMEINSINN in the spring of 1990.[11] On one side of the medal is the image of the wall being smashed apart, with two hands reaching across the old death-space border – one from the West, the other from the East. Framed by the Brandenburger Tor and the inscriptions 'with one another' and 'for one another'[12] the imminent handshake illustrates the repair of the rent in the fabric of the German nation. The German nation would shake its own hands, in matt relief.

The highly-polished reverse of the medal offers an inscription spiralling down to an image of a half-eagle fused with a half-hammer and dividers – the arms of the two states combined with the dates 1989, on the left, commemorating the fall of the wall, and 1990, on the right, anticipating the GDR election of 18 March.[13] The chimerical emblem is framed above and below with the curved words 'Deutschland Deutschland', naming the two Germanies, but also citing the first words of the German national anthem 'Deutschland, Deutschland über alles' – two Germanies *über alles*.

The vertiginous inscription surrounding this incongruous scene of German unity in difference reads 'Einigkeit und Recht und Freiheit für das deutsche Vaterland, danach lasst uns alle streben, brüderliche mit Herz und Hand' ('Let us all strive fraternally with heart and hand after unity, law, and freedom for the German Fatherland'). A strange combination of words, splicing together the Federal Republic's motto, 'unity, law, and freedom' and the words of the GDR's

Jugendweihe or secular state confirmation ceremony in which 14-year-olds pub-
licly dedicated themselves 'with heart and hand' to socialism: 'Dem Sozialismus
unsere Herz und unser Hand' The two formulas of Germany unity, the Federal
Republic's formal unity of law and freedom and the Democratic Republic's
affective unity of heart and hand are awkwardly fused into the higher unity of
the German Fatherland.

Yet the emblems of national unity issuing from this period are hesitant and
indeterminate, indicating uncertainty over the character of future German unity.
Was it to be the chimerical rebus of eagle, hammer and dividers, or the shared
'D' in BRDDR? The open question of future German unity is indicated in the
Aktion Gemeinsinn medal in which the hands reach across the wall, but have
not yet closed upon each other. This indeterminacy also featured in constitutional
debate of the period, in which the constitutional future of Germany was by no
means a foregone conclusion. The extra-parliamentary GDR 'Round Table'
comprising representatives from the SED and other parties, the revolutionary
citizens' movements, and the Church, which flourished in the early months of
1990, proposed a new constitution for the GDR, one which would, in the words
of the draft preamble, 'build on the revolutionary renewal'.[14]

With the victory in the elections of 18 March 1990 of the conservative
'Alliance for Germany' committed to rapid unification of the two German states,
the Round Table constitutional proposal changed its significance, as did the
nature of constitutional debate. At issue in the spring and summer of 1990 was
the nature of the handshake which would seal the unification negotiations
between the two states. This resolved itself into a debate concerning the future
of the German constitution.[15] The Federal Republic's *Grundgesetz*, or 'Basic
Law' of 1949 was a self-consciously provisional document, its preamble stating
that the constituent *Länder* of the Federal Republic acted 'on behalf of those
Germans whose participation was denied', and calling in future on the 'entire
German people ... to achieve in free self-determination the unity and freedom
of Germany'.

In spite of the preamble, the Basic Law was ambiguous concerning the
constitution of a unified Germany. Article 23 on the 'Jurisdiction of the Basic
Law' foresaw its promulgation 'in other parts of Germany ... on their accession'
to the existing Federal Republic, while the final article (146) on the 'Duration
of the Validity of the Basic Law' proclaimed that 'This Basic Law shall cease
to be in force on the day on which a constitution adopted by a free decision of
the German people comes into force.' In the first case, unification is thought in
terms of accession, with one party agreeing to relinquish its constitutional
identity in the other, while in the second case, the German nation as a whole
freely agrees to reconstitute itself, surrendering its existing constitutional identities and creating a new one. However, events dictated that the first route was
taken, and the representatives of the two German republics shook hands on the
two state treaties which dissolved the German Democratic Republic: the first,

of 18 May 1990, agreed the economic and social union, the second, of 31 August, the political and social union.[16]

With the dissatisfaction in the Eastern *Länder* of the extended Federal Republic with some of the economic and social consequences of unification, it seems as if once again the German handshake has left one party in the grip of the other. It is too early to speak of the success or failure of unification, which culturally, economically and politically may require generations,[17] but it may be timely to conclude with a fragment from Kafka's second octavo notebook. The writer's hands are fighting, and the left is being vanquished by the stronger right:

> If, confronted with this misery, I had not got the saving idea that these are my own hands and that with a slight jerk I can pull them away from each other and so put an end to the fight and the misery – if I had not got this idea, the left hand would have been broken off at the wrist, would have been flung from the table, and then the right, in the wild recklessness of knowing itself the victor, might have leapt, like a five-headed Cerberus, straight into my attentive face. Instead, the two now lie one on top of the other, the right stroking the back of the left, and I, dishonest referee, nod in approval.[18]

Notes

1 H. W. Koch, in his *Constitutional History of Germany in the Nineteenth and Twentieth Centuries*, London: Longman, 1984, writes: 'the Frankfurt assembly, in spite of its failure, had ... laid the practical and constitutional foundations for Germany's unification' (p. 77). As a non-Imperial model of unity it continued to haunt the Reich after 1871 and influenced subsequent liberal constitutionalism. It is still considered as the first and exemplary modern German constitution, and is widely reprinted (see the paperback edition of *Deutsche Verfassungen*, ed. Rudolf Schuster, München: Goldmann Verlag, 1989). The 1991 constitutional proposal for a unified Germany from the *Kuratorium für einen demokratischen Bund der deutscher Länder* cites this precedent in its prefatory *Paulskirchnerklärung* – see Bernd Guggenberger *et al.*, *Eine Verfassung für Deutschland*, München: Carl Hanser Verlag, 1991.

2 For revolutionary developments in Leipzig see Bernd Lindner, *Zum Herbst '89: Demokratische Bewegung in der DDR* Leipzig: Forum Verlag, 1994.

3 Jürgen Habermas, *Die nachholende Revolution*, Frankfurt-am-Main: Suhrkamp Verlag, 1990, especially pp. 179–223.

4 The first article of the constitution defines the essence of the state, which is inseparable from its emblematic representation in its capital city, its flag, and its coat of arms.

5 The 'Admiral Palace', or Metropoltheater, at Friedrichstrasse 101/2, was an incongruous site for the meeting. The decorative giant doric columns of its façade, punctuated by an extravagant frieze, masked a bathing establishment.

6 Order no. 2 of the *Sowjetische Militäradministration in Deutschland* (Soviet Military Authority in Germany – SMAD) of 10 June 1945 legalized the re-establishment of anti-Fascist political and trade union organization in the Soviet Zone, which at that point included the whole of Berlin. The KPD was refounded on 14 June and the SPD on 15 June.

7   An incongruous combination of *gravitas* and operetta, probably appropriate for the occasion, although the choice of Lortzing (1801–51) composer of 'The Tsar and the Carpenter' does seem, in retrospect, somewhat inauspicious.

8   For an example, see H. P. Schaeffer, *East Berlin*, Berlin: Informationszentrum, 1988, p. 16.

9   Perhaps the musicians should have been playing the climactic scene from *Don Giovanni* at this point, as the Commendatore pulls the Don to his doom?

10 See Hans-Peter Stiebing's photograph of such a banner, reproduced in the *TAZ DDR Journal*, 1, Berlin 1990, p. 78.

11 *Aktion Gemeinsinn* was, in its own words, 'an association of independent citizens whose aim is to acquaint the citizens of our state (*Staatwesen*), by means of advertising and publicity, with the tasks which must be achieved in the interests of all, but which cannot be left to the authorities alone' (prospectus). The association, based in Bonn, produced a pamphlet entitled *We are your Homeland*.

12 This motto is also represented as two interlocking circles, with each part of the phrase forming half of each circle.

13 This juxtaposition of the two states was represented in a number of ways, notably in the oval car-bumper stickers containing the initials BRDDR (signifying Bundesrepublik Deutschland/Deutsche Demokratische Republik) with the central 'D' larger than the flanking 'BR' and 'DR'. This was a popular conceit, also reproduced in postcards from this period.

14 For the protocols of the Round Table see Helmut Herles and Ewald Rose, *Vom runden Tisch zum Parlament*, Bonn: Bouvier, 1990.

15 See the articles collected in Bernd Guggenberger and Tine Stein (eds), *Die Verfassungsdiskussion im Jahr der deutschen Einheit*, München: Carl Hanser Verlag, 1991.

16 See Geoffrey K. Roberts, 'Constitutional and political problems of German reunification: their relevance and impact on European unification', in Preston King and Andrea Bosco (eds), *A Constitution for Europe*, London and New York: Lothian Foundation Press, 1991, pp. 93–107, and David Southern, 'The constitutional framework of the New Germany', *German Politics*, 1(1), pp. 31–49.

17 The issue of the new German identity has been the subject of vigorous debate, with two notable contributions being Manfred Riedel, *Zeitkehre in Deutschland: Wege in das vergessene Land*, Berlin: Siedler Verlag, 1991, and Wilhelm Schmid, *Was geht uns Deutschland an?*, Frankfurt-am-Main: Suhrkamp Verlag, 1993.

18 Franz Kafka, *Wedding Preparations in the Country and other Posthumous Prose Writings*, trans. Ernst Kaiser and Eithne Wilkins, London: Secker and Warburg, 1954, p. 68.

Bad girls? Feminist identity politics in the 1990s

> It's not just nostalgia that keeps calling me back to the pioneering feminist art of the 1970s, but the ever more obvious affinities with what's going on in the 1990s. It seems politically and aesthetically crucial that the work done then not be forgotten now and that its connections to the succeeding decades be clarified (Lucy Lippard, 'In the flesh: looking back and talking back').[1]

How in the 1990s, after twenty-five years of intensive feminist debate about women's art practice, the status of Theory and the politics of feminist art practice, can we speak of feminism's identity politics? For a time, in the 1980s, identity politics seemed displaced by a focus on difference. The most pressing question, it seems to me now, is not just about going beyond a (singular) identity for feminism, since it has become all the more pressing to speak of feminisms in the plural, but about the levels of identification amongst different generations of women with the bodies of feminist knowledge which have emerged in the last twenty-five years. This is a question about historical knowledge and conscious political affiliations as things change and yet the repetitive character of sexism remains. The necessity of speaking about the complex plurality of feminist practices and theories exists in the face of the narrow and negative perceptions of what feminism is seen to represent in a male-dominated art world which remains protective of the status quo. Feminism itself has become increasingly defined by an agonistic politics, by recognition of itself as operating through specific strategic interventions.[2]

Central to defining these issues is how we understand the last twenty-five years of feminist art practice. The stake in identity for feminist art practice now is as much about identification with a feminist past – the women's art movement – and a theory about feminist political activism, as it is about the mobilization of collective identities to make change for the future. It also concerns whether we regard feminism as an umbrella coalition of women which since the 1970s continues to operate within a continuum of shared beliefs and values, even when realized through different forms, political alliances or strategies, or whether we see feminist politics as divided by generational differences, sites and moments of emergence which are discontinuous and disjunctive and without possible unity or common political goals. This dual sense of identity politics marks feminist cultural politics as much as it represents the fundamental paradox within feminist politics itself. As Rosalind Delmar suggests, the paradox for feminism lies in the 'generality of feminism's categorical appeal to all women as potential participants in a movement, and on the other hand ... the exclusiveness of its current internal practice, with its emphasis on difference and division'.[3]

The 1993 and 1994 *Bad Girls* exhibitions in London, New York and California[4] provide a focus for exploring how competing definitions of feminism operate in the art world and how identification with an image of feminism from the early 1970s was problematically reclaimed by several women curators in the 1990s. The staging of several *Bad Girls* shows in Britain and America was intended to relabel and potentially to reinvest in a revised form of feminist politics for the 1990s, but was its role simply to mark a different generation's terms of engagement? However, did it succeed in identifying a new set of strategies in feminist art practice?

The curating of these shows on either side of the Atlantic was not related, though the *Bad Girls* exhibition at the Institute of Contemporary Arts in London (ICA) preceded the exhibitions at the Museum of Contemporary Art, New York (MOCA) and its sister show at The University of California, Los Angeles' Wight Art Gallery. While the 'borrowing' of the title (believed to be from New York to London) and the presence of Sue Williams (in New York) form the superficial connections between the shows, the curatorial arguments advanced in each catalogue are marked by a similarity of theoretical ideas or resources but sharp differences in how they declare the stake for feminism.

Both catalogues positioned their 'bad girls' as 'bad' with reference to the Black American slang for 'wicked' (where the word's meaning is the opposite to its normal usage) and to a definition of 'nice' or 'good girls' in the sense of obedient would-be wives and mothers. While the MOCA show included a few male artists, 'good boys', whose works questioned identity, it largely presented American artists (with a view towards a multicultural perspective); by contrast the ICA show offered a transatlantic combination of three Americans, two British and one Irish women – all white/young(ish)/cosmopolitan. All three exhibitions traded on the significance of transgressions performed by the work of the 'bad girls', largely through the shock value contained in the subject-matter addressed – rape, transsexuality, lesbianism, pornography, abuse and violence against women. Though the ICA show presented only the conventional forms of drawing, painting, sculpture and photography, the MOCA exhibition also presented videos and installation work. In all cases, the representations of 'taboo' subjects supposedly paralleled early feminist work which focused on women's experience from the 1970s, and yet displaced it by what was regarded as a 1990s-style engagement with cynicism and irony, using humour as a 'strategy of subversion'.[5] Tempting though it might be to take the claims of humour as a subversive tool at face value and portray a new set of feminist art practices emerging in the form of Donna Haraway's blasphemous and irreverent cyborgs, seeking to displace and highlight 'contradictions that do not resolve into larger wholes' (a tactic adopted in the MOCA catalogue),[6] I want to ask what kind of rhetorical strategies, what kind of political ideas did the exhibition and the works included actually seek to address?

For the subversiveness edge of *Bad Girls* was presented not simply as anger at the ruses of patriarchy – the eruption of an angry, passionate group of women responding to sexism, similar to the first wave of feminists – but was directed at a perceived legacy of feminism. As Susan Dyer wrote of *Bad Girls* in New York, this 'sense of humour [may have served as] relief in the chaos of identity politics', but 'in sticking out their tongues, have they literally blocked their ability to speak?'[7] Why did the American shows present the 'bad girls' ' feminism as somehow 'politically incorrect within feminist art activity',[8] even going so far as to suggest that its transgressions were not political? As Dyer asks, 'Is there feminist art which isn't aligned with feminist politics? If so, are these 'bad girls' 'bad' because they'll do as they please no matter whose house they dismantle along the way?'[9] Although the humour in their work was regarded as 'irreverent' to contemporary politics, and even declared non-ideological, Marcia Tanner, in the New York/California catalogue, nevertheless mapped a history of foremothers to the 'bad girls' through the figures of Artemisia Gentileschi, Meret Oppenheim, Yoko Ono, Louise Bourgeois, Faith Ringgold, Lynda Benglis and Cindy Sherman, as well as the representation of women in Hollywood movies, pop songs, and through media images of women who fought back. In spite of this attempt to recognize connections with other dissenting voices, this was a set of artistic foremothers who, in the late twentieth century, have had a largely ambivalent, if celebrated, relationship to contemporary feminist art practice in America.

In Britain, the subversive power of 'bad girls' humour was characterized differently. Their irreverence, though regarded as caustic and bold, was positioned in opposition to a negative image of early seventies feminism, but with a sexiness which, to a large extent, derived from the fashionable hype surrounding the exhibition and its venue. Cherry Smyth argued in the ICA catalogue that '*Bad Girls* celebrates the multiplicity of feminisms in the nineties, resisting and undermining the tendency towards the essentialist and didactic voices of early feminist work. Sly, in-your-face, disturbing, provocative, haunting, subtle, sensual, shocked, sexy – the bad girls have come.'[10] However, instead of the proposed 'heteroglossia' – signalling a multiplicity of mixed voices and a pluralism within feminist perspectives, the ICA exhibition appeared more like one of the titles of Helen Chadwick's pieces – a 'glossolalia' – a speaking in tongues, an incomprehensible babble (Figure 4). Thus Michael Archer, writing in *Art Monthly*, argued that the ICA show represented 'a deliberately up-front concoction – of what? – which made claims for the existence of a new authority of expression among women artists, they raised the question, "what's changed?" The tag is different –

FIGURE 4. Helen Chadwick, *Glossolalia*, 1993

feminism/post-feminism – but the prefix in itself conveys little beyond the fact that we are looking at different generations.'[11] He continued: 'the least interesting thing to do is to wonder whether the work of Nicole Eisenman, or Sue Williams, or Dorothy Cross is somehow more shocking than, say, Judy Chicago's *Red Flag* (the image of her removing a tampon, for those who weren't there at the time), or the exhibition mailers or art magazine adverts of Lynda Benglis'.[12] Archer's least interesting question, it seems to me, is the only interesting question for any feminist cultural analysis to ask. Why did the ICA catalogue and exhibition produce this kind of repression of an earlier generation of feminist politics, negatively stereotyping them as didactic, essentialist and collectivist? Why was there a wish to mark the London exhibition of women artists as having no relationship (except for denegation) to the broader history of over two decades of (American) feminist art practice? Reducing all past feminist practice to a version of essentialist feminist neatly enabled the presentation of these six women as post-feminist, as something new, but then what happened to the feminist art practice of the 1980s? For, according to some critics, it was only in the 1980s that feminism emerged as an avant-garde political force in postmodernism. In fact, the 'pluralism' of the 1970s and 1980s was marked by the emergence of feminist art practice(s). All three exhibitions were struggling to represent contemporary women's work as a new trend. In spite of the fact that the American exhibitions offered 'a continuum' from foremothers to 'bad girls' (and boys), thus potentially validating a matrilineal tradition, it also distinguished this new trend as representing a generational break from what was perceived as 'orthodox' feminism. This closed down upon more obvious parallels in the works as feminist variants and critiques of current male mainstream practice. As Laura Cottingham, however, did remark as an aside in the ICA catalogue, an appropriate male counterpart to *Bad Girls* would be an exhibition of Mike Kelley, Jeff Koons and Richard Prince, called *Stupid Idiots*.[13] Might feminism here become recognizable, to parody Frederic Jameson's terms, as the political unconscious of the late consumer capitalist art world?

References to how *Bad Girls* relates to feminist politics of the 1980s were short-circuited and excluded by this parallel with the 1970s. This played, perhaps successfully, on the inadequacies of male critics' engagement with feminist issues and ideas in the 1980s, but the implications of this move also suggested that the transgressions enacted by the works came from a libertarian individualism rather than a liberationist politics. The ICA catalogue declared that 'What distinguishes it from previous feminist work is the use of humour as a strategy of subversion. And it operates outside the bounds of feminine propriety. It is not ideological, though it is operating from positions of power and liberation.'[14]

Freedom to act, even transgressively, relies upon occupying a privileged position – liberation here is recast as women 'making it' and saying what they like. It is impossible, however, to claim that humour is 'non-ideological', because in order to laugh one has to be able to recognize what one is laughing at. The very process of laughter, the recognition of a knowing irony depends upon naming and knowing the position adopted by the joke. The knowing smile marks one's particular appellation into a specific set of ideologies, however much the effect of that ideology 'is to erase its own traces completely, so that anyone who is "in ideology", caught in its web, believes "himself" to be outside and free of it'.[15] As Theresa de Lauretis argues, following Althusser, there is nowhere in the construction/representation of gender outside ideology, no position of power or liberation outside ideology,[16] even if it were possible to claim that for a few white Western women at the end of the twentieth century that liberation – economic, social and sexual – had been achieved. Similarly the ability to act from a position of power or 'liberation' – including the ability to subvert – means that one is acting from an already-inscribed ideological position, while identifying one's ideological opponents. The identification of a libertarian impulse, defined above, became the keynote of the London show. It presented an attempt to escape both 'politics', seen as a constraining, not an empowering force, and history, in so far as the humour, wit and compassion attributed to the works carried with it a desire to supersede/wipe the slate of history and tradition clean in a satirical gesture. The transgressions within *Bad Girls* operated at the level of the 'shock' content of the images, but as Lippard suggests, since the 1980s defined 'retrochic', there are many artists who play with a 'dialectic between acceptable surfaces and unacceptable content(s)'; the question remains:

> Now we have to figure out whether it's satire, protest, or bigotry ... when a woman artist satirises pornography, but uses the same grim images, is it still pornography? Is the split beaver just as prurient in a satirical context as it is in its own original guise? What about an Aunt Jemima image, or a white artist imitating a black's violent slurs against honkies?[17]

For satire and puns, while provoking laughter and making fun, notoriously have the aftermath effect of reinforcing the old, not the new. As Annette Kuhn suggests, there remain some very basic questions about the status of any art practice as feminist: 'Is the feminism of a piece of work there because of the attributes of the author (cultural interventions by women), because of certain attributes of the work itself (feminist cultural interventions), or because of the way it is "read"?'[18] Given this, how, or did the works in *Bad Girls* engage with perhaps a broader project of critiquing gender identities as fixed or natural and present representations of identities as ideological and psychically or socially constructed? What are the stakes in Nicole Eisenman's drawing *Betty Gets It*, which parodies the happy heterosexuality of *The Flintstones* characters Betty and Wilma as a lesbian couple in a 'hilarious expression of dyke camp'? Is it possible to say that Nan Goldin's work (also shown at the ICA), photographs of her friends and their lifestyle, succeeds in doing this as a textual operation? Or is it only because of the context, the documentary memorial framing of a subculture of trans-sexuals, inside and out of the gay community, that these works of people in 'private moments' acquire significance? In the catalogue these works were situated alongside Rachel Evans as the product of personal experience, a form of art as autobiography – but one which was not referenced against feminist artists using the personal as political. Or is this an extension of modern art's role as private production made for a market, rather than feminist concern for changing modes of engagement with an audience? As Lucy Lippard has noted, 'Mobility within representation, especially when it is controlled from within, is a subtle form of resistance. Art, especially avant-garde art (now called "cutting edge"), is expected to be unexpected.'[19] Claims about the radical edge to this work were made by outlining the subjects addressed, not through providing contexts for understanding and speaking about the issues in a broader politics. In so far as the ICA show celebrated the individual works and artists, it denied the relevance of politics and history in their subservience to the aesthetic. The 'references' alluded to were through contrasts between the artists in the show, as parodies of Picasso, Meret Oppenheim or Richard Prince, and their departures from feminist artists like Kruger/Holzer/Levine, Chicago/Spero.

Feminism in the 1980s invested heavily in critical analysis of difference, but as Teresa de Lauretis's analysis also productively suggests: 'if the deconstruction of gender inevitably effects its (re)construction, the question is [remains], in

whose interest is the de-re-construction being effected?'[20] De Lauretis productively suggests a means to consider feminist analysis as 'the space not visible in
the frame, but inferable from what the frame makes visible' – a 'space-off' by/in
representation, discourse and the sex/gender system.[21] What feminist analysis
aims to bring into view through its cultural interventions is both the desire to
affirm the historical condition of the existence of feminism (bodies of feminist
thought and ideas) and its continuing theoretical conditions of possibility.

In art school culture in Britain, in spite of nods towards pluralism (for
feminism is an area which must be catered for because of student demand),
feminism is still perceived (by staff and students) through a number of clear
stereotypes which trade on both popular and academic models of feminism,
largely as a means by a male-dominated administration to 'police' women
employees and students. Popular assumptions about feminism are used to close
down on discussions of more complex issues by stereotyping anyone who raises
feminist issues along the lines of: 'feminists just hate or have problems with
men'. Three populist assumptions about feminism continue to operate: first,
that feminism is equivalent to women 'making it' or women in power, or sexually
independent women (and with an increasing number of women in the workforce
this includes anyone from Mrs Thatcher to the only woman lecturer in a
department to any female who can be stigmatized/identified as a dyke). In the
second stereotype, feminism is limited to the Women's Liberation Movement of
the early 1970s and, as with hippy culture, it is now outdated, outmoded and
has had its day. Feminism can, then, be presented as a form of essentialist
separatist feminism dating from the seventies, associated with bra-burning,
male-hating castrating viragos, or a monstrous female superiority identifiable in
any discussion of women's culture, as part of a radical 'outdated' politics. What
interests me about these two stereotypes is the way that they close down upon
any possibility for women to identify with feminism, since to do so brings down
torrents of personal abuse or a barrage of negative criticism. A third stereotype
of feminism emerges in the way it also signifies the holding term for all and any
discussion of women, gender politics, or gender in politics; conceived entirely
as the radical separation of male from female and as sex antagonism between
two camps. More 'sophisticated' versions of the idea that feminism = gender =
women is the identification of all feminist theory with one – albeit currently
hegemonic – camp in feminist debate, French feminism, through its principal
proponents Kristeva, Irigaray or Cixous. This stereotype marks the move into
anti-essentialist gendered forms of analysis of the 'feminine' beyond the con-
juncture of Althusser/Lacan, Marxism/psychoanalysis which dominated debate
in the late 1970s and early 1980s. This third stereotype has become the most
academically acceptable form of feminist praxis in the academy and the confer-
ence circuit; the identification of feminism with Theory. Feminism's existence
as synonymous with developments in French feminism is given a place, but in
such a way that it can be dismissed as a variation of no particular importance,

and one which does not necessarily carry with it a commitment to looking at the work of women artists. This development and its currency I do not bemoan, but nevertheless its confinement to certain forms of discussion, to 'appropriate' areas of work (scripto-visual, film, video, photography) creates immense problems for younger women students working in studios where the ethos in practice is defined by an almost exclusive 'male' tradition, and where beginning from a consideration of either issues or ideas remains anathema. In each of these stereotypes feminism is invoked in the singular as the ground which needs to be acknowledged, but something constantly disavowed. These problems are reinforced by the limited teaching time given to feminist lecturers to provide a bridge for students into often complex theoretical debates.

The third stereotype also led to a development where, under the rubric of postmodernism, it became almost routine for women artists and academics to declare themselves fashionably 'post-feminist', and declare a belief in an aesthetic/textual politics of the feminine as the carrier of all and any potential for subversive Otherness, while neatly distancing themselves from identifications with anything that could be identified as essentialism. Post-feminism also carried with it a media perception in the late 1980s that careerist women succeeded in direct proportion to how loudly they could denounce the continuing relevance of feminism to women today. But as with postmodernism, all those wishing to declare themselves post-feminist have to make clear which version of feminist politics they position themselves as moving beyond. If they follow Kristeva's characterization of the three moments of feminism, (1): equal rights, (2): advocacy of a separate women's culture, or (3): total re-evaluation of both masculine and feminine, post-feminists might be happy to dismiss the first two, but this ignores Kristeva's own stress on their simultaneous existence.[22] For, in spite of the fact that essentialist feminist politics had already become the object of substantial criticism through the last fifteen years,[23] declaring oneself post-feminist may actually be about embracing and identifying with the negative view of the irrelevance of all or any feminist politics in the company of male poststructuralists who desire to embrace the discursive space of 'woman' while ignoring the cultural production of women.

The repetitive ways in which these three stereotypes about feminism operate in art school culture in Britain certainly fed into the critical reception of the ICA *Bad Girls*. From the hungry excitement of women students to identify with an exhibition of contemporary feminist art in a mainstream venue which was 'setting a new trend' to the 'reinventing the wheel' attitude of older women artists involved with feminism since the early 1970s, mixed with their amazement at the hype surrounding the show. Or the bored, cynical male critic Michael Archer, who regarded the exhibition as 'doing over again' early seventies feminism, but where the 'impact dulls, meaning dissipates ... because somebody wasn't there at the time, and they want to know what it was like ... cynics who would have us believe that they've seen it all before, and it corsets the already comfortable, who are convinced that it was better, because truer, more authentic, back then. But they haven't, and it wasn't.'[24] The 'bad girls' signalled a 'feminist' interventionist strategy if one regards lesbianism, shrieking viragos, and parodic irreverence as symptoms of contemporary feminism. What is disavowed, however, is also the theoretical work of the 1980s, with its emphasis on sexual/textual practices, speaking subjects, and écriture.

It would be very easy for a curator to assemble a visually compelling set of formalist parallels between 1970s and the 1990s positioning: Lynda Benglis's lumps of polyurethane, *Modern Art No. 1* (1970–4) against Laura Godfrey Isaacs's acrylic excesses, *Monstrous Alien Blobs* (1993–4): or Lee Bontecou's *Untitled* (1961) steel and canvas constructions with Cathy de Monchaux's metal and velvet fetish-like sculptures, *Defying Death, I ran away to the Fucking Circus* (1991); or Ava Gerber's installation of intertwined aprons, *Sisterhood* (1992) with Miriam Schapiro's quilt installation, *Anatomy of a Kimono* (1976) and Zoe Leonard's museum installation, substituting photostats of vaginas for historical paintings at *Documenta IX* in 1992 compared with Judy Chicago's drawings developing 'core imagery' from *Rejection Quintet* (1974) or Susan Santoro's artist book, *Towards a New Expression*, which contrasted vaginal photographs with flowers, shells and Ancient Greek figurines. The strategic questions feminism raises about knowledge production, its insistent challenges made about the gendering of all discourses, about masculinity and femininity as psychosocially constructed, cannot be so easily side-stepped by feminist critics: 'Feminist art, for instance, cannot be posed in terms of cultural categories, typologies, or even certain insular forms of textual analysis, precisely because it entails assessment of political interventions, campaigns and commitments, as well as artistic strategies.'[25]

Feminist art does not exist as a stylistic/formalist entity – even parodic forms of retrochic. Feminist art practice was never a homogeneous movement or art world trend, defined by characteristics of style, favoured media or subject-matter. The parallels with Lynda Benglis's mailers, however, would be found not in *Bad Girls* but in the *Guerilla Girls*, Fanny Adams or the poster campaigns and protests of the Women's Action Coalition.[26] Feminist art practice is widely recognized to exist through interventions in visual codes and in the relation art has to its audience or as an avant-garde politics of reintegrating art into life. This, as Mary Kelly insists, is the feminist problematic in art, and why there is no single theoretical discourse of feminism.[27] Feminist cultural politics have always been more than a set of textual/formal strategies engaging a broader political context, as both Lucy Lippard and Griselda Pollock have, in different ways, insisted:

> Feminist opposition to Modernism has therefore been more complex than the substitution of pluralism for formalism, of critical engagement for abstraction and apparent neutrality, of photography, video or scripto-visual art forms for pure painting. It has entailed a political assessment of the relations between a range of potential practices and the sites of their effective deployment.[28]

Feminism's political goal has been to change the character of art, changing both the nature of art and impacting upon the representation of women's experience of the world. It is possible to see the parody and pastiches within the *Bad Girls* show as not only parallel to other postmodern phenomena but also as continuing feminist strategies of role reversal (for example, Nicole Eisenman's substitution of castrating amazons for Picasso's rapacious minotaurs in her mural *The Mino- taur Hunt*, or Sue Williams's parody of Richard Prince in *Spritual America*, 1992). As Rosa Braidotti has argued, early 1970s feminist writing is also marked by precisely witty role-reversals, parodies and irony (consider, for example, Mary Daly's verbal puns).[29] If political feminism was regarded as humourless, what about other more engaged feminist work which also uses humour, the perform- ance artist Bobby Baker, or the comedians French and Saunders? Being a 'bad girl' in the sense of not conforming to social stereotypes about obedience to patriarchal expectations was, for me, always a definition of being a feminist, since it meant asking troubling questions and speaking 'out of turn'. The question remains, in what way does the work selected relate to other feminist work which was routinely described in terms of feminist postmodernist strategies in the 1980s?

The indifference to sexual difference in postmodern criticism so neatly characterized by Craig Owens, or, as Martha Rosler pointed out, the collapse of all difference to the marker of one difference, be it feminism, sex, race, creed or sexuality, continues because most critics remain indifferent to any historical conception of feminist art practice since the 1970s.[30] For, in spite of the impression that the number of women artists exhibiting in the mainstream is increasing, critics still refer women's work largely to male peers rather than to feminist mothers. For many male and conservative critics in the 1980s, feminism was seen as an irrelevance to 'Bad Painting' (neo-Expressionism), retrochic, or post- minimalist work – at best a minor, brief episode, or a colouring of a particular woman's work which could be read (preferably) in non-feminist/formalist or even psychoanalytic ways. This is often coupled with the idea that either feminist art practice, identifiable only with core imagery, Lippard's early notion of a feminine aesthetic[31] or the reintroduction of crafts or traditional craft media, was somehow over and finished with, or that feminist analysis of representation should be curtailed to certain forms of discussion – like a concern with images of women, discussions of sexuality, or, in its most recent incarnation, as a minor branch of queer theory. Where feminism is seen to ally itself with postmodernism, it still remains all too frequently marginalized as peripheral in the development of art. Feminism merits a chapter or slight reference, but is rarely placed as central to the discussion or its terms of reference. Whether, as Owens rightly suggested, postmodernism is another masculine invention to exclude women, remains a pertinent question,[32] since women still remain marginalized by the mainstream which, in spite of a few incorporations, continues with business as usual. Business as usual is constructed around marginalizing women artists as second-class citizens. In this regard, it is striking how few women who have been working for the last twenty years have been given major retrospectives, for to do so would of necessity foreground a re-evaluation of the negative positioning of feminism in the art world.

Owen's definition of the apparent crossing of the feminist critique of patriarchy and the postmodernist critique of representation is marked by his prioritizing of feminist deconstructive works (e.g. Mary Kelly, Barbara Kruger, Laurie Anderson, Martha Rosler, Dara Birnbaum) because of their affinities with (male) post-structuralist textual strategies – of Lyotard, Foucault, Derrida, Deleuze and Guattari (another version of the third stereotype).[33] More sceptically, as Susan Rubin Suleiman has noted, there is an element of mutual political opportunism amongst feminist postmodernist artists (the same identifiable group), while less fashionable feminist work goes unnoticed. For 'Feminism brings to postmodernism the political guarantee postmodernism needs in order to feel respectable as an avant-garde practice', and postmodernism, in turn, brings feminism into a certain kind of theoretical discourse on the frontiers of culture, traditionally an exclusively male domain.[34] While Owen's analysis is/was widely endorsed by feminists as an important critical intervention, it remains one of the few serious analyses by male critics of the role of feminism in the contemporary visual arts.

Owens argues that postmodern strategies – in line with Hal Foster's anti-aesthetic kind – demonstrated an awareness of the hegemonic aspects of cultural texts; art objects read as texts and practices. The counter-practice of intervention involved (1): a critique of official representations, (2): alternative uses of informational modes (like photography), (3): a recovery of the history of others, and (4): scepticism regarding separation of fields of expertise – resulting in a merging of disciplines.[35] While this fitted well the group of largely American artists described in Owens's argument, it cannot be taken as prescriptive of all feminist art practice in the 1980s, still less of the 1990s. Analyses of the postmodern condition and feminist politics are now seen to overlap at particular conjunctures rather than to coincide or fit as assimilable to one another, but the implications for feminist cultural politics are only just beginning to be analysed. Donna Haraway in 'Manifesto for cyborgs' was well aware that 'taxonomies of feminism produce epistemologies to police deviation from women's experience'[36] and such taxonomies as Owens's inevitably excluded much less fashionable feminist work which did not use scripto-visual, photography, video and performance.

It also remains highly questionable whether Lyotard or Jameson's discussion of the loss of authority in and disillusion with the grand narratives of modernity as symptomatic of postmodernism actually applies to feminist thought, beyond potentially the discrediting of the term 'sisterhood' in the 1970s.[37] This also does not fit the other characterization (by male postmodernists) of the women's liberation movement after 1968, which used 'sisterhood' as its rallying cry, as an example of one of the large number of 'local' liberation movements which emerged as symptomatic of the moment of postmodernism (dated from the 1970s).[38] Such definitions are dependent on whose shifting periodization and characterization of postmodernism you subscribe to, and whether or not you are prepared to cast women's liberation as a 'local' movement, even while you may be prepared to admit that feminists' insistence on consciousness-raising and the 'personal is political' recasts other/older notions of political activism. Does feminism share Lyotard's loss of authority in a single narrative (its critique of patriarchy) to describe women's condition, to legitimize women's position, and compel consensus, which is regarded as symptomatic of postmodernism? Do feminists, in spite of the discrediting of the word 'sisterhood' and its replacement by networks (even electronic world-webs) or contingent alliances truly see themselves as subjects of the postmodern condition in the sense of having lost the 'ability to locate ourselves historically [where] schizophrenia replaces meaning and life is characterized by a collapsed sense of temporality'?[39]

Most feminists still insist on the need for strategic political alliances amongst women, without invoking sisterhood, because of women's unequal, low-status, or subordinate positioning within institutions, discourses and practices as 'women'; however fractured by generation, creed, race or sexual orientation, it is now recognized that it is crucially necessary for such alliances to accommodate. Feminism, under the broader rubric of the 'movement of women', can legitimately position itself since the early nineteenth century as having been engaged with a critique of the enlightenment project and a critique of humanism confined to the male of the species, with women seen as representative of 'nature', the 'irrational', 'the body' or 'emotion'. As Robin Morgan has suggested:

> If I had to name one quality as the genius of patriarchy, it would be compartmentalization, the capacity for institutionalizing disconnection. Intellect severed from emotion. Thought separated from action. Science split from art. The earth itself divided: national borders. Human beings categorized by sex, age, race, ethnicity, sexual preference, height, weight, class, religion, physical ability, *ad nauseam*. The personal isolated from the political. Sex divorced from love. The material ruptured from the spiritual. The past parted from the present, disjoined from the future. Law detached from justice. Vision dissociated from Reality.[40]

In this sense, feminism can argue that the project/promise of modernity remains an incomplete project[41] as regards women's status as citizens or cultural producers. Analysis of the inadequacy of binary oppositions within patriarchal thought to account for women's experiences of the world, even recast in terms of phallologocentrism or the play between power and knowledge, remains central to feminist critique in the 1990s.

The *Bad Girls* presentation as a spectacle/a carnival in just the sense described by Stallybrass and White, 'the repeated parodic celebration of the grotesque body-fattening food, intoxicating drink, sexual promiscuity, altered ego-identity, the inverse and the heteroglot'[42] is thus extremely apt, for the carnival is a ritual regarded as separate from everyday life. The food and wine, in this case, being that of the media, fashion, and its representation of subversion in terms of all or anything that can be immediately recuperated or repackaged as an 'object' without meaning–effect. Can feminism afford to disregard the incredible debt of these women to very obvious feminist strategies of role reversal and montage? Can we afford to collude in the dismissal of previous generations of women artists? This is not to suggest that an interrogation of stereotypes in behaviour and attitudes, from feminism itself (in Sue Williams's work), to male violence against women, or the languages of romance in Rachel Evans, or the attention to bodily metaphors, are unimportant. Or that parody and jokes are irrelevant to feminism. They highlight some of the absurdities of masculinity as well as undermining their claims to sexual power. But, how does Sue Williams's piece sit by comparison with the 1970s performances and media-staged consciousness-raising of Ariadne's *In Mourning and In Rage*? Are we back in the limiting institution of the fine art market and its identifications, however temporarily 'shocking' a few 'bad girls' might appear to the mainstream?

Notes

1 Lucy Lippard, 'In the flesh: looking back and talking back', *Women's Art Magazine*, September/October 1993, p. 4.
2 See Rosi Braidotti, *Patterns of Dissonance: a Study of Women in Contemporary Philosophy*, Cambridge: Polity, 1991; Judith Butler and Joan W. Scott (eds), *Feminists Theorise the Political*, London: Routledge, 1992.
3 R. Delmar, 'What is feminism?', in J. Mitchell and Ann Oakley, *What is Feminism?* Oxford: Basil Blackwell, 1986, p. 11.
4 *Bad Girls*, London, Institute of Contemporary Arts, 7 October–5 December 1995; New York, Museum of Contemporary Art, Part 1: 14 January–27 February 1994, Part 2: 5 March–10 April 1994. MOCA shows included around ninety artists. *Bad Girls West*, Wight Gallery, UCLA, 25 January–20 March 1994.
5 Marcia Tucker in the MOCA *Bad Girls* catalogue made it clear that the 'bad girls' mockery was an antidote to silence: 'Women's humour at its best creates solidarity within and between groups, challenges traditional roles, defies stereotypes, is seductive, inclusive and, most important, is based on the idea that any and all systems of exploitation, not just those that exploit women, can and must be changes for the better' (p. 41).
6 Donna Haraway, 'Manifesto for cyborgs', in Linda Nicholson (ed.), *Feminism/Postmodernism*, London: Routledge, 1990, pp. 192–3.
7 Susan Dyer, 'Blowing the house down', *Women's Art Magazine*, 58, May/June 1994, p. 29.
8 *Ibid*, p. 28.
9 *Ibid*.
10 Cherry Smyth, 'Bad girls', ICA *Bad Girls* catalogue, p. 12.
11 M. Archer, 'What's in a prefix?', *Art Monthly*, 173, February 1994, p. 4.
12 *Ibid*.
13 L. Cottingham, 'What's so bad about 'em?', ICA *Bad Girls* catalogue, p. 59 (note 3).
14 Marcia Tanner, quoted in Susan Dyer, 'Blowing the house down', p. 28.

15 Theresa de Lauretis, 'The technology of gender', in T. de Lauretis, *Technologies of Gender*, Basingstoke: Macmillan, 1987, p. 6.

16 *Ibid.*, p. 9.

17 Lucy Lippard, 'In the flesh: looking back and talking back', p. 8.

18 A. Kuhn, quoted in R. Parker and G. Pollock, *Framing Feminism: Art and the Women's Movement 1970–1985*, London: Pandora, 1987, p. 93.

19 Lucy Lippard, 'In the flesh: looking back and talking back', p. 9.

20 Theresa de Lauretis, 'The technology of gender', p. 17.

21 *Ibid.*, pp. 25–6.

22 Julia Kristeva, 'Woman's time', in Nannerl O. Keohane, Michelle Z. Rosaldo and Barbara C. Gelpi, *Feminist Theory: a Critique of Ideology*, Brighton: Harvester Press, 1982, pp. 36–8.

23 See, amongst many others, Rosi Braidotti, *Patterns of Dissonance: a Study of Women in Contemporary Philosophy*; Judith Butler, *Gender Trouble: Feminism and the Subversion of Identity*, London: Routledge, 1990; Diane Elam, *Feminism and Deconstruction: Ms. En Abyme*, London: Routledge, 1994.

24 M. Archer, 'What's in a prefix?', p. 4.

25 Mary Kelly, 'Reviewing modernist criticism', *Screen* 1981, 22(3), p. 58.

26 See N. Broude and M. Garrard, *The Power of Feminist Art*, London: Thames and Hudson, 1995.

27 Mary Kelly, 'Reviewing modernist criticism', p. 58.

28 Lucy Lippard, 'Sweeping exchanges: the contribution of feminism to the art of the 1970s', *Art Journal*, 39 (Fall/Winter 1980), pp. 362–5; R. Parker and G. Pollock, *Framing Feminism: Art and the Women's Movement 1970–1985*, p. 104.

29 Rosi Braidotti, 'Assessing the second wave', in *Patterns of Dissonance: A Study of Women in Contemporary Philosophy*, pp. 151–67.

30 C. Owens, 'The discourse of others: feminists and postmodernism', in Hal Foster, *Postmodern Culture*, London: Pluto, 1985, pp. 61–2.

31 Lucy Lippard, *From the Center: Feminist Essays on Women's Art*, New York: E. P. Dutton, 1976, p. 49.

32 C. Owens, 'The discourse of others: feminists and postmodernism', p. 61.

33 *Ibid.*, pp. 64–5.

34 Susan R. Suleiman, 'Feminism and postmodernism: a question of politics', in C. Jencks (ed.), *A Postmodern Reader*, London: Academy Editions, 1991.

35 C. Owens, 'The discourse of others: feminists and postmodernism, pp. 64–5.

36 Donna Haraway, 'Manifesto for cyborgs', p. 198.

37 C. Owens, 'The discourse of others: feminists and postmodernism', pp. 57–8, 64–5.

38 C. Jencks, 'The post-modern agenda', in C. Jencks (ed.), *A Postmodern Reader*, pp. 10–24.

39 C. Owens, 'The discourse of others: feminists and postmodernism', pp. 57–8.

40 Robin Morgan, *The Demon Lover: on the Sexuality of Terrorism* (1989), quoted in Somer Brodribb, *Nothing Mat[t]ers: a Feminist Critique of Postmodernism*, Melbourne: Spinifex, 1992 p. xix.

41 J. Habermas, 'Modernity: an incomplete project', in Hal Foster, *Postmodern Culture*, pp. 3–15.

42 Peter Stallybrass and Allon White, *The Politics and Poetics of Transgression*, Ithaca, NY: Cornell University Press, 1986, quoted by Marcia Tucker in 'The attack of the giant ninja mutant barbies', MOCA *Bad Girls* catalogue, p. 22.

PART 3

Refiguring identity
in art

More and less than objects: unapproachable alterity and the work of Jana Sterbak and Rosemarie Trockel

Tout autre est tout autre (Jacques Derrida, *Aporias*).[1]

Before me stands a metal structure. It resembles a dummy; yet, by resembling a dummy, by being a dummy dummy, it seems to dissolve that space and zone of rehearsal which dummies support and sustain, of being the assistant in some process of trial and error in manufacture. It also resembles a dress, that which is left behind once the dummy has been discarded. Yet, given its outstretched arms and, in particular, those lower portions which rise from where the elbows may be imagined to be – as if in a gesture imploring recognition, but rendering it impossible – the structure further resembles a body wearing a dress. And coiled around the inelegant lines of the bodice, and descending below the waist, turns a live wire, glowing with the light and heat transmitted from two mains electricity sockets behind the figure. Approaching this figure, which seems to gesture to me in supplication, would nevertheless entail risk and danger: if I tried to close on this thing, to respond to its open arms as an invitation, perhaps my flesh would not return as mine. As if my flesh might become the substance of the skeletal structure before me.

These fictions of the elements and space of Jana Sterbak's *I Want You to Feel the Way I Do* ... (Figure 5) are not necessarily common. Yet they are guided by what may prove to be the necessary, if hardly sufficient, senses of space and location that are required for us to become aware of the existence of the bodies of others as other bodies. The metal structure can be said to be 'before me' in the sense of 'opposite me' (such a position of viewing is given by the photograph of it reproduced here). Yet, before this, before I can take up my position, opposite its suspended gesture, it has had to be put in place, set up (in the gallery; in an image) to perform its mute imitation of imploring my attention. Like a dummy, it may conform to my expectations or desires for expression, for an acting out of positions, but only at the risk of seeming to want to take on my very materiality in order to convince. And who would want to be convinced? None other than the very spectator who, in moving into this space, and coming across this figure in the light, had transferred to it something of the excess of that movement which had been guided and arrested by the figure which was both more and less than just some other gesturing figure; more and less than something animated as if by some obscure power-source which feeds the possibility of cutting a figure in space; more and less than the occasion for an identification of, by and for the viewer.

'Before me', a spatial identification, apparently the very act of auto-opposition by which an object is figured as an object for a subject, as other than a subject, is, however, also a phrase of temporality.[2] In being a phrase, it is also a phrase *as* temporality. Thus, in temporalizing, as well as spatializing, as phrase, the phrase also remarks the time before this use of this phrase. And, further, it suggests a question of the before of any 'before', the before of any spatial or temporal determination. Inaccessible as such, this before nevertheless haunts the space and time of any particular 'before' and, in particular, any 'before me'.[3] In principle, therefore, any figure may come to fall out of place, out of the here and now, and out of the then as a prior here and now, as the co-operation of time and space for a subject. In so far as this is organized through the determination of objects, by and for a subject, then so-called 'object-based' visual artworks – named as such in order to reassemble a categorial field which the

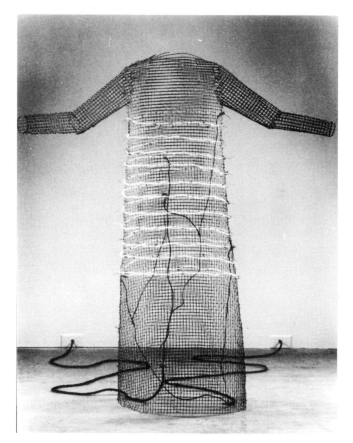

FIGURE 5.
Jana Sterbak, *I Want You to Feel the Way I Do ...* (*The Dress*), 1985–6

criticism of art is losing, with the waning of the logic of sculpture as a rationale of and for the production of so-called art objects – tend to promise and threaten to undermine and replay – undermine, perhaps, *by* replaying – the conditions of objecthood as such. Compelling and repelling, they proffer up the space, and time, of objects as already haunted by something more and less than the positions of and for subjectivity.

As if at once to confirm the strands of this argument and go beyond it, the figure in wire of this piece is accompanied by a text, projected from a slide on to the wall, behind and more or less above the figure. How may this text be read?

> I want you to feel the way I do: There's barbed wire wrapped around my head and my skin grates on my flesh from the inside. How can you be so comfortable only 5″ to the left of me? I don't want to hear myself think, feel myself move. It's not that I want to be numb, I want to slip under your skin: I will listen for the sound you hear, feed on your thought, wear your clothes.
>
> Now I have your attitude and you're not comfortable any more. Making them yours you relieved me of my opinions, habits, impulses. I should be grateful but instead ... you're beginning to irritate me: I am not going to live with myself inside your body, and I would rather practise being new on someone else.[4]

Before me, as well as the figure in wire, there appears this text, with its several 'I's. What links them? That which reading forgets, as it reads: namely, the inscription of the text, as site and process, as the process of site, forgotten in reading's movement to transcend the mark as mark, for the sake of signification. The determination of a mark as a signifier, as 'that which represents the subject for another signifier',[5] as an account of signification, repeats the movement of the transcendence of the figure; as if before me there was nothing other than another me, seeking to communicate its me-ness, tragically alienated in the 'I', in the armature of that image.[6]

But let us try to read this text as if it were such a communication, the communication of the figure which stands before us. What doesn't fit? The figure in wire does not have a head. The text would thus seem to complete the figure by describing its missing head. Headless and faceless, the figure in wire appears to address us only on condition that it lacks its head and face. In having the 'I' assumed for it, it cannot present itself as one who looks. In assuming the other to be another 'I', the head of the other appears to go missing, its torture in the field of the look, with 'barbed wire wrapped all around', cannot be seen; nor the embedding and the abrasion of the skin *in* its flesh. As if the other were in its skin; as if the other as another 'I' was in its own body. And consequently, desiring no more than a silence of itself to itself, a silencing of thinking, as well as an end to feeling movement, feeling itself on the move. If the other is the other 'I', that 'I' does not want any of this; instead, in a movement of violent substitution, it wants you too, wants your skin to get under, your hearing and thinking. And whatever the want of fit here, it won't care; it'll get into your body and into your clothes, taking not only your wardrobe, but its codes, an attitude, along with opinions, habits, impulses, dispossessing you even of what seemed, on occasion, to take possession of you from elsewhere. And, what's more, this process will seem interminable: assume the other as another 'I', and you will always have begun to irritate the other; who will, furthermore, always seem to be in the process of leaving something behind in you; always threaten to depart, leaving you with a trace of an alterity which you will not be able to reassign to the other, who wants to get away from its identification as such, renew itself for itself.

By doing exactly what you did to it. Figure of revenge of the very processes of identification. And this cannot be avoided, even if I read myself as the 'I' represented in the text on the wall. As an account of the 'I' of the spectator, the text predicts and accuses, representing the viewer as the one who seeks to take up a position opposite some figure or other, position in which the figure may come to relieve the one who looks of pain, thought, feeling and movement. To become the 'I' of the text here is thus to want to be occupied by the figure, forgetting noise and feeling; perhaps, indeed, feeling as noise, as interference in and beyond indentification. Even to the point of undressing, the one who wants to see the other as for itself, wanting, apparently, to disrobe and enrobe itself in the figure as other. And in this movement, which Freud might have described as the shift from voyeurism to exhibitionism, with a consequential exchanging of the object of a drive,[7] the viewer projects the other as itself, as the one who has suffered as it has done. Guilty, sensing obscurely an obligation of gratitude, the viewer nevertheless gets irritated. Some want of fit between the seer and the seen is sensed, but all that the viewer-as-subject can think of is to disentangle and renew 'itself' in a rehearsal with some other figure.

The lesson of these interpretations, if there is one, would be that this moving on to the other figure, to the other as figure, will always fail to overcome the work and play of the figure, its operation as the possibility of representing something other than ourselves, along with the want of fit, the wearing (out), of its operation as such. Reiterating the figure may thus seek to show that, and how, it has been reinscribed differently; how the figure has been more and less than a figure, something other than figure 'itself'. Sterbak's piece, as a staging and an occasion of different processes of figuration, prompts and jams the exit from these processes, becoming less the display of certain objects and more a temporary taking-place: the gallery as scene of a set-up of the viewer for these processes, of an expenditure of energies, for projection and illumination, in which matter, including the viewer as matter, comes to play a part. Apparently threatened with sacrifice, as witness and as victim, the viewer may be understood instead as the play of the figure, even if – and necessarily – setting him- or herself up in a movement in which the otherness of the figure has been transcended.

Such a set-up brings us round, apparently, to a question of gender. And is it not rather too late? 'I don't know whether sexual difference is ontological difference', ventriloquizes Lyotard in a portion of a text attributed to a 'SHE'.[8] And he goes on to suggest that the question of gender may always come around too late: initially 'outside our control', sexual difference, working according to a Freudian conceptualization of *Nachträglichkeit*, 'inscribes effects without the inscription being "memorized" in the form of recollection'.[9] Thus, according to Lyotard, thought and the thinking subject would be that which co-operated on pain of this effect of an inscription, a figure, which brings with it 'fields of perception and thought as functions of waiting, of equivocations'. Gender and its identifications would thus be a way of seeking to transcend the operation of the figure, of overcoming the 'waiting' and 'equivocations', waiting for the effects of the figure which bring their inevitable equivocations.

Lyotard develops this questioning of sexual difference – which is not 'just related to a body as it feels its incompleteness, but to an unconscious body or to the unconscious as body' – in a way which, for me, outlines something of the attraction and pain – indeed, attraction to the pain – of the play of the attributes of gender in the works of Jana Sterbak and Rosemarie Trockel. He writes of the 'waiting' and the 'equivocations' brought about by a split between the senses of being a body and of being a gendered body, of being 'programmed' by the representations of sexual differences as gender, of lining up as a girl or boy, of seeking correspondences according to the programming of and by these representations:

> This quite probably defines suffering in perceiving and conceiving as produced by an impossibility of unifying and completely determining the object seen. To that which without gendered difference would only be a neutral experience of space–time of perceptions and thoughts, an experience in which this feeling of incompleteness would be lacking as unhappiness, but only an experience producing a simple and pure cognitive aesthetic, to this neutrality gendered difference adds the suffering of abandonment, because it brings to neutrality what no field of vision or thought can include, namely a demand. The faculty to transcend the given that you were talking about, a faculty lodged in immanence indeed finds a means to do this in the recursiveness of human language – although such a capacity isn't just a possibility but an actual force. And that force is desire.[10]

Desire is thus the relay of a force, felt by the subject of thought, feeling, representation, one which, as it operates through thoughts, feelings, representations, works to transcend the immanent precisely by means of a return to inscription, the work of the figure as language. And – I would say – as visible figure, one which plays across the imagined zone of 'a simple and pure cognitive aesthetic', which has never existed, even while it may seem to have taken place for a subject. The sufferings of abandonment, perceiving and conceiving – indeed, of abandonment in perceiving and conceiving, as one might trace them, for example, through Lyotard's work on the sublime – lie latent, as possibility, in any return to a figure.[11]

Hence the structure of appeal of Sterbak's *I Want You to Feel the Way I Do ... (The Dress)*, to give it its full title. This title seems to represent the figure as already given in a zone of the representation of gender. As if dresses were, *de jure* and *de facto*, only for women. Yet it does so in a way which recalls a sense of abandonment, and its different evaluations: between putting on the dress and the possibility that this gives of taking it off, Sterbak's piece, like her other pieces which play on the meanings and values of clothes, finds a play of the figure of the veiling by clothes, the obscurity of the effects of sexual difference in play. But played out is the promise of the conclusion of such obscurity in enlightenment, in unveiling. Thus, whatever the claims and effects of gender to rule and regulate the field of representation, there remains a residue of the work of the figure which haunts the violence of its conceptualizations, including those of gender, which will always have been a mode of a transcendence of some alterity or other. Otherness will not be unveiled as a gendered other.

Something of this is conveyed, along with the uncanny violence of the drive to overcome the veiling of the other in the same, by Sterbak's *Vanitas: Flesh Dress for an Albino Anorectic* (Figure 6), a piece which needs to be considered in its several, unstable and unstably related instances. As designed and assembled meat, *Vanitas* invokes curatorial activity as care of decay and of danger: locus of a switching of meat, from potential nourishment to infection and poison, the piece haunts its photographic representation, hung on a hanger, displayed on a chain, with an anteriority, the time before it was photographed becoming both an occasion of mourning for the dress as meat and a representation, if not recollection, of the struggle of the meat dying as dress. And these two relations complicate each other, to the point of suggesting that *Vanitas* presents the viewer with scenarios which lead to a thought of dying and death which can never quite be objectified. Always already preying on examples, the relation of non-relation to 'my death', death as mine, exceeds any finality of representation such as might, once and for all, assure us of the meaning, value, value of meaning and meaning of value of death. As Derrida puts it, there is a 'mineness of dying or of being-toward-death, a mineness not that of an ego or of an egological sameness', one which may be retraced through relations with objects *as* the means of the ego's always deferred – *nachträglich* – self-relation. 'Originary mourning' as the fundamental possibility of the ego, defended against by some objects, threatened and recovered by others as traumatic wound.[12]

Meat offers up a finality of dying which would always have something of the other about it, even if it were of what might be claimed as my 'own' body. 'Me' approaching becoming-other, as dead, as meat, perhaps as animal; but without ever being able to be, to exist, as other simply for myself, my 'I'. There is no relation to death as such, argues Derrida; it is, from the beginning and

FIGURE 6.
Jana Sterbak,
*Vanitas: Flesh Dress
for an Albino
Anorectic*, 1987

without end, a relation 'to perishing, to demising, and to the death of the other, who is not the other':

> It is like the experience of mourning that institutes my relation to myself and constitutes the egoity of the *ego* as well as every *Jemeinigkeit* in the *différance* – neither internal nor external – that structures this experience. The death of the other, the death of the other in 'me', is fundamentally the only death that is named in the syntagm 'my death', with all the consequences that one can draw from this.[13]

And, no doubt, there are many effective denials of this, many imperatives to recognize the death of the other as *the* other, and hold us together in a community of mourning. The *vanitas* tradition has perhaps never had another promise, and, in the variety of its instances and their articulations, another failure. Sterbak's piece might well be cited as a plea for animal rights, for animals as something

like non-signifying, but significant others, the victims as material of and for
'our' processes of signification and survival. And the interruption of oral assimilation, signifying whatever carnivorousness may, as the possibility of this piece
(it is made of flank steak), demands some relation to these questions. The
paradox, however, of being able to grant rights to the other only as the same,
the same *as* the bearer of rights, remains.

And what would be missed, in this redemptive movement to represent this
aspect of this piece, would be the loss of whatever had become this meat. The
mourning of the dress as meat, mentioned above, would thus be the problematic
substitution for the mourning of the other – the other animal – as dress and as
image. The representation of the meat as dress thus returns as the haunting of
meat by the other who is no longer. Perhaps this is the position given and taken
by the woman who wears the dress: this woman, identified as such, no longer
simply other, haunts the haunting of the dress. Wearing a dress as a woman
thus suggests the risk of flesh becoming meat for her spectators; and the meat
dress becomes the presentation of an unpresentability of the otherness of *this*
woman, an image of a promise and threat of her becoming nothing other than
animal, meat, dead. Posed for and by the camera, the woman models a becoming-
woman as a necessary and yet finally impossible-to-guarantee transcendence of
flesh. Strangely pathetic, the woman also models herself as the risk of a failure
to become *this* woman. The trail of blood left by the dress, perhaps as the model
moved herself into position for the camera, offers also an appearance of a loss
of a limit of the woman's body. Of menstruation fantasized and feared as a
wound; of a wounding perhaps fantasized as menstruation. The marking of
other limits to the woman's body, however, finger- and toe-nails with nail polish
and lips with lipstick, stalls and re-routes this question of limits, becoming a
body always having lost itself to something other than itself.

Allure as horror of a loss of limit, the look thus mourns its captivation by
the image; and what has been photographed is lost and returns as less and more
than objects for the look. Perhaps there is no more strict and risky representation
of a woman as other than meat. Meat as garment risked, like all garments, as
veil – as if something needed to be hidden – in turn risks provoking the
identification of what might be unveiled as meat, or as dead flesh. But this 'or'
is perhaps the turn here, away from the risk of becoming meat, held and framed
as photographic image, as anteriority haunting any sense of a 'now', a reminder
of death and of dying which might supervene to prevent the threat of becoming
meat from ever taking place. Meat put on as garment, never to be undressed as
meat. To imagine unveiling this woman would thus be to unveil her as other
than meat and, indeed, as more than any mere possibility of being identical with
herself.

This difficult process, of the look losing its objects as its objects and
becoming instead the impossible search for something other than what it sees
(the look as drive and pulse, as impulse; the work of visual art as more and less

than object of and for scopophilia), is perhaps more economically set in motion by some of the works of Rosemarie Trockel.[14] Attributes of gender replayed to the echoes of the violence of any identification of an object with them. *Untitled (Dress)* of 1986, machine-knitted in wool with long sleeves and a roll-neck, bears in its surface two 'Woolmark' logos. *In* a surface thus recalls the look's aim beyond its objects and the tendencies to identify what lies beyond its limits. For where are these logos? Where breasts might be; but only if another object, a woman as object, is imagined as the wearer of this dress. Invoked by the breast, representable as totality of part-object, as a body traced and retraced as a site of violent identifications, the woman as object for any subject; and any woman subject to such a look for an object. The logo thus returns as a making recognizable, the visible become all but legible, which echoes misrecognition of the visible as a tissue separated into objects for some subject or other.[15]

Similarly and differently, other textile pieces offer the opportunity to retrace the becoming-interpretable of a mark. Like *Vanitas*, *Untitled (Pullover)* is used to name the work of art both as garment and as photograph. As garment, a pullover patterned with hammers and sickles; as photograph, a figure of a man, wearing the same, face turned away from our look to the right, left hand raised, index finger of his right hand in his right ear. Smiling, as if addressing – as if having been addressed by – someone, the man's gestures come to seem like attempts to block that very possibility of address: left arm raised to guard him from the direction of his look; index finger of right hand as if seeking to block the orifice of the ear. At the same time, the finger plays with the limit of the body, thus echoing the very play of a garment. As if a garment only ever obscured something or other. Showing, here, man as model – perhaps model man – dressed, once again, as an avant-gardism of, if not apparently for, the working class.

Perhaps the avant-garde will always have sought to dress itself anew, putting on the clothes of others as its own? Trockel's clothes pieces are haunted by traces of possible pasts and become, as a consequence, difficult to put on with hope of renewal. *Schizo-Pullover* names a pullover with two roll-necks, but also two photographs, which are (of) more than one. In 'one', the heads of two different women; in the other, heads of the same woman. 'The' print is thus – perhaps on both occasions – of more than one exposure, more than one time before the time of their viewing, a 'now' deferred by the interruption of a misrecognition, or two, and a stealing up of fantasies of bodies merging and dividing without achieving identity in visibility. As if before your eyes, the figure of the other has already been cloned, becoming more or less the same other, the other as more or less the same as herself. Such a fiction, sustained by the image, gives way, before the image, to a sense of otherness as more and less than any particular other.

Perhaps clothes are prone – and not especially if prone – to provoke and perturb identifications. Put on to protect against something or other, as if to produce something as other, to attract, to distract, retract from something or other as other, they are also attached to by what becomes detached. Who is

haunted by the remnants of such a process? Writing of the differences of view
of Heidegger and Schapiro over paintings by Van Gogh of shoes, Derrida puts
in question the processes by which these paintings, detached and reproducible,
are treated to a variety of reattachments. Schapiro – pro-history of art, historian
of art as pro – claimed that the shoes could not be those of a peasant woman,
as Heidegger appears to claim, but were, in their apparently indubitable existence, before the picture, and are, in the picture, as their apparently indubitable
representation, the shoes of an inhabitant of the city; for, when he painted them,
Van Gogh was himself an inhabitant of the city. He was, and he was no more
nor less than such a city dweller, and the shoes he painted were his shoes. Even
if now they might belong, as painted, to one and all. Not only did they seem
to Schapiro and to Heidegger to belong, but to belong to someone or other,
someone who, by reason of one projection or other, would put them on.
Identification of the shoes thus goes by way of some projection or other; usually
of the other as another 'me', by which something or other may return as
belonging, at least, to *a* 'me'. As Derrida notes, this detour through something
or other to return to a 'me' would be essential, were it not always already to
have included something other than 'me': 'Supplementary, since identification,
like attribution, has a *suppplementary* or *parergonal* structure. And supplementary because this demand for reattachment is by definition insatiable, unsatisfied,
always making a higher bid.'[16] The demand for a return from what is seen of
what is seen thus implicates any process of knowledge of the visible and of
visual art. As objects, works of art are always already added on to something
other than themselves. Examples, therefore, of haunting by being haunted, even
if only as a consequence of the very identification of them as works of art.

The works by Sterbak and Trockel considered above double this identification of them as works with the provocation to and problematization of
identification, of getting dressed up in them. As works, they may not be addressed
in another way. Yet, in being addressed, in being taken as objects to be seen
and known, these works return as more and less than such objects: something
seems to have been added to them, which they did not lack; and in not lacking
what they receive, they exceed their identifications. Perhaps, if you are not
convinced, it will only seem as if I have been raising the stakes of my identifications and attributions. Perhaps the following words, taken from an interview
given by Rosemarie Trockel, will tend against this inevitable risk, of trying to
address what may not be addressable. Asked about an affinity between her work
and that of the surrealists, she replied:

> Yes, sometimes, appalled, I detect a 'distant nearness'. But contrary to the belief
> in the omnipotence of dreams, of images from the depths of the subconscious,
> embellished with Freudian psychoanalytic theory, which the Surrealists used to
> impose their fantasy images upon us, I look rather for the plainness and
> simplicity of the objects, their simple beauty.
>
> Take the so-called long-necked heads from *Comaland*. They're a fusion of

FIGURE 7. Rosemarie Trockel, *Comaland*, 1988

phallus and vagina into a head. But it's not the psychological, ethnological or anthropological background of these heads which fascinates me; it's the total strangeness and uniqueness of the object. Also the wit in it. The meaning, though, remains totally open and unclear.[17]

As if there was one. And as if, with the things hung suspended in stockings from the wooden and metal support in *Comaland* (Figure 7) modelled on these 'head' objects, there was still a 'total strangeness and uniqueness of the object'. Yet this latter 'as if' is not so impossible: no matter how many times the object becomes another object, it does not become another object. At least, so it seemd to Trockel. Something of the 'plainness and simplicity' of the objects perhaps survives, whether they are taken as objects of fear or delight, or some combination of the two. Confirmation of logics of castration? The prick is a nose and the vagina eyes, the medusa-effect reflected back. Face of some other, which is not a face, but something suspended in a stocking, something secreted in a garment, showing as a face – if at all – of one who might steal something from you and who might be punished by a species of decapitation. Thief of several fetishes, returning as another possible fetish, 'of the psychological, ethnological or anthropological'. More and less than the tokens of subjects as gendered others, of some culture or other *as* other, gifts, false feet, playing out an occupation of a garment, and a descent without touching the floor.

A little geopolitical and politico-ethical disorientation perhaps accompanies this piece, then, at least if it were anticipated that what were presented as works of art were always going to line up to tell us what we might become. As if we could always, and without end, make and remake ourselves from what appears to lie before us.

Notes

1 J. Derrida, *Aporias*, trans. T. Dutoit, Stanford: Stanford University Press, 1993, p. 22. While any translation of this phrase would miss its idiomatic economy, the play in and between 'tout autre' as meaning 'every other' and 'completely other' would approach the effect of that idiom. Hence the phrase gives, as well as the speculative identities 'The completely other is completely other' and 'Every other is every other', the chiasmus of 'Every other is completely other' and 'The completely other is every other'. The phrase thus generates different deconstructions of the positing of the other as such, suggesting a necessary reiteration of Derrida's stricture from an earlier text: 'If the alterity of the other is *posed*, that is *simply* posed, doesn't it amount to the same, in the form, for example, of the "constituted object", the "informed product" invested with meaning, etc. From this point of view I would even go so far as to say that the alterity of the other inscribes something in the relation which can in no way be posed' (*Positions*, Paris: Éditions du Seuil, 1972, p. 132.)

2 For an account of 'auto-opposition' which details its conditions of possibility as its conditions of impossibility and outlines the *consequences* of this ('I must be other than myself, and that other must be another myself'), to which my chapter returns, see M. Borch-Jakobsen, 'Ecce Ego', in *The Freudian Subject*, trans. C. Porter, Basingstoke: Macmillan, 1988, p. 85.

3 Cf. 'Presence is made possible by the race, which makes pure presence impossible: each present moment is essentially constituted by its retention of a trace of a past moment. This is just as true of the "first" present moment as of any other, which thereby has a relation with a past that never was present: absolute past' (G. Bennington, 'Deconstruction is not what you think', *Art and Design 'The New Modernism: Deconstructionist Tendencies in Art'*, 1988, p 6.)

4 See National Gallery of Canada, *Jana Sterbak: States of Being*, Ottawa, 1991, pp. 13, 26–7, 66–7.

5 J. Lacan, 'The subversion of the subject and the dialectic of desire in the Freudian unconscious', in *Écrits*, trans. A. Sheridan, London: Tavistock Publications, 1977, p. 316.

6 Cf. M. Borch-Jakobsen, 'The Statue Man', in *Lacan: The Absolute Master*, trans. D. Brick, Stanford: Stanford University Press, 1991, pp. 43–71, linking Lacan's theory of signification with the determination of the 'imago' of the 'I', the 'I' *as* imago, in his conceptualization of 'the mirror phase'.

7 Hinting, perhaps without wanting to, at the breakdown of the analytic oppositions of activity and passivity, Freud writes: 'Analytic observation, indeed, leaves us in no doubt that the masochist shares in the enjoyment of the assault upon himself, and that the exhibitionist shares in the enjoyment of [the sight of] his exposure. The essence of the process is thus the change of the *object*, while the aim remains unchanged. We cannot fail to notice, however, that in these examples the turning round upon the subject's self and the transformation from activity to passivity converge or coincide' (S. Freud, 'Instincts and their vicissitudes', in the Standard Edition, ed. and trans. J. Strachey, London: Hogarth Press, 1953–/4, 14, p. 126.) Thus the subject seems to become itself again by taking itself as object; but the aim, in having to leave the subject to return, threatens analysis with ceasing to become an *aim* at all, offering rather an echo of a process of radical expenditure.

8 J.-F. Lyotard, 'Can thought go on without a body?', in *The Inhuman: Reflections on Time*, trans. G. Bennington and R. Bowlby, Cambridge: Polity Press, 1991, p. 21.

9 *Ibid.*

10 *Ibid.*, pp. 21–2.

11 For example: 'Matter does not question the mind, it has no need of it, it exists, or rather *insists*, it 'sists' 'before' questioning and answer, 'outside' them. It is presence as unpresentable to the mind, always withdrawn from its grasp' (Lyotard, 'After the sublime: the state of aesthetics', in *The Inhuman*, p. 142.)

12 Derrida, *Aporias*, p. 39.

13 *Ibid.*, p. 76.

14 For further details of this piece and the others considered here, see S. Stich, *Rosemarie Trockel*, New York: Prestel, 1991.

15 Cf. P. Weibel, 'From icon to logo', in Kunsthalle Basel, *Rosemarie Trockel*, Basel: 1988, pp. 25–35, which rather confirms the domination of the 'logo'; for example: 'Trockel's pictures, by contrast, maintain a state of *semiotic ecstasy*, because they deomonstrate the transformation of a sign space into a logo space' (p. 35), missing the question of the picture as object for a 'subject' of ecstasy, the picture which appears to 'maintain' some state or other.

16 J. Derrida, 'Restitutions', in *The Truth in Painting*, trans. G. Bennington and I. Macleod, Chicago: Chicago University Press, 1987, p. 368.

17 Interview with Rosemarie Trockel, J. Harten and D. Ross, in *German Art of the Late 1980s*, Cologne: DuMont, 1988, pp. 282–3 (translation and punctuation modified).

Unfold: imprecations of obscenity in the fold

Included in the category of things folded are draperies, tresses, tessellated fabrics, ornate costumes, dermal surfaces of the body that unfold in the embryo and crease themselves at death ... styles and iconographies of paintings that hide shapely figures in ruffles and billows of fabric or that lead the eye to confuse different orders of space and surface.[1]

I

This chapter has been produced from a combination of documents. It began with a short descriptive text that I wrote about seeing two works of art placed, I thought, purposefully and provocatively, together in a gallery. That is not in itself an unusual occurrence, but I wanted to record the brief conversation I had with their curator/dealer about the comparison that was set up by their juxta-position. Then I include a sequence of quotations from other conversations. Both within themselves and in their interaction in the text these are intended to reflect the theme of dialogue between unexpected protagonists, or between positions that cannot be resolved, that is central to this piece. Finally, my commentary upon those quotations, in which I attempt to analyse and situate the surprise I felt at seeing these works so harmoniously together.

Surprise itself reflects on expectations imposd by the regulations of etiquette, sensibility, judgement, that comprise 'identity': the science of boundaries and limitations that governs who or what may be related in dialogue and the terms and conditions under which relation may occur. This chapter investigates the aesthetic concerns that surround judgements of identification and difference through seeing what emerges from placing together these two very differently identified works 'in conversation'. They appear like a visual version of a Shaw play, in which drama is heightened when a pair of the most unlikely characters has been brought together in a strange and capricious combination: a considered literary device whereby something not normally spoken of becomes the unavoid-able centre of attention and a cause for anxious speculation about what may result. The spectator now has to face the consequences and work through the cultural and ideological implications both of surprise at seeing these two together, and of fascination with the possibilities of how this relation could develop.

The dialogues included here use different voices, timings and relationships. Within the process of dialogue, distinctions emerge that may form the basis for oppositional frameworks to be expressed. However, they may also be subverted by contextualization, so that opposition is rarely as complete as it may appear, and, under certain circumstances, may be capable of reversal: not opposition at all.

II

In the gallery there are two works: one on the floor, a plaster cast of an inflated airbed by Rachel Whiteread (Figure 8), the other a painting by Bridget Riley (Figure 9). Between them there is a striking visual rapport: references to wave patterns, similar scale, neutral colour, highly tensioned surface and calm, luminous presence. Superficially their physical presences are well matched, the painting and the sculpture look good together, for obvious reasons. However, there seems to be nothing that could be identified about these works that could bring them together within the kinds of coherence normally expected in proposals of relationship made in exhibitions: their individual histories, their genre (genetic) denomination, or their aesthetic/ideological/theoretical background. Instead, within the discrete space of this gallery the simplest of surface references become so important, and their import suggests that this is the most significant aspect of looking at these works. I want to indulge my pleasure in seeing the closeness of these two together, but I am also aware that I feel quite guilty about this. In response I question this closeness by investigating these superficial comparisons in more detail.

In the Whiteread bed the plaster retains its pristine self, straight from the mould. It is not modified with the touch of handiwork, but displays the unquestionable authenticity of time and imitation that inheres to the mechanics of casting. This permeates the work and reproduces intimately the surface of inflated fabric and its internal structural dynamic. The sense of liquid origins in the slight signs of pouring and bubbling transforms these physical references. They also refer to the lost container/matrix that leaves the positive form of the bed in negative and mentions an underside/undesired that had been uppermost as the plaster coagulated, but now forms the base, the hidden sign of the fragmented nature of the casting process. The bed is strongly present, but, in reality, it is the very thing that is absent, an anti-bed that is the opposite of the expected image. It remains a disarmingly accurate commentary on the appearances of beds while incorporating other material references, cloth, liquid, waves, air (this is an airbed) and the tensions under which they coexist.

Riley's paint is flat: its original fluidity may be residually referenced in the flowing pattern of the drawing, but now it lies in a fine layer across the picture in an even continuous film, its own texture subordinated to a plastic ideal of perfectly smooth consistency. Phenomenal painterly content is totally rationalized into a predetermined scheme: the flawless surface seems to have arrived through automatic procedures. Paint is literally a skin, divided by sharply delineated streams of black/grey/white. The closure of their edges is absolute: not a layering but a suffocating continuity in the surface. The perfection of the skin reveals and reproduces the hidden structure of the underlying support, a surprising reference to cloth, evenly woven, stretched but elastic, subject to pressure: an estimated depth of movement paralleled in the imaginary depth of the undulation of the painted pattern. The image, in the design of a wave pattern, suggests continuity, duration and distance. However, Riley's pattern is cut at a random edge, and brought up close by its unvarying ratio. Like the patterning of textile or wallpaper, it implies the function of a cover or a blanket/obliteration.

Both artists refer to what may lie below the surfaces of their work in an involuntary reading of soft against hard, warm against cold, porosity against impermeability. Both artists use rigorously mechanical methods of construction as a distancing device and as a way of producing a perfection of surface 'untouched by human hand'. Both works suggest themselves as whole, while, unsettlingly, they turn out to be fragments; both have an area of unseen content that is powerfully present yet invisible. On the one hand suggesting tragic and elegiac possibilities, on the other, a permanent and frustrating inevitability.

III

When I spoke to the curator of this show about the presence of these works together he coined the two expressions 'postmodern' and 'late formalist modernist' in order to speak of how the works came from distinct practical and aesthetic traditions, and to acknowledge his understanding of their difference. For him the postmodern Whiteread seemed to offer the possibility of a free range of poetic connotation, not in any way limited or proscribed by the work itself, while the Riley was to be taken on its own materialist terms: its specific alterity of appearances. There was no speculation about any depths to be interpreted. By adding the term 'late formalist' he seemed to imply that the rules that formed the Riley were already known and well defined, and the painting should be viewed in relation to that canon. This was a possibility that might apply to all works made under the regimes of modernism, while the postmodern was less determinate. The words 'post' (in 1992) and 'late' (in 1965) spoke not only of a difference in time, but also of a more profound difference that may inform critical distinctions that could be made in describing these works.

Apart from these two works, the gallery was blank. Signs of contextualization that usually attend exhibitions to establish that this work is historical, circumscribed and validated by its alignments to other works of art, or that this work is radically trying to establish a space for itself by refusing all that baggage, were not on view. (As an arch-demonstration of curatorial neutrality?) The even disposition of the works in the space and the minimal labelling refused to offer directions, presumably in order to facilitate their dialogue on equal terms. The lack of indications seemed to make the works closer, to permit a freer play of resemblance. If there were to be limitations to the degree of their being together, the spectator would have to manufacture them speculatively in a situation that would comment reflexively on the spectator's own needs.

What could representatives of postmodernism and modernism have to say to each other? Did their exhibition here imply more, maybe a problematizing commentary on the art-historical/curatorial need to demonstrate awareness of identifications and categorizations which would usually ensure that different kinds of work would be seen in different spaces and under different contextual conditions? The curator said not. They were just placed together: the superficial appearances had been the main consideration: 'It is the very superficiality of their resemblance that is so important, so fascinating.' Any other sense of dialogue was incidental, and there could be no projection of intention or resolution to that dialogue.

IV

I am reminded of another irresolute dialogue between irreconcilable personalities, that of Naphta and Settembrini in Thomas Mann's *Magic Mountain*. In an epic attempt to play out the polarities and positionings that he observed in European culture during the period leading up to the First World War, Mann brings together a pair of characters: Naphta, the Jesuit priest, and Settembrini, the republican reformer. He makes no point of contact between these two, no similarities except perhaps a willingness to join in debate, and a shared health problem that sites them both as patients in the same sanatorium. They were there for treatment, but the 'accidental' predicament of their proximity is an imposition made by Mann so they may be driven to discuss cultural, scientific, political and religious themes with no possibility of agreement. For the utilitarian Settembrini, the world can be organized for the good of the greatest number, providing the health, welfare and leisure that it is assumed they desire. For the priest, these concerns can provide only a thin veneer over a depth of evil and suffering that continually impinges on his consciousness and to which spirituality is the only appropriate response:

> 'Say it!' [Settembrini] cried to his opponent, '... say straight out, that the soul is – disease! Verily you will thereby encourage them to a belief in the spiritual. Disease and death as nobility, life and health as vulgarity – what a doctrine whereby to hold fast the neophyte to the service of humanity! ...'. And like a crusader he entered the lists in defence of the nobility of life and health, of that which nature gave, for the soul of which one did need not to fear.[2]

With Riley's painting, as with Settembrini, there is no caprice. Rules are devised, then soberly carried out to specific ends. A utilitarian symbolism of pattern, order, hygiene suggests a radical exclusion of undesirable elements. This painting does not attempt to represent or stand in for anything in the world, and cannot be given meaning through any other form of function than that of being a painting: its surface takes up a measured area of space on the wall and has a measured depth and edge in relation to that wall. Abstraction, stylized devices and seamless facture are used here to deflect attention from reference to human activities or the workings of the artist, and attest only to the painting's own reality and order: there is no need to fear for its soul; it has the radiant beauty and simplicity of the automatic, whose origins are secretively embedded within its own appearances.

Iconography and the imagined play of resemblance was always more readily at the service of the Jesuit, who keeps a potent and terrible medieval carving of Christ in agony on the cross as a sign of the real: that which is incapable of being symbolized, a condition of which he must always be mindful. Morbidity attaches to Whiteread's airbed, which breathes only outward in one long expiring sigh. Her casting is mechanical rather than automatic, you sense how it was done in the detail of the materials and the surface, the pressure of contact with the faithfully reproduced bed. This is closer to the 'convulsive beauty' of the surrealists, a beauty discovered in the transformation of the 'real' that takes place between the memory/thought of the original and the sight of that original in representation (in this case, casting). The real becomes a subconscious trace, a forgotten dream, no longer quantifiable in practical or material terms, but suggestive of a powerful but inadmissible desire. These are the revelations latent in the transformations of the plaster bed. The bed has an equivocal presence, stone-cold and rock-hard, a contradiction to its suggestion of providing comfort. It is absent, but in its negative form it exists as a 'stand-in' that differs from the real bed in its ambivalent proximity. We animate it from our own fears of its dire passivity. It seems warm.

With Settembrini and Naphta the degree of their difference is modulated by the fact that they are both dying from consumption. Mann remarks on this throughout the narrative by the authority given to the doctor in charge of the sanatorium, who is the intimate observer of their physical condition. Mann also imposes their shared literary dependence on a narrator, Hans Castorp, who disposes of the rhetorical passion of their dialogues through his earnest attempts to understand them and through his self-conscious obsessions with social predicaments that threaten to overwhelm his studious attention to the argument.

V

Despite their physical rapport, the works of Riley and Whiteread seem to make very different approaches to the spectator. Plaster is an ancient and homely substance, and Whiteread's pink bed suggests a natural colour of stone. Its gentle horizontal gravitas and self effacing openness about how it came into being makes accommodation for the presence of the spectator and allows associations. There is some comfort in this permission to engage in introspection and the invitation to dream.

Standing before the imposing verticality of Riley's impeccable optic surface, logic takes over from reverie. The painting, with its modern acrylic paint and its synthetic colour scheme of grey, white and black, systematically modulated, seems coldly indifferent to the spectator's gaze, and the spectator must struggle to coexist with the perfection it exudes. Spectators become a dark, confused shape in front of its brilliance and order, their space challenged by the animation of painted geometry.

Why does the Whiteread feel so familiar while the Riley looks so austere? At this point it seems necessary to choose between the two, to make a judgement like Hans Castorp pondering the arguments of Naphta and Settembrini. If I want the space to dream, then I cannot have the certainty of that order. If I decide to lie down, maybe I won't be able to get up. The oscillation that the spectator must play out in the theatre of vertical and horizontal positionings set up by bed and canvas forcefully symbolizes the difficulty of the predicament: a charged space of movement in which identity is challenged and identification must be painstakingly worked out. A moral predicament emerges that does not allow for equal enjoyment of both possibilities, a rule against the confusion of resemblances, that insists that differences in quality or rationale must be responsibly taken into account. This rule vests significance in the sequences of reference to what these works differently resemble, their pre-existing models that go beyond what can be seen in the gallery, rather than in what resembles: the presence of the works themselves.

VI

I am reminded here of another dialogue based on a comparison of resemblance: in Kleist's short story, 'On the marionette theatre', two friends meet and discuss the relation between dancing movements of the human body and those of some marionettes they were observing in the market-place. One friend, a popular and famous dancer himself, has been studying the action of the marionettes and finds it more free and perfect in its mathematical and mechanical origins than the self-conscious effort of interpretation that he has observed to inflect other dancers' movements:

> He smiled and said he was confident that if he could get a craftsman to make a marionette according to the specifications he had in mind, he could perform a dance with it which neither he nor any other skilled dancer of his time ... could equal.
>
> [...]
>
> my reply was that, no matter how cleverly he could present his paradoxes, he

would never make me believe a mechanical puppet could be more graceful than a living human body.[3]

The dancer proceeds to point out the subtle harmonics of movement that arise from the relationship of the action of the puppeteer's fingers and the limbs of the attached puppets, 'something like the relationship between numbers and their logarithms or between the asymptote and the hyperbole', or 'a more natural arrangement of the centres of gravity'.

Kleist's protagonists are barely characterized. Their conversation is carried out in the disembodied tone of documentary report, recollected at a distance. Both voices are the same, as if, in reality, this is Kleist talking to himself. There is no resolution; the only requirement is that the speaker, originally so shocked by the comparison of the human and the puppet, should see the point. He need not agree to the universal principle of perfect movement suggested by the dancer, he need only make the concession 'certainly the human spirit cannot be in error when it is non-existent'.

However, 'that the human spirit can be in error' and a cause of lack in 'grace' is a point of concurrence in the text. This is exemplified by the story of a young man whose body had a 'natural' grace which he knew was noticed. One day he discovered, in a mirror at the baths, the resemblance of a movement of his body to the pose of an admired classical statue. He proceeded to strike that pose deliberately, but with unfortunate results. The response he wished to provoke, one of delight in his effort to please, disappeared in humour at his affectation. The young man's problem is that he attempts to achieve grace through knowledge of what is graceful, when it can only be achieved by either no-consciousness or infinite-consciousness. The fact that the movements of the puppets resemble the human without being human intensifies their grace and offers a fantasy of the human, as partially composed of movement and posture, without the problems of the body or of the self-consciousness that attends it. For Kleist's dancer the aesthetic choice is based on signs of all or nothing: total innocence or god-like comprehension. For the other speaker a doubt remains: maybe this grace can exist only under conditions of an absence, and those may not be desirable conditions.

VII

Both the Whiteread and the Riley share a reference to the potentially mobile surface of cloth. In both the sculpture and the painting this reference seems to have the status of an incidental detail, but it imposes on their form with unexpected force, since in both, the image of the cloth is embedded in another surface (plaster or paint) to the point where it nearly disappears. The residual image of the cloth resonates with the patterning of waves, informing and intensifying the sensation of surface movement. However, the fluidity of plaster and paint make their own references to waves, which inflect the movement of the cloth with a different mathematical ratio. The surfaces ripple, part of the illusion of the painting and the structure of the sculpture; but these reticulations are immediately contradicted in the stretching of the canvas and in the reversal of the casting. The potential fold in the surface is immediately flattened, its recess revealed, and yet the hidden aspect of the fold remains permanently present as an imagined possibility.

This is a continuous folding and unfolding that is out of the spectator's control: a simultaneous display of two positions, so that there is a perpetual relay between two opposed visual messages. This process puts the content of the fold on display, returning its hidden nature to a surface which cannot settle into place and immediately hides it again. This refusal to keep still leaves the spectator with literally 'nothing to hold on to', deflecting the spectator's gaze through the permanent defeat of closure to a surface that seems always on the verge of opening up, an unconscious movement of logarithms and numbers, not to be controlled by conscious design.

This perpetual sense of movement, the perpetual promise to reveal continuously countered by the imposition of concealment in a mutual tension that gives ground equally to all possibilities and none whatsoever, parallels the structure of the space of phantasy, a space of shifting identifications that will not settle and which offers no definable form, nothing to hold on to. Kleist's bewildered interlocutor, trying desperately to find a manageable image for the mystery into which he has just been initiated, asks if this means that we must eat again of the tree of knowledge, to which the dancer replies, 'of course ... but that's the last chapter in the history of the world', or: a space of phantasy that cannot be occupied.

VIII

The movements of these folds conjure the enlightenment spectre of the automaton, at once more perfect, more functional, and, with the fascinating innate grace of lack of sign of how they come into being, provoking the same question as the marionettes: 'can you believe in this simplicity?' Beauty without poetry, memory, dream or desire, all the more intimidating because it seems to lack the need for those investments, even though the spectator may feel the involuntary need to make them.

Another reference to folding, and I am indebted here to Joan Copjec's account, can be found in the work of Gaetan de Clérambault the psychiatrist, and his fascination with cloth.[4] Clérambault taught a course in 'drapery' at the École des Beaux Arts, which suddenly, after some years of supporting the course, the college authorities decided to close. In remonstration, Clérambault tried to explain the importance of his course. He wrote to the college stressing that he aimed not 'merely at a comprehension of the drapery, but also an exact rendering of the FOLD'. In fact the suddenness of the action of the authorities and the recoil they felt it necessary to make, in order to disassociate themselves from that very concern with FOLDing, demonstrated the degree of their embarrassment. It was important to mark not just disapproval, but the stronger emotion of disgust, a visceral revulsion to which there could be no adequate response from Clérambault, who wanted his course to be reinstated.

Copjec sees the completeness of this recoil or repudiation as a feature of the utilitarian regime: the registering of shock or surprise is itself a recoil 'from the principle that the moral law must be founded on a recoil from the neighbour':

> The utopian dream of a society in which the relations of exchange would be harmonious and universal was dreamt up in the nineteenth century as an evasion of the failed – and forbidden – relation of the individual subject to its terrifying, superegoic other – its Neighbour. Rather than recoiling from the obscene/sublime part of itself, utilitarianism refused to recognise it, setting itself up on the erasure of its self-contesting aversion.[5]

The guilty content of Clérambault's cloths is that while they are ostensibly a simple demonstration of how cloths function, they simultaneously offer a surplus of pleasure for the enjoyment of the spectator, that goes beyond what is needed for the functional purpose recognized by the utilitarian college authorities, and thus become suspect of belonging in that oppositional realm of forbidden relations:

> By not converting the Other's supposed pleasure into an image useful to utilitarianism, by laying the two alternatives side by side, the photographs taken by Clérambault expose what the phantasy [of practical purpose] obscures: its strict supposition of the Other's obscene enjoyment. Not an enjoyment that can be corralled by use, but one threateningly outside the bounds of utility.[6]

Copjec here analyses the content of the dialogue of Clérambault and the college authorities: their awareness of the obscenity of his pleasure in offering photographs of figures draped in folded cloth, knowing that dubious spectatorial speculation about unfolding would be aroused; his assertion of an important academic research project with scientific credibility based on detailed empirical observation of the folding action of cloth. The assumption of neutrality and objectivity in the process of recording was an important device here. For Clérambault there could be no indications of actual sexuality in his obsessively detailed photographs, or any indication of his own pleasure in offering the photographs as documents to be studied. His passion was strictly limited to the very surface of the cloth, the twisting, tying, wrapping, draping actions, and to scientific record-making. It was not apparent that he knew that his research would fuel the phantasies of his spectator. However, the utilitarian authorities became suspicious of an unpleasant secret, a possibility of obscenity, and needed to put a stop to his activities.

Copjec points out that it is this very blankness of Clérambault's figures, often underlaid by simply structures of wood and wax with no bodily indications, that indicates the possibility for obscenity in the simultaneous awareness, in phantasy, of both the folded and the unfolded figure.

The automatic/mechanical distancing techniques of Riley and Whiteread, and their non-committal presence in the gallery, have a similar effect. The pristine nature of the painted and cast plaster surfaces, and their shallow rectangular form determined purely by function, strictly refuse to hint of any specific bodily presence, although their surfaces suggest underlying structure/facture. The automatic action of the illusion of folding and unfolding does not reveal but remains blank. It functions here to make lack of reference to the body a poignant sensation, a pleasure in loss. However, the question remains as to how these mechanics are intended to function in relation to this ulterior intimate suggestion of a degree of pleasure that is surplus to requirement, and surplus to the simple physical facts of the 'superficial comparisons'.

Liam Gillick, writing about Whiteread's work, hints at the sense of absence that haunts the imagery of cast plaster and the references to our knowledge of the use of plaster in the reproduction of antique sculpture (the drapery of which Clérambault subjected to detailed scrutiny). He also mentions plaster's association with body casts, and remarks that 'Taking an impression of the surface brings forward information that could otherwise remain hidden.'[7]

Modern acrylic paint lacks these connotations, but the nature of its use in the Riley painting presents not only its own nature, but also that of its underlying support, for speculative examination. Both the Whiteread and the Riley have disarmingly calm and beautiful surfaces which offer subliminal readings, subtle inflections to this folding/unfolding, bodied forth by the actions of stretching and inflation. They offer a highly tactile sensation, not only the desire to press, but a response to that pressure, to be pressed back: a sensation that hints of desire and relation in excess of the contemplative utility of art.

IX

Bryan Robertson, writing in the catalogue to Riley's Hayward exhibition of 1971, has recourse in his practice as an art critic to two kinds of experience, his feeling for what it is to be a man, and his connoisseurship based on his study of art. In this piece of writing, these aspects of his consciousness are placed rhetorically in dialogue, in order to make a comparison between the apparent coolness of Riley's paintings and the warmth of his response. Most of the writing is in his professional voice and describes the progress of her work with reference to training, personal history, use of materials, influences, and evolution of motif. Occasionally he uses a more informal address to speak of his response to her work:

> What Riley's paintings are about is quite different to what on close inspection their apparently unyielding surfaces suggest. Like the way in which a man may

be relaxed, through analysis, after being inhibited from being fully himself or true to his inherent personality by the interference of an enforced rule, thrust upon him by the suppositions of society, so Riley is intent on laying bare with absolute accuracy the fundamental energies ...'[8]

This sequence of references: 'apparently unyielding surfaces' through 'liberated male' to 'laying bare fundamental energies' represents an eroticization of this surface felt with a passion and a tenderness that culminates, later in the same text, with the statement 'finally it is not a matter of reason, it is a matter of love'.

When Liam Gillick writes about *Ghost* that 'to cast the whole space inverts the entrances',[9] he precisely sums up the ambivalent erotic proposition of the plaster surface of Whiteread's work, and clearly states the invitation to phantasy current in the reversals she creates.

In Whiteread's bed the touch of the plaster is even, over the whole surface; no emphasis or sequence is implied. The mechanics of its operation parallel what Riley refers to as an 'infinitely subtle grid', an elastic overall structure that the eye continually tests for depth, openings, spring. Riley describes her paintings as a 'multi-focal' space that refuses to let the eye settle, and which will not compose itself to allow a sense of right position or a consuming gaze. As Deleuze observes, 'That we were always perceiving in folds means that we have been grasping figures without objects.'[10] The 'multi-focal space' does not question 'focus' itself but the focal point, the moment of judgement of function for the entire edifice of the picture's composition. The multi-focal space invites pleasure in the activity of focusing, but supplies no answer to the question of what to focus on: an uncertain pleasure that might also be experienced as a deprivation. The automatic nature of this work's production has a poignant function here: it disavows the body in itself and serves to deflect all reference to experience of the body back on to the spectator, indicating that this pleasure in the loss of object is produced as a function of spectatorial needs.

When Robertson notes, in reference to Riley's work, that 'in good art the creative gift ... recognizes the complete interdependence of masculine and feminine elements', there is an echo of the undefinable play of sexuality current in Gillick's brief remark. This mutuality threatens the identification of speaking positions and compresses differences in a simultaneity of possibilities that permits no polarization of opposites. Robertson's ambivalence is represented in this text: on the one hand needing to demonstrate his awareness of the correct historical and cultural references for the work, to relate it to what it resembles, in a way that the director of the current exhibition does not feel obliged to do; on the other, wanting to speak of his response to the work more naturally, on a one-to-one basis that he can justify only by reference to his own experience: his sense of 'what resembles', a feeling of rightness about the 'fundamental energies'. 'The folds in the soul resemble the pleats of matter, and in that fashion they are directing them.'[11]

X

The eye confuses different orders of space and surface on account of the visual stimulus of folding and unfolding. The action of the folding breaks down the separation of categorizations, the kind of separation that is laid out as a play of exclusive oppositions that subtend the ideal forms of identity: the included and the excluded, the abject and the desirable, the obscene and the seen. The confusion of the eye, the fact of the intimate presence of the fold within the unfold, questions the need for decisions about mutual exclusivity. In the visual research of the fold there is the voluptuous desire to see everything that can be seen in a scenario of perpetual frustration of vision. As Gillick writes about the experience of looking at Whiteread's work: 'There is a link with forensic gathering', an impartiality about the acceptance of what is seen in an attempt to see everything, 'reminiscent of an enquiry followed with possible aim yet without pre-judgement'.[12] This is where the 'superficial resemblances' of the Riley and the Whiteread as they are displayed in this gallery become so important, so fascinating. A space is created for intense study of traces, residues, minute details, in suspension of awareness of the indications that would permit judgement.

The process of utilitarianism, on the other hand, deliberately sets up its own oppositions in order to create prejudged scenarios of acceptance and refusal. Identification confers presence and place while difference is deferred as absence. It is the shifting play of these values that I have tried to record in the arrangements of the folds of this chapter:

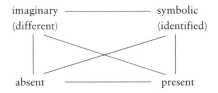

This schema charts a disturbance to 'identity' by proposing a possible reversal of expectations of presence and absence in the symbolic function of cultural presence in the utilitarian scheme. The very process of erasure, making absent, supports concepts of ideal presence: beauty, value, hygiene, usefulness, concepts that demand evaluation and judgement. Erasure is justified and dramatized when absence is accompanied by imprecations of obscenity, morbidity, revulsion and excess to usefulness.

This is where the social agenda of utility approaches the aesthetic arena in which the terms 'postmodernism' and 'late formalist modernist' function, and the possibility that one term could cast the other as an obscenity, an absence or a presence, depending on the context of identification. These terms intimate another form of presence, that of how authorial intention is signalled in the work, the consequent theorization of the relation of author to reader/spectator through the work, and the critiques of autonomy, expression and subjectivity they entail. Here the sculpture and the painting differ: Whiteread withdraws indications of authorial intention through the reference to 'ready-made' and the mechanical relationship of casting to bed. Riley's painting is the opposite, showing signs of total control in the strict design and application of the painted surface, even if the surface was designed to exclude signs of the author's activity. In this difference lies the potential for scandal in the Riley and the Whiteread being seen together and to the balance and poise of their equivalence in relationship: identity as difference in presence.

The gallery is impassive and the curator gives no reassurance about his own sense of there being significance in the placing of these works together. In fact the opposite: he is purposefully offering only superficial resemblances, and that is what is so important. This gives rise to unease about irresponsibility: if they are together because they just happen to look good/get on together, that suggests an excess of 'pleasure' over reason or 'function', and not the appropriate workings of 'judgement'. Certainly these works look wonderful together, but there is something troubling: that pleasure was too easily obtained. Aesthetic suspicions are aroused: 'can you believe in this simplicity?' What critical grounds could there be for exercising discretion? The indeterminate nature of resemblance asserts itself: could there be imprecations of obscenity in 'the fold'?

Notes

This chapter originated as a lecture for the MA Textiles course at Goldsmiths College, University of London, at the invitation of Janis Jefferies, and I am indebted to her for the original context in which this theme could be developed. My thanks also to Karsten Schubert at whose gallery the two works referred to here were exhibited, 27 May–26 June 1993.

1 Translator's introduction to G. Deleuze, *The Fold, Leibnitz and the Baroque*, trans. T. Conley, Minneapolis: University of Minnesota Press, 1993, pp. xi–xii.
2 T. Mann, *The Magic Mountain*, trans. H. T. Lowe-Porter, Harmondsworth: Penguin Books, 1979, p. 466.
3 H. Von Kleist, 'On the marionette theatre', trans I. Parry, *Times Literary Supplement*, 20 October 1978, p. 1211.
4 J. Copjec, 'The sartorial superego', *October*, 50, pp. 56–95.
5 *Ibid.*, p. 82.
6 *Ibid.*, p. 94.
7 L. Gillick, *Rachel Whiteread – Ghost*, London: Chisenhale Gallery, 1990.
8 B. Robertson, *Bridget Riley, Paintings and Drawings 1951–71*, Hayward Gallery Catalogue, London: The Arts Council, 1971.
9 Gillick, *Rachel Whiteread – Ghost*.
10 Deleuze, *The Fold, Leibniz and the Baroque*, p. 94.
11 *Ibid.*, p. 98.
12 Gillick, *Rachel Whiteread – Ghost*.

Beyond identity?
The beyond in *Beyond Japan*

This chapter will explore two particular instances of an inscription of an *other than* or *beyond of* identity, in both cases of identity/otherness in the name of Japan; the exhibition *Beyond Japan*[1] and Roland Barthes's *Empire of Signs*.[2]

Jacques Derrida has written on the conceptions of the Other in terms of the psyche – that is, on the dialectic of identity – and the possibility of 'invention' therein, through 'speech act' theory.[3] In this schema Derrida stituates 'two poles'. One, the 'constative', involves 'discovering or unveiling, pointing out or saying what is'; i.e. the realm of 'truth', or at least the already, the pre-existing. The second 'pole' is that he terms 'the performative – producing, instituting, transforming'.

According to my dictionary, the performative designates 'a statement or verb [action], that itself constitutes the action described':[4] typically the constitutive statement 'I name this ship'; or, 'it's a boy!' The point here is that, whilst Derrida is often critical of such speech act theory, he confers that the psyche *vis-à-vis* inventions of the other – of 'the other' *as* invention – operates 'between these two poles'. That identity, whether framed as totally mutable and adoptable/droppable as masquerade, necessarily also negotiates the 'constative pole'. That is, identity – dependent as it is on a relation with an other, both fixated and partially unknowable, is bound to this economy; of the stasis of 'fixity' and the dynamic of 'play'. The dynamic term 'performative' has recently been appropriated in theories which aim to produce or propose 'radical' subjectivities.[5]

However, I would wish to employ Derrida's assertion in order to argue that the very possibility of a kind of 'absolute' performativity is a logical impasse; to render gender-identity if not impossible; then in an impossible relation to 'itself': gender-identity is not identical to identity. Identity is bound to that already (im)possible negotiation between 'fixity' and 'play'; between other-self or self-other as a limit condition.

I will aim to demonstrate that both *Beyond Japan* and *Empire of Signs* risk becoming embroiled in the very metaphysics that they attempt to go beyond, tied to the very paradox of the *other than*, itself predicated on a conception of the *one* that renders *other than* and *identity* equally impossible. Not that these sites or texts are peculiarly embroiled, otherwise, their very vigilance demonstrates the extent that (re)inscribing *identity* is fated to negotiate this relation

between 'fixity' and 'variability' – whether represented topographically, temporally, psychically or as (constituting) a body; the erotics of the *other*.

I also aim to show that – dependent on a logic of the *other* – identity/counter-
identity thinking would also be an erotic project, in the construction of the
rhetoric of an imagistic body, an imaginary or phantasmic embodied other.

The topography – temporality of the Beyond

The exhibition *Beyond Japan: A Photo Theatre* takes its place in a genealogy
of curatorial events within which the exhibition becomes a mass spectacle, that
is, it stakes a claim on the hegemonic culture of the 'popular imagination',
contests a claim within the topos of ideology (the term 'art exhibition', with its
connotation of a collection of images/texts gathered under the sign of a canon
or an *œuvre*, seems insufficient here to denote the programmatic of *Beyond
Japan*). *Beyond Japan* shares with exhibitions such as *Tutankhamun* at the
British Museum in the 1970s the sensibility that I am calling the curatorial event;
the exhibition as something Beyond, that is more than, art. The 'curatorial event'
presents or produces an archaeological exploration of a culture, a discrete and
unique time-space, hitherto buried beneath the surface of Occidental consciousness; a bringing into the open, that is into post-enlightenment Occidental
aesthetic consciousness.

In the course of this chapter the paradigmatic terms Occidental/Oriental
will appear, both in particular citations and in an endeavour to exposit the
economy of thought within which they are sustained. I hope that their use may
be understood as provisional and cautionary – that their reinscription here may
avoid the continuity of dichotomous terms that are understood as absolute and
mutually exclusive, whilst positing a 'first term' against which the other is judged
and positioned as secondary and, accordingly, insufficient.

Beyond Japan is also an art exhibition, and as such the pre-publicity and/or
curatorial guide must explain itself, must articulate its own (curatorial) logic,
must formulate the ways in which the images cohere into a corpus, an ideological
imagistic body. To this end visitors to the exhibition are presented with a leaflet
containing a text written by the curator, Mark Holborn. At its opening the
leaflet asserts that

> No country in modern times has been subject to such transformations as Japan
> since 1945. From the rubble of the immediate post-war years to economic
> domination, Japan has experienced an unprecedented rise to the status of a
> world power.[6]

Immediately it is apparent that we are dealing with modernity, with the modern
as a condition, and Japan as a symptom of that condition – a representation
through semiology (the study of signs and/as symptoms). As a condition we can
speak of modernity – and, similarly, Japan – as having a within, a body, with

an outside, an other, an after or before. Japan, seemingly, both finds its identity *in* and is troubled *by* these 'transformations'. Yet this very identity (of Japan as modern) is itself challenged. The 'transformations' will, ultimately, make or break Japan. The *Beyond* of the exhibition title is configured by a temporal and epistemological scission identified with 1945, a scissiparity constituted politically and geographically as 'post-war' and marked, in the exhibition, spectacularly, as post-Hiroshima.

The writing on the first section of the exhibition – this ordering is constructed both by the instructed route through the exhibition and by the structure of the leaflet – describes a

> long sequence of photographs of a devastated world, focusing on the scorched concrete of the Hiroshima dome ... He [Kikuji Kawada] was evoking a memory, using photography not as a means to record the present, but to retrace the past.

In *Beyond Japan* an event, which takes its name from a town on which a nuclear bomb was dropped, is identified precisely with this geopolitical and epistemological break. The modern Japanese sensibility is identified as *post-Hiroshima*.

Is the Beyond of *Beyond Japan* the cultural identity of Japan 'before-Hiroshima'? Is the Beyond of *Beyond Japan* the cultural identity of Japan 'after-Hiroshima'? For the answer to either of these questions to be affirmative would be to imply that in 'Hiroshima' Japanese culture transgressed its own identity; an instantaneous cultural fission of massive proportions. We should expect the pursuit of this drifting sign of the *Beyond* to be complex. After all, 'For a generation of artists, designers and photographers who have grown up in these years, the question of "Japanese" identity is complex.' Complex indeed, as questions of identity are, yet we get the impression that they are somehow more complex for the image-makers of *Beyond Japan*, who 'wish to resist the simple categorization of the label "Japanese" with its implied homogeneous identity'.

'Japanese', then, refers to both a complex identity and a simple, homogeneous identity. 'Japanese' is a sign that has undergone a transformation. Do we then speak of an identity 'Japanese' that has undergone a transformation post-Hiroshima; wherein post-Hiroshima also indicates a Beyond Japaneseness? In this way *Beyond Japan* becomes a time-space. And, curatorially, the locus of this time-space of Japan-Beyond-Japan is Tokyo; the axis of the post-Hiroshimaesque cultural capital – which we begin to recognize as the postmodern in the modern.

Tokyo is the term assigned to the interstice of Occidental–Oriental influence. Tokyo – in its (re)emergence, in its renaissance in the post of Hiroshima – is both a limit point (or condition) and Japan in its essence in its Beyondness: 'Tokyo emerges as a creative axis for both East and West with many Western artists and photographers working in Japan who in turn inspire or influence the Japanese.' Tokyo *is* Japan-Beyond-Japan, existing in a topic-temporality identified as both Eastern and Western cultural capital.

The image-making of Japan or *Beyond Japan*, that is Japan in the post-Hiroshima postmodern, is both simply Japanese and universal; 'a specific Japanese experience and extending into the nineties with a view that is more universal'. Without dwelling on the metaphysics of this plea for universality, we may question the structure of this identity, both one-in-the-many and many-in-the-one. A subjectivity that is not impossible, as this *is* the subjectivity of the *Beyond Japan*, Japan beyond Hiroshima, beyond the modern, the subjectivity of *Beyond Japan*, structured as a general condition. In the light of this, a visitor from the occidental modernity can only experience Japan as an absolute Otherness: 'He [William Klein] arrived in Japan as if on another planet.'

The fashion label *Comme des Garçons'* installation in the exhibition uses 'the British photographer Brian ... Griffin's photographs in a way that is even suggestive of Russian sacred space – the antithesis of Japan'. These images, reminiscent of Russian sacred space – as Russian, pitched in another in-between of East and West, as sacred, inherently pre postmodern – find themselves in a dialectical relationship with Japan. Japan here is used as an adjective, to signify 'Japaneseness'. Tokyo is the locus of this synthesis of antithetical images: in texts cited in the exhibition the precise form of this temporal-topographical schism – configured as something other than this atopic impact of 'Hiroshima' – is delimited within the economics or metaphysics of *the sun*.

For the notorious writer, militarist and seppuku suicide Yukio Mishima, the sun denotes the summer, which itself is a borderline state, a frontier awaiting a devastating transgression that inscribes the subduing of the Empire of the Sun. For Mishima this luminosity is reduced to a terrible, material frontier: 'A relentless sun blazed down on the lush grass of that summer that lay on the borderline between the war and the post-war period – a borderline, in fact, that was nothing more than a line of barbed-wire entanglements.'[7] For the architect Arata Isozaki the borderline is inscribed as that of 'the day Japan surrendered'. That day is itself identified with the spectacular luminosity of the sun. This day also marked, we read, 'the end of history': 'The day Japan surrendered. The summer sun threw sharp black shadows on the ground. There was a marvellous silence; the passage of time halted; more, it was the end of history.'[8]

The sun becomes the privileged signifier in this metaphysics of the end. The blast of Hiroshima, like Japan's surrender, sees the Empire of the Sun put in the shade. Whilst we might sympathize with the tendency of this thought, I would urge a caution around the graphics of 'Hiroshima' as a Holocaust which determines a terminal moment of Japan in relation to which the very 'transformations' invoked earlier are seen as a renaissance of Japan Beyond Japan; of an identity as other to an anterior, original – and as such authentic – identity. The mutual influence of Japan (the Other of its Other) and 'the West' (as Other) is not Beyond Japan but Japan beyond itself: or not even that, as it would not then be 'Japan', but Japan inside–outside itself; facilitating that exteriority to contain its interiority – Japan. This is the logic of the Beyond.

In Freud, the Beyond (of) the Pleasure Principle involves the Pleasure Principle's own annihilation, its beyond within itself, its interiority its own exteriority.[9] If the Pleasure Principle is understood as a drive formation as categorization of the subject, then the Beyond (of) the Pleasure Principle involves the annihilation of the subject; the effacing of the first term in the very logic of the Beyond. In the context of an overview of a perceived 'moment' in a cultural imaginary, such a conceptualization seems bound to a nostalgia for an original presence (that of tradition in the modern) in regard to a polyglot and dystopic imaginary of a particularly 'complex' identity (that of diasporic pluralism in the postmodern); within which the sovereignty of the Empire of the Sun is foreshadowed by the tyranny of the Empire of the Sign.

The theatre of the body

For Roland Barthes – in his *Empire of Signs* – the structure-in-difference between the so-called Western and Oriental theatres is that of an interiority/exteriority division or decision. However, this is a decision which does not immediately slide into a logic of the Beyond:

> Take the Western theater of the last few centuries; its function is essentially to manifest what is supposed to be secret ('feelings', 'situations', 'conflicts'), while concealing the artifice of such manifestation ... The stage since the Renaissance is the space of this lie: here everything occurs in an interior surreptitiously open, surprised, spied on, savoured by a spectator crouching in the shadows ...
>
> We must recall that the agents of the spectacle, in *Bunraku*, are at once visible and impassive ... tinged with that mixture of strength and subtlety which marks the Japanese repertoire of gestures and which is a kind of aesthetic envelope of effectiveness ... offered to the spectators to read; but what is carefully, preciously given to be read is that there is nothing there to read; here again we come to that exemption of meaning (that exemption *from* meaning as well) which we Westerners can barely understand, since, for us, to attack meaning is to hide or to invert it, but never to 'absent' it. With *Bunraku*, the sources of the theater are exposed in their emptiness. What is expelled from the stage is hysteria, i.e., theater itself; and what is put in its place is the action necessary to the production of the spectacle: work is substituted for inwardness (Barthes, *Empire of Signs*, pp. 61–2).

Barthes's discourse on the discourse of a generalized 'Western' theatre suggests a structure of perversity, one dominated by secrets, by surprise, by fascination, by the unveiling or opening of an unveiling or opening – in short, a structure of fetishism or a repetition (a rehearsal) of a primal scene. This body is then a hysterical body acting out its own spectacular symptomology, its *semiology*.

In contrast – or in its very Otherness – the 'Oriental' theatre, the specifically named *Bunraku*, is the spectacle of the already revealed; yet marked by this elliptical and enigmatic 'aesthetic envelope of effectiveness'. This openness is the sign of a non-sign, a cipher, a reading more and/or less than reading. A sign in the logic of the Beyond; a sign and/or reading that absents itself in its appearance, a theatre which establishes itself in its own effacement, its annihilation.

For 'we Westerners' – a category itself which Barthes here inhabits and transgresses, goes beyond, in his semiology – the loss of meaning is a violence; for the 'Oriental' a bearable, even desired, abstention from the signifier. This lack is the possibility and drive towards the spectacle and yet the restoration of a proper interiority. Would then the sequential logic suggest a return of the manifestation of this interiority in a scene of fascination, an unveiling? Or are we, or 'they' beyond all that? I have dwelt some time on this *tropographics* of the theatrical sign because *Beyond Japan* sustains a curatorial 'metaphor' of theatre.

The first section of the exhibition-spectacle-event is entitled 'Fragments on the Map', within which the post-war, post-Hiroshima, tempero-topography is configured. The second, third and fourth sections are, respectively, 'The Theatre of the Body', 'The Theatre of Revolt' and 'The Theatre of the Street'. Whilst my intention is not to compare the efficacy of Barthes's characterization of the 'Japanese' theatre with the use of the term in *Beyond Japan*, another question comes to mind. Why is the section of *Beyond Japan* that focuses on the theatre as such entitled 'The Theatre of Revolt' and not 'The Theatre of the Theatre'? Why? – what then of the status of the metaphor of the theatre in (the) *Beyond*; because to insist on this unsustainable ellipsis would be to collapse the possibility of the spectacle? Besides (or Beyond?) *Beyond Japan* is also an event, is a spectacle and a performative utterance, in short – it is in its totality (its interiority–exteriority) a work of art, an invention. In this relation the curator, Mark Holborn, becomes an author, his name a signature. And as Barthes writes:

> If I want to imagine a fictive nation, I can give it an invented name, treat it declaratively as a novelistic object ... so as to compromise no real country by my fantasy (though it is then a fantasy itself that I compromise by the signs of literature). I can also – though in no way claiming to represent or analyze reality itself (these being the major gestures of Western discourse) – isolate somewhere in the world (*faraway*) a certain number of features ... and set out these features deliberately to form a system. It is this system which I shall call: Japan (Barthes, *Empire of Signs*, p. 3).

In this paradoxical, elliptical (and possibly unconvincing) schema we may identify an image of how *Beyond Japan* configures its relation to Japan. Is Japan a name that *Beyond Japan* borrows for its invention? What then of the topos of identity in the leaflet's opening remarks? The possibility of identity loses its ground inasmuch as Japan might lose identity in the other's fantasy – the necessary structure of identity–otherness, in which each term is dependent on its other, which means that the very possibility of identity is radically atopic.

Beyond Japan is, then, Japan Beyond, that is, more than *as* less than itself – its own annihilation-in-exorbitance. We are left, like Barthes, with a fantasy of the 'faraway', of a fantasy of alterity, an Otherness 'compromised by the signs of literature', by the signs of signification. *Beyond Japan* effaces its topos, its project, its fantasy, itself, in its spectacularization: 'If I want to imagine a fictive nation, I can give it an invented name' (Barthes, *Empire of Signs*, p. 3); 'If Japan did not exist, Barthes would have had to invent it'.[10]

I will dwell a moment on this structure of the inventive. Jacques Derrida writes:

> the concept of invention distributes its two essential values between these two poles: the constative – discovering or unveiling, pointing out or saying what is – and the performative – producing, instituting, transforming. But the sticking point here has to do with the figure of co-implication, with the configuration of these two values.[11]

For Derrida, in the realm of invention, the statement (of truth or falsity) is identified with an *unveiling* – which for Barthes is bound to Western theatricality, to the hysterical exteriorization of a cryptic interiority.

Another question – one intended to elucidate the fantastic, transformative 'pole' of the performative theatrical identity of and in *Beyond Japan*: Why does Antonin Artaud feature in the section entitled 'The Theatre of Revolt'? Artaud is heard on an audiotape and cited from the text *The Theatre and Culture* (1938). Is Artaud an honorary Japanese, at least within the conceptualization of this identity in *Beyond Japan*? Or is he the *other* through which this identity is constituted?

Imaging translation

> but photography creates a visual language that requires little translation (Mark Holborn, *Beyond Japan* leaflet).

> The dream: to know a foreign (alien) language and yet not to understand it: to perceive the difference in it without that difference ever being recuperated by the superficial sociality of discourse, communication or vulgarity: to know, positively refracted in a new language, the impossibility of our own: to learn the systematics of the inconceivable; to undo our own 'reality' under the effect of other formulations, other syntaxes: to discover certain unsuspected positions of the subject in utterance, to displace the subject's topology; in a word, to descend into the untranslatable, to experience its shock without ever muffling it, until everything Occidental in us totters and the rights of the 'father tongue' vacillate – that tongue which comes to us from our fathers and which makes us, in our turn, fathers and proprietors of a culture which, precisely, history transforms into 'nature' (Barthes, *Empire of Signs*, p. 6).

To suggest that photography requires no translation would be to disassociate photography from culture–language – no anchorage, no reference, no doxa; no signification. The argument of culture transformed into nature is familiar; it is the argument of ideology. I am aware that the text reads 'little translation', but prefer to read this qualification around translation, a less and more of translation, as a denial of a problematic. How can one quantify translation? Or does photography require 'little' translation because in the theatre of our performativity of the image one internalizes the language of the other?

Barthes refers to the way in which his own photograph, reproduced in a Japanese newspaper, is transformed by the process/production of translation in a cross-cultural reproduction, 'Japanned': 'This Western lecturer, as soon as he is "cited" by the *Kobe Shinbun*, finds himself "Japanned", eyes elongate, pupils blackened by Nipponese typography' (Barthes, *Empire of Signs*, p. 90). In this process of reproduction-as-translation/translation-in-reproduction, the body (Barthes's) is hystericized, Barthes becomes a cipher or palimpsest on which the semiology of otherness is acted out. Yet 'this Western lecturer' recognizes himself in his own otherness or otherization, the theatre of himself as his own other. The question, then, of the subject to the image of and as cultural translation as hysterical theatre of the body may be (to modify Freud's articulation) 'What nationlity am I?'[12]

This procedure also marks out the body as a written space, a topology, which returns me to a section in the lengthy Barthes quote above that I passed over, possibly, too hastily:

> to know a foreign (alien) language and yet not to understand it: to perceive the difference in it without that difference ever being recuperated by the superficial sociality of discourse ... to know ... the impossibility of our own ... to undo our own 'reality' ... to discover certain unsuspected positions of the subject in utterance, to displace the subject's topology; in a word, to descend into the untranslatable ... until everything Occidental in us totters and the rights of the 'father tongue' vacillate.

For Barthes the encounter with the language of the other – that is, with the other to the extent that we may *name* the *other* – is to be valorized as an encounter with a radical, irrecoupable alterity beyond discourse. Barthes seeks a displacement of the discursive doxa, of the subject, and a relinquishing of the paternal signifier – the 'father tongue', that is, of the Signifier.

I would also suggest that this move in Barthes is also a desire finally to do away with the aspect of the ideology that interpellates the subject as the (paternal) guardian of a culture that, as naturalized, must be defended and protected from the other, fantasized as a phantasmic and threatening alien. Additionally, I bear in mind that for Barthes this is a dream, a fantasy; and my thesis might be precisely that Barthes bears this precaution – that of the fantasy of the other as such *as* a fantasy – more successfully than *Beyond Japan* achieves.

In the section 'Introduction: this/that/the Other' of his recent book *The Infection of Thomas De Quincey*[13] John Barrell describes the phantasm of 'oriental imagery' that haunted De Quincey's opium-inspired dreams, within

which the 'oriental' – a phantasmagoria of images and undifferentiated faces –
came to represent a 'bad other'. In addition to providing a lucid exposition of
the structural logic of the non-dialectical self/other binary, Barrell complicates
this by defining the paradoxical logic of the Beyond in and of the other, which
at once produces an undifferentiated synthesis of the two terms whilst reinscrib-
ing and breaching an impasse between them.

Barrell describes a 'process' which 'begins by identifying an apparently
exhaustive: there is a self, and there is another, an inside and an outside, an
above and a below'. For Barrell, this process of identifying an other implicates
an interiority/exteriority relation, as well as a hierarchy of forms as values.
However, the 'self is constituted by the other, and it requires that other to mark
out its own limit, its own definition; yet the two are implacably hostile, and
their confrontation appears unavoidable, for there is no third term, no other
identity possible, nowhere to go'. As such, the 'self' is both dependent on the
'other' and in a position where antagonism is unavoidable. Accordingly, some
form of synthetic reconciliation is achieved by the constitution of a third term –
the negation of negation as compositely negative – wherein 'the difference
between them ... is as nothing compared with the difference between the two
of them considered together, and that third thing, way over there, which is truly
other to them both'. Barrell refers to Gayatri Chakravorty Spivak's distinction
between a 'self-consolidating other' and an 'absolute other' – which appears,
itself, to draw on Jacques Lacan's psychoanalytic distinction between the object
of desire which takes the (projected) form of a part of the subject's body and
an Other that remains phantasmic, perhaps schematizable as a heterogeneity/
alterity distinction.

However, Barrell aims to emphasize the geopolitical ramifications of such
psychic processes, in order to

> dramatise how what at first seems 'other' can be made over to the side of the
> self – to a subordinate position on that side – only as long as a new, and a
> newly absolute 'other' is constituted to fill the discursive space that has thus
> been evacuated.
>
> There is a 'this', and there is a something hostile to it, something which lies,
> almost invariably, to the east, but there is an East beyond that East, where
> something lurks which is equally threatening to both, and which enables or
> obliges them to reconcile their differences.[14]

In the light of this it may be possible to say something like: *Beyond Japan*
repeats a familiar structure of negotiation in the logic of the one and the other,
within which 'Hiroshima' takes the place of the other beyond the other – the
East beyond the East – in and through which the differential relations – of East
and West – may be synthesized, reconciled or reduced to a minimal value.
Hiroshima as the beyond of Japan-in-itself in *Beyond Japan* is the spectral figure
of a potential threat lurking over both East and West, in the face of which they

find their common value, an identity forged in the face of the nuclear threat as a geopolitical fetish object, a 'little translation'.

This beyond beyond the beyond, in the logic or fantasy of *Beyond Japan*, is the potential for economic and cultural exchange, with little translation, a fantasy of a loss of difference beyond the differential moment.

The un/differentiated body of the Beyond

in Japan the body exists, acts, shows itself, gives itself, without hysteria, without narcissism, but according to a pure – though subtly discontinuous – erotic project. It is not the voice (with which we identify the 'rights' of the person) which communicates (communicates what? our – necessarily beautiful – soul? our sincerity? our prestige?), but the whole body (eyes, smile, hair, gestures, clothing) which sustains with you a sort of babble that the perfect domination of the codes strips of all regressive, infantile character (Barthes, *Empire of Signs*, p. 10).

For Barthes the Japanese body is differentiated (from the 'Western'?) according to an 'erotic project' where the so-called 'whole body' is engaged. Immediately one may detect here something of a fantasy of completion, the un-lacking body of the other that indicates an undifferentiated – the other does not lack – (a)sexuality. The Japanese body, for Barthes, is not constituted in relation to the Law, is not the somewhat haphazard collection of *petits objets* that is characteristic of the Lacanian subject of desire. However, in Barthes this subtly discontinuous whole body is one made up, precisely, by a catalogue of (parenthesized) parts. Barthes – as if he (mis)recognizes (or disavows) the pre-Oedipal nature of this fantasy of the completion of the other – is hasty to return the Japanese body to speech, to a speech that is a babble, a plethora of tongues and chains of signification, but one that is *not* infantile. The term that he will have recourse to, to counter suggestions of infantilism, is 'domination'.

These fantasy scenes – of the other as not-lacking, of infantilism, of the babble, of master–slave dialectics – are recurrent tropes in the history of the sexual imagery of *Orientalism* in which the Oriental is structured as the other, whose lack is substituted by a partial object or explained away through a dialectic of plenitude. In this topos the body finds its proper identity and sexuality its proper place. Barthes also says: 'in Japan in that country I am calling Japan – sexuality is in sex, not elsewhere; in the United States, it is the contrary; sex is everywhere, except in sexuality' (Barthes, *Empire of Signs*, p. 28).

Or, in a description of a present brought back from a visit by a child, the gift to the one he loves (I say '*the* gift' rather than '*a* gift' because, in Barthes's reading of the Japanese, the specific takes on the economy of the general). Or the gift of Japaneseness as gift. (Barthes describes in detail the presentation of such a gift.) And it might be significant that the giver of this gift in his phantasm called 'Japan' is a male child. He details the seemingly endless series of envelopes, which, like the gift scene itself, are 'often repeated'. This 'unwrapping', which seems to go on 'forever', Barthes writes, 'postpones the discovery of the object it contains' like a scene of sexual discovery, revealing that little thing which 'is often insignificant', a 'vulgar "souvenir" ... wrapped with as much sumptuousness as a jewel'. This procedure, apparently, is one undertaken by 'hordes of schoolboys', who, all of them young, all of them boys, discover the 'ecstasy of the package'. Thus it is not the contents that are of significance, but the revealing/unveiling process which performs (as) the signifier:

> the box acts the sign: as envelope, screen, mask, it is *worth* what it conceals, protects and yet designates: it *puts off*, if we can take this expression in French – *donner le change* – in its double sense, monetary and psychological; but the very thing it encloses and signifies is for a very long time put off until later ... the signified flees, and when you finally have it (there is always a little something in the package), it appears insignificant, laughable, vile: the pleasure, field of the signifier, has been taken (Barthes, *Empire of Signs*, p 46).

All this unveiling, this deferment of the signifier, of this vulgar, insignificant little (no)thing behind the veil, this substitution of the veil for the signifier; does this not produce an ideal metonymy, a substitution for the scene of fetishism, a substitution for the very act of substitution for the lack of the signifier–phallus? Or describing Japanese food: 'on the side of the light, the aerial, of the instantaneous, the fragile, the transparent, the crisp, the trifling, but whose name would be *the interstice* without specific edges, or again: the empty sign' (Barthes, *Empire of Signs*, p. 26).

This is from a short chapter (of some two pages) called 'The interstice'; my dictionary reads: 'interstice, *n.* a small space between things, or between parts which compose a body'. And describing the capital: 'The city I am talking about (Tokyo) offers this precious paradox: it does possess a center, but this center is empty. The entire city turns around a site both forbidden and indifferent' (Barthes, *Empire of Signs*, p. 30). In Barthes, here, the lack or emptiness at the centre is named 'indifference'. I am not wishing to *accuse* Barthes of some violence under the sign of cultural or sexual difference (could such a loving text end in violence?) but to suggest that in this beautiful book, his self-avowed fantasy of the other place or scene, this difference (or, here, indifference) is at least partly sexual, as is the fantasy. And that this sexual fantasy is one in which Japan becomes a (or *the* maternal) body, and the body of the other yields to him, and lack is substituted, or even desired; a fantasy of the plenitude of *the other*.

The Beyond of the Japanese body

This configuration in Barthes, involving a certain, or uncertain, 'slippage' – of the signifier, of identity, of the signifier of and as identity – is, at least, in tension with 'colonial discourse' as defined in Homi K. Bhabha's oft-cited essay, 'The other question':

> colonial discourse produces the colonised as a fixed reality which is at once an 'other' and yet entirely knowable and fixable.[15]

> An important feature of colonial discourse is its dependence on the concept of 'fixity' in the ideological construction of otherness. Fixity, as the sign of cultural/historical/racial difference in the discourse of colonialism, is a paradoxical mode of representation: it connotes rigidity and an unchanging order as well as disorder, degeneracy and daemonic repetition.[16]

Moreover, for Barthes 'Japaneseness' is characterized by the operations through which it is precisely not entirely knowable and visible. Precisely, Japan, *the* Japanese subjectivity, and accordingly Japanese sexuality – lies 'elsewhere', Beyond even.

And, as Bhabba has adequately demonstrated, (the phantasm of) *the other* – and, I assert, accordingly the fantasies of *identity* and a going *beyond* of *identity* – must negotiate that very 'fixity' on which it is both predicated and that it seeks to overcome.

Notes

1 *Beyond Japan: A Photo Theatre*, at the Barbican Art Gallery, London, 11 July to 22 September 1991, part of the Japan Festival, was one of the most publicized exhibitions in London in recent years.

2 Roland Barthes, *Empire of Signs*, trans. Richard Howard [from *L'Empire des signes*, 1970], New York: Hill and Wang, 1982. Subsequent references in the text are to this edition.

3 Jacques Derrida, 'Fables: beyond the speech act', from 'Psyche: inventions of the Other,' in *A Derrida Reader: Between the Blinds*, edited with an introduction by Peggy Kamuf, London: Harvester, 1991.

4 *Chambers English Dictionary*, 1988 edn.

5 See, for example, Judith Butler, *Gender Trouble: Feminism and the Subversion of Identity*, New York: Routledge, 1990.

6 Mark Holborn, Leaflet to accompany the exhibition *Beyond Japan: A Photo Theatre*, London: Barbican Art Gallery, unpaginated. All other unreferenced citations herein are to this leaflet. See also the catalogue by Holborn, *Beyond Japan: A Photo Theatre*, London: Jonathan Cape, 1991.

7 Yukio Mishima, *Sun and Steel*, 1970, as cited by Holborn (see note 6 above; catalogue, p. 37).

8 Arata Isozaki, in Ryuji Miyamoto, *Architectural Apocalypse*, 1988, as cited by Holborn (see note 6 above, catalogue, p. 38).

9 Sigmund Freud, 'Beyond the Pleasure Principle' (1920), Standard Edition, 18, London, 1961.

10 Edmund White, *New York Times* book review, as cited on the back cover of Roland Barthes, *Empire of Signs*.

11 Jacques Derrida, 'Psyche: inventions of the Other', p. 206.

12 Jacques Lacan, following Freud, suggested that the question that 'the Hysteric' is
    asking could be summarized as 'what sex am I?'
13 John Barrell, *The Infection of Thomas De Quincey*, New Haven, Conn.: Yale
    University Press, 1991.
14 *Ibid.*, pp. 10–11.
15 Homi K. Bhabha, 'The other question', *Screen*, 24 (6), Nov.–Dec. 1983, p. 23.
16 *Ibid.*, p. 30.

Painting another: other-than-painting

At first glance the scene reminded me of a paradise: a luscious garden enclosed by a monumental building at the top of a cliff. Exotic trees and foliage are silhouetted against a brilliantly coloured sky which is heavy in the intensity of its colour. There is a pool reminiscent of a grotto. The picture harks back to Giorgione's *La Tempesta*, refers to a landscape passage in *Good Government* by Lorenzetti, is reminiscent of Gauguin even. I look again more closely; now my pleasure stops. I see that the sky is too dark and black above the roof-top which is full of foreboding. The sunset is too lurid, the yellows are too acid: a sour taste prevails. What first appeared to me as a paradise becomes a blighted, disordered garden, a reversal of Matisse's *Joy of Life*. The duality of the picture is like the Fall itself: nature, purity, primitive bliss are evoked, but consolation is quickly transformed into anxiety. The discovery of knowledge, of good and evil, of nature and culture, mark the first diaspora. R. B. Kitaj's *If Not, Not*, the name of the picture (Figure 10) was inspired by T. S. Eliot's poem *The Wasteland*, those 'fragments shored against (his) return'.[1]

Kitaj's project has been to create anew a narrative painting informed by the rigours of modernism. His art tests the limits of narrative painting and is provocative, unsettling and disturbing. There is an ever-growing literature which now attends to it and to which Kitaj himself contributes.[2] The images are surrounded by words, labels abound: narrative painting, material fragments, Jewish art, prefaces, diaspora manifesto.[3] Despite all these explanatory texts, face to face with his paintings I am uncertain. The reflective act of interpretation is always risky, and I feel the fear which comes from not knowing where the work will take me, or more, even, whether it will take me anywhere. All that I can be sure about is that meanings are provisional, ambiguous and ambivalent. Ambivalence, as Zygmunt Bauman suggests, is 'indeterminate and unpredictable':[4] as the Other of order, it is the unknown component of the known.

If Not, Not initiates a game between signs. The landscape is scattered with unrelated incidents – a broken figure; a classical head (referring to a Matisse bust) which has been knocked off its pedestal.[5] This broken sculpture could suggest the fragility of art and even of representation itself. Another head emerges, belonging to a body which has been swallowed up in a stagnant swamp. There is a man with a hearing-aid, who may refer to Walter Benjamin. Indeed the form of Kitaj's work has been compared with Benjamin's writing; it has been described as fragmentary, elliptical and open-ended, rather than as complete and closed. *If Not, Not* offers a site of open readings in which visual clues may be revealing and misleading. It is not that the work itself is endlessly open, rather, there is an openness within the picture. It provokes certain themes which may touch upon European history, literature, art history, and politics, yet prompts the awareness of the existence of the blind spot, of the 'I don't know' which emerges out of each one of the possibilities.

Inscribed in the very language of Kitaj's painting and use of imagery is the defiant impossibility of fixing a single meaning. *Jewish Rider* presents a man on a train. The train here may sustain a double connotation: the idea of Jew as wanderer, uprooted and dislocated, and Jew as victim, being transported to the camps. Neither one of those possible interpretations can be collapsed into the other. Inside the carriage primary colours masquerade, as bright as Van Gogh's palette. The man appears relaxed, urbane, dressed in a lemon-coloured jersey, red trousers, casual white shoes: assimilated. Whilst the situation itself

FIGURE 10. R. B. Kitaj, *If Not, Not*. Oil on canvas, 1975–6

may be calm and innocuous, the paint handling and the colours are turbulent. Kitaj's overtly Jewish themes created a response in form: the paint became thicker and more loaded, more *expressionistic* than hitherto. The window has a view – a second reality, a sepia-coloured landscape, blighted ravines: deep blacks against soft translucent brown. A chimney burns – an evocation of the spectre of the camps, perhaps? The smoke is drawn, as if by a wind, towards a cross upon a hillside – another Passion? A third reality, a steeply rising corridor, chimney-like, reveals at its end a uniformed guard who wields a whip and represents, perhaps, authority itself, diminished yet ever present.

The title, *Jewish Rider*, refers to Rembrandt's *Polish Rider*. Does the reference to Poland point us to Auschwitz? In Kitaj's picture the head and tail of a horse also figure. To what do these refer? Is the association with a horse meant to evoke a sense of movement? Could it also be a reference to Ernst Gombrich's *Meditations on a Hobby Horse*? The sitter for the painting is already known to be Michael Podro, who was a pupil of Gombrich, and is himself an art historian. Is the picture to be understood solely as an art-historical riddle to be solved? Or does it provide a comment on the precariousness of assimilation? Or again, are we being invited to think of those journeys which took the Jews from their homes to the death camps? Long after the threat to annihilate all Jews, many would or could not believe that possibility. They were deceived by possibilities of resettlement, work camps or special provisions. Is it plausible to describe the image itself as a deception: a deception akin to the deception played on the Jews? Learning to live with the possibility of deception, with the provisionality of meanings – thereby refusing the lure of certainty – is, for me, the work of Kitaj's work.

Can facing a painting be seen as an event akin to Emmanuel Levinas's description of the originary encounter? Such a moment marks the discovery of the responsibility for the existence of the other: perceived neither as a negation, nor as an affirmation, nor as a narcissistic projection of the self.[6] Painting inaugurates a play between the materiality of the object (presence) and the image (absence): always other-than-other, it is a sign dependent upon presence, absence and loss. My concern is to think *If Not, Not* through Levinas's notion of the other, aided and abetted by Jean François Lyotard's own reading of Levinas. Inescapably, my chapter touches on questions of identity which themselves revolve around the constitution of self and other, and carry with them ethical implications.

Levinas offers a way of thinking the other which challenges the logic of identity thinking, which is merely, in his words, 'a reconciliation of contradictions: from the identical and the non-identical, identity! It is still the philosophy of the intelligibility of the Same, beyond the tension of the Same and the Other'.[7] The other cannot be assimilated to the same. Levinas offers a critique of Hegelian alterity, showing it to be, as Lyotard explains, a 'caprice of identity': 'The absolutely other, is not the other of the same, its other is the heart of that supreme sameness that is being: it is other than being'.[8] Levinas, Lyotard suggests, attempts to 'break this reversible totality and to discombobulate speculative dialectics by reinforcing the dissymmetry of the ethical instances'.[9] The idea of the other, as an enemy of the same, is an abuse of the notion – as, indeed, perhaps it is of *notions* as such.

Kitaj paints a *Self Portrait as a Woman*. Here a heroic figure, who has defied the Nazis by consorting with Jews, is pictured, stabbed by violent brush-marks. At once, she is appropriated and affirmed *and* obliterated and negated. Such violence marks the traces of an impossible identification: an overidentifi-cation with Woman, another, which the artist desires to incorporate. The picture swings around conflictual emotions of desire and disavowal, identity and differ-ence, but always bounded by the regime of the same: here Woman becomes a sign of deviance.

However, Levinas proposes that we should go beyond understanding which is the same, equal and which seeks to assimilate, incorporate and possess the other. Instead, he suggests we might think about the Same (echoing Kant) as 'drowsy in identity', as hibernating, as self-enclosed: waiting (and needing) to be woken by the other.[10] Such an awakening is the possibility of consciousness and of love. Can facing *If Not, Not* be likened to an awakening, and thus be akin to witnessing otherness? Between the painting and me lies a mysterious gulf.

Mystery, for Levinas, is the unbridgeable gap between myself and another: 'The other as other is not here as object that becomes ours or becomes us; to the contrary, it withdraws into mystery.'[11] Mystery is neither mystification nor romance. It does not expel clarity; rather, it demands greater intensity. Levinas argues it is not vision which describes the authentic relationship with the other. For the other who faces a face with a face is not other in so far as a face is shown. Rather, it is a response or responsibility which wakes the ego from its sluggish sleep. For Freud, Eros is the other of the ego: the other of mastery and control. Love, the urge to identify and merge, is always in tension with self-preservation. Levinas keeps absolutely separate and distinct the *exteriority* of the other and the *interiority* of the self. The other, for him, is not an affirmation or a negation, but a *mystery*. Eros is the situation of pure otherness:

> The pathos of love consists in an insurmountable duality of beings. Love is a relationship with that which is forever concealed. This relationship does not neutralize alterity, but conserves it. The pathos of desire rests in the fact of being two. The other as other is not as object bound to become mine or become me; it retreats on the contrary into its mystery.[12]

Eros maintains otherness: it is a relationship with what always slips away. It seeks neither to consume, devour, know nor possess the other. For if one consumed, devoured, knew or possessed the other, the other would no longer be other. Respect for the other in this sense admits difference, but difference without mastery. Mystery involves acceptance of the impossibility of mastery and consequently is marvellous.

Returning to *If Not, Not* as a text of otherness, a text *as* otherness, I notice a ram and a bush, and am reminded of the story of Abraham and Isaac recounted in Genesis, chapter 22. In the biblical story Abraham is ordered by God to sacrifice his son. The Law is invoked through a threat of imminent violence. Abraham hears: 'That Isaac die, that is my law',[13] and he is prepared to obey the command: 'And Abraham stretched forth his hand, and took the knife to slay his son'.[14] The picture does not figure Abraham. The Jew is himself unrepresentable. Yet, as Andrew Benjamin notes, this is one of Kitaj's 'most dramatic biblical references'.[15] The painting can be thematized around issues of obedience and obligation, the Law and ethics.

Lyotard asks if the command received by Abraham is any more intelligible than those which ordered 'round-up, convoys, concentrations, and either slow or quick death'. How can we know, he asks, if Abraham is, or is not, a 'paranoiac subject to homicidal (infanticidal) urges? Or a fake?'[16] Lyotard argues that in order for the command to be answered or resisted, it must first be understood as a call rather than a 'fantasy'. The call is obligatory if, and only if, its addressee is obligated. Abraham only obeys *because* it is God who gives the order. As all God's commandments are just, Abraham is obligated to obey them. Abraham is woken by the imperative to obey: obedience is irreducible. However, Lyotard cautions: 'alone by itself, this implication is a crime against ethics: the people would be obligated by an order because they could understand its sense!'[17] If the law is already established and known, then the ethical is no longer a question, but is presented as fact. Obligation cannot result from an already legitimated authority, for obligation takes hold immediately and before understanding. Being obligated depends on being receptive: the receptive other hears the command and is both bound by and obligated to it. There is an authority beyond the *self*, and through which the self is made responsible and confronts freedom and its limits. Levinas argues:

> My very uniqueness lies in my responsibility for the other; nobody can relieve me of this, just as nobody can replace me at the moment of my death. Obedience to the Most High is defined for me by precisely this impossibility of running away; through this, my 'self' is unique. To be free is simply to do what nobody else can do in my place.[18]

Obedience here is not understood as subservience to the Law, but as the necessary condition of freedom. The Law is not absolute. In the uncertain space between obedience and freedom, receptivity and alterity lies the possibility of self-knowledge and ethics.

The ethical relation is the responsibility to respond to the other. The message comes from the outside and can only be heard when the identity of the subject is splintered. The ego, argues Lyotard, does not proceed from the other;

the other 'befalls the ego'; the other can only happen to me through a 'break-in' or a 'revelation'.[19] From the beginning, Jewish revelation, Levinas explains, is commandment. The other commands: Abraham responds. Ethics occurs in the demand for a response. The impossibility of Abraham's predicament questions the rationality of reason. There is a form of truth that is totally alien: 'And Abraham lifted up his eyes, and looked, and behold behind *him* a ram caught in a thicket by his horns: and Abraham went and took the ram, and offered him up for a burnt offering in the stead of his son'.[20] Abraham had been subjected to and been the subject of (which for Levinas is *subjectivity*) absolute alterity. The alterity of the other places the subject in a relation of severe responsibility.

The receptive ear is the me that can hear the other.[21] Obligation is an aspect of time, and its organ is the ear. Unlike sight, which fixes and is static and dogmatic, sound is unexpected and is open to endless possibilities of change. The angel calls, Abraham hears: 'And the angel of the LORD called unto him out of heaven, and said, Abraham, Abraham: and he said, Here *am* I.'[22] This encounter is the 'Here am I' of the man welcoming his neighbour.[23] Each person is a chosen one: the one who can respond to the call, 'Here I am', but more with the reply, 'Here I am for the Other.' Perhaps Levinas asks, is there not a way of 'losing one's soul' which comes from something better, or higher than the soul? He suggests that it is through the act of deference that the very manifestations of *better* or *higher* are articulated and that 'seeking, desire and questioning which come are better than possession, satisfaction and an-swers'.[24] Revelation is not received wisdom but an awakening. Responsibility for the other gives me over to the other. Surely, Levinas asks, 'our model of revelation must be an ethical one?'[25]

Ethical obligation comes about not from logic and reason, pre-established rules, but from the uniqueness of the situation itself, as the story of Abraham, that most violent of fathers, shows. However, it must be that some orders are to be refused. So how can we recognize what might be the legitimate and ethical responses to a command? The *sign*, for Lyotard, is injustice, yet there can be no constant, enduring, overbearing notion of justice – it can only be judged in the fullness of the instant. Lyotard cites the case of Ishmael, who will later be unjust.[26] When he was dying of thirst, God chose to save him because at that moment he was neither just nor unjust: he was dying. Each person is judged for what he or she is now. It is unjust to judge what will be the future in order to judge what is now. Through his critical reading of the Kantian notion of the sign of history, Lyotard advances the idea of the necessity to judge without determinable laws.

The work of Barnett Newman offers Lyotard another sign, evidence, of a response to the originary order to be. It represents for him the one who speaks, the one that utters the 'Here am I'. Its message is a presentation, presenting nothing save presence: 'Presence is the instant which interrupts the chaos of history and which recalls, or simply calls out that "there is", even before that which has any significance.'[27] The painting does not give us anything that has to be deciphered or decoded. It takes to an extreme the rebuttal that has been the central concern of avant-garde modernist practice. It just is. The time invoked is *now*. There is no before or after. Through Lyotard's writing it may be possible dimly to glimpse something beyond the dialectical trap. It affirms an ethics of being in which the 'I' can only exist on a terrain of other 'I's. Here the 'I' always bears responsibility in excess of itself. Extreme particularism is universalized and marks the passage from individual responsibility to justice.

Judgement is a critical activity, a way of determining the mode of presenting and establishing the reality, rather than a re-presentation where something (a pre-constituted subject) already presents something to itself. Lyotard claims that the problem of judgement is twofold, given the impossibility of avoiding conflicts (the impossibility of indifference) and the absence of a universal genre of discourse to regulate it. The issue, then, is 'to find, if not what can legitimate judgement (the "good" linkage), then at least how to save the honor of thinking'.[28] To judge is to open the abyss between phrases by analysing their *differend*: the *differend* marks a point of disagreement, of dispute or difference, where narratives fail and no criteria exist for judgement. The critical task is to find ways of phrasing the *differend*, and it must always be kept unresolved.

If Not, Not is crowned with the Gates of Death, Auschwitz; there is neither a redeeming nor an avenging Angel. What can the picture reveal of the ethical? The name 'Auschwitz', Lyotard reminds us, became for Adorno the model for negative dialectics. Lyotard argues that 'what meets its end there is merely affirmative dialectics'.[29] And he tears apart the edifice of dialectics, describing it as a 'magical affirmative farce'.[30] Lyotard presents the proper name, 'Auschwitz', as an abyss in which the genre of dialectics is repudiated: 'Then, it will have awakened the despair of nihilism and it will be necessary "after Auschwitz" for thought to consume its determinations like a cow its fodder, or a tiger its prey, that is with no result ... We wanted the progress of the mind, we got its shit.'[31] The crime signalled by the name is real. The name marks the limits of knowledge and understanding. In that abyss narratives fail. Between the SS and the Jew, Lyotard argues, there is no shared phrase or common idiom; the dispute cannot be phrased. The inability of dialectics to conceptualize Auschwitz questions knowledge. Auschwitz tests the possibilities and limits of thought itself.

Critical thought has less to do with knowledge than with its limits. For Lyotard, it is the very name with which the *differend* is identified which signals crisis. Speculative dialectics are stuck in the 'genre of mythic narrative'. According to Lyotard, the latter yields 'only identical repetition'.[32] Everything remains in place after all. He argues that speculative logic is jammed, condemned to disarrangement. Negative dialectics stay within, do not disrupt the logic of *identity thinking*: identity-in-difference remains the discourse of Other and of Same. This is the trap of the 'yes/no' of *identity thinking*, and a trap into which some of Kitaj's work seems unwittingly to fall.

In his writings and some of his paintings, Jewish identity has, for Kitaj, an
a priori existence which is indelibly shaped and marked by anti-Semitism. When
he utters 'Jew' he seems to mean 'victim': someone trapped, someone imprisoned
in and by an identity. Yet 'Jew' is itself unrepresentable: it is only through the
title of a picture, such as *Jewish Rider*, that we can assume that we are looking
at a *real* Jew. The identity of the 'Jew' is already figured in and by the idea of
displacement: the Jew as contaminating virus who has been forced to make
endless departures. A chimney as a symbol occurs in Kitaj's pictures in different
forms: sometimes overtly, as in *Jewish Rider*, at other times obliquely – evoked
perhaps by the shape of the canvas, as in the right-hand panel of *Germania (the
Tunnel)*. The chimney, which sets up a chain of possible associations which
may lead to a de Chirico painting, to a factory, to a crematorium, to the death
factory at Auschwitz – can be understood to function as an indictment of
Christianity. Jewish identity in these works is achieved only in opposition to
Christianity. It can only be realized through reiterating the Christian/Jew opposition. Such an identity can only be accomplished through violent negation.

None the less, it may be possible to avoid the seductions and entrapments
of *identity thinking*. The possibility that this could be so is held out in *If Not,
Not*. The handling of the paint is loose, the surface glazed and opulent. Yet
those oversaturated colours might seep away, evaporate, disappear at any instant.
The image never coalesces: its spaces never arrest. Its very tight formal arrangement of pictures-within-the-picture is also random. The boundaries between
each incident are not fixed, but endlessly seep into one another. Everything
which is observed can take on other identities. The *essence* of ethics is precisely
not to have an essence: it is to disturb essences and undo *identity*.

In *Todtnauberg*, a poem by Paul Celan, any attempt to crystallize difference
into identity is subverted.[33] The title refers to the place where Martin Heidegger
lived, and where Celan visited him after the war. Celan was himself a survivor
of a Romanian work camp; both his parents died in the internment camp at
Trasnistra. The poem is indirect, allusive, and evades decoded understandings.
In its own way it displays the consideration of ethical problems in the more
general questions of identity and interpretation. *Todtnauberg* seeks neither
answers nor solutions. It creates images which are in constant disarray. It is
infused by a refusal to thematize that moment of history in terms which affirm
one meaning or identity at the expense of another.

The poem does not elicit judgements. It neither retreats into affirmative
idealizations (justification), nor into indictments (accusation), but simply recognizes that there are some things which cannot yet be said. In this way, *Todtnauberg* may be understood as a figuration, as Philippe Lacoue-Labarthe
suggests, of 'silence'.[34] Everything that has yet to happen, has happened, is still
happening. It offers no consolation.

If Not, Not – the title – proposes a double negative which cancels itself out
to accomplish yet other identities. It exists as a constantly shifting play between

aggression and counter-attack, between affirmation and negation; neither reducible to the other. It provokes us to think about the Holocaust, yet is not assimilable to its narration. *If Not, Not,* while risking identity, fails to secure it. The image is a combination of beauty and terror; the one does not conceal the other. *No-certainty,* not uncertainty, is its condition. Abraham is an absence whose presence cannot be presented. In the allusive space between presence and absence the subject is realized as if – and now to borrow Bill Reading's description of Lyotard's own work – 'directed towards the immemorial, to that which cannot be either remembered (represented) or forgotten (obliterated). A history which evokes figures that haunt the claims of historical representation, haunt in the sense that they are neither present to them nor absent from them.'[35]

The image initiates a play between history and its making, between the painting and the discourses which seek to speak of it, between Western (Christian, modernist) and Jewish thought. This play takes place in the hazy site of ambivalence. But which ambivalence? Ambivalence concerning representation – of Abraham, of the Holocaust, of the ethical object, of the disaster demanding an ethical response? Or, again, perhaps such ambivalence instructs us of the necessary breach in, or even failure of, the face-to-face encounter in the awakening of the ethical.

A man in the picture flees from the embrace of a nude woman. She stares intently into his short-sighted (spectacled) eyes. Here both sight and hearing are shown as impaired. A mutilated figure, with a bandaged arm, carries what could be a bag of explosives. The headless body of a man in the foreground creates a visual dynamic which brings us back into the picture to look again. What history creates and narratives dissimulate will meet again; *If Not, Not.*

Notes

1 R. B. Kitaj, 'Prefaces', in Marco Livingstone, *R. B. Kitaj*, Oxford: Phaidon, 1985.

2 See Richard Morphet (ed.), *R. B. Kitaj: A Retrospective*, London: Tate Gallery, 1994, for a full (if not complete) bibliography.

3 See, for examples, Richard Wollheim, 'Kitaj: Recollections and reflections', in Morphet, *R. B. Kitaj: A Retrospective*, p. 37 and R. B. Kitaj, *Diaspora Manifesto*, London: Thames and Hudson, 1989.

4 Zygmund Bauman, *Modernity and Ambivalence*, Cambridge: Polity Press, 1991, p. 7.

5 Kitaj, 'Prefaces', p. 150.

6 Emmanuel Levinas, 'Philosophy and awakening', in E. Cadava, P. Connor and J. -L. Nancy (eds), *Who Comes After the Subject*, London and New York: Routledge, 1991, p. 214.

7 *Ibid.*, p. 208

8 Andrew Benjamin (ed.), *The Lyotard Reader*, Oxford: Basil Blackwell, 1989, p. 276.

9 Lyotard, *The Differend: Phrases in Dispute*, trans. G. Van Den Abbeele, Manchester: Manchester University Press, 1988, p. 113.

10 Sean Hand (ed.), *The Levinas Reader*, Oxford: Basil Blackwell, 1989, p. 209.

11 Emmanuel Levinas, *Time and the Other (and additional essays)*, Pittsburg: Duquesne University Press, 1987, p. 86.
12 *Ibid.*, p. 86.
13 Lyotard, *The Differend*, p. 107.
14 Genesis 22: 10 (Authorised Version). Originally Abraham was called Abram: his name was changed after he received the covenant (Abraham means 'father of the multitude'; Isidore Epstein, *Judaism*, Harmondsworth: Pelican, 1973, p. 14).
15 Andrew Benjamin, *Art, Mimesis and the Avant-Garde: Aspects of a Philosophy of Difference*, London: Routledge, 1991, p. 92.
16 Lyotard, *The Differend*, p. 107.
17 *Ibid.*, p. 109.
18 *The Levinas Reader*, p. 202.
19 Lyotard, *The Differend*, p. 110.
20 Genesis, chapter 22, verse 13.
21 *The Levinas Reader*, p. 206.
22 Genesis 22: 11.
23 *The Levinas Reader*, p. 206.
24 *Ibid.*, p. 207.
25 *Ibid.*, p 209.
26 Lyotard *The Differend*, p. 109.
27 *The Lyotard Reader*, p. 247.
28 Lyotard, *The Differend*, p. xii.
29 *Ibid.*, p. 90.
30 *Ibid.*
31 *Ibid.*, p. 91.
32 *Ibid.*, p. 106.
33 Paul Celan, *Selected Poems*, trans. M. Hamberger, Harmondsworth: Penguin, 1990, p. 293.
34 Philippe Lacoue-Labarthe, *Heidegger, Art and Politics*, trans. C. Turner, Oxford: Basil Blackwell, 1990, p. 117.
35 Bill Readings, *Introducing Lyotard: Art and Politics,* London and New York: Routledge, 1991, p. 62.

Disappearing acts:
an impossibility of identity

Janine Antoni's *Lick and Lather* has a significant impact before you enter the gallery, before you *see* anything of her artwork, which is made of malleable materials – soap and chocolate.[1] The fragrance leaves you salivating, awash in an invisible sea of thick cocoa and scented fat; where are these smells coming from? Excretory, oral and hygiene fetishism associated with this pungent aromatic admixture acts to produce an overdetermination in the work, advances a tension to it, a riddle – clean or unclean? Our olfactory senses are giving us something to chew on from behind the door. Led by the nose, the eyes follow the visual aspects of the work. Seven busts of dark chocolate set high on white box plinths, forming the left-hand side of an aisle, facing seven creamy soap busts set high on white box plinths, forming the right-hand side of an aisle. All the work stands at the same height, each plinth equidistant to each other in a row. Every bust appears to have been cast from the same head and shoulders, the same mould, and to this extent the work appears to conform generically to a classical mode, even whilst its figuration is 'distorted'. Consequently, the work can be read allegorically, as a ruin of the classical genre with its implications of perfection, idealism.

Reading the curatorial notes to the exhibition, themselves essential supplements to it, we understand that the busts are cast from the artist's head. One significance of these notes for this chapter is that they act to collapse the distinction between artist and artwork, in the way that the dancer is the dance. Arguably, therefore, we may consider *Lick and Lather* a display of objects which are explicit remainders of a performance: the making, the maker and the object of the work combine, apparently, here, the a priori concept 'artist' is rendered questionable, questioned too, disappearing along with the work, at the end of each performance – meltdown is a material inevitability. The work has been licked and lathered to render the busts 'disfigured' or 'transfigured', or, in the instance of the uncanny soap bust figured here (Figure 11), it almost disappears. It is both familiar and unfamiliar, is it or is it not a bust, as it appears?

The figures are pulled, rubbed, licked until they are more *or* less perfect casts, more *or* less ideal, more *or* less not at all; big foreheads, elongated chins, flattened craniums, remnants reduced from a proto-cast, all reminiscent of a rogues' gallery where nineteenth-century physiognomic categories of identity are dubiously paraded or parodied. Do these freakish mutations of cast(e), however, poke fun at, critique or affirm the conceit of unity, of self-presence or homogeneous identity as a sustainable art/curatorial practice? Do they act as a critique of predeterminately collapsing politics to identity to a judgement of priority – *more* or *less*; radical, modern, inevitable?

The process of producing self-similar busts from one's own head and shoulders not only emphasizes a temporal dimension to the work, but also renders the unified category 'self-presence' at least partial, if not derisible. Importantly to us here, the self-similarity of the busts can be read in part as a critique of the self-sameness of identity categories. That is, she/they are not themselves; any guarantee of an original, along with the fantasy of a hard-edged subject, is thrown out with the soapy bath-water.

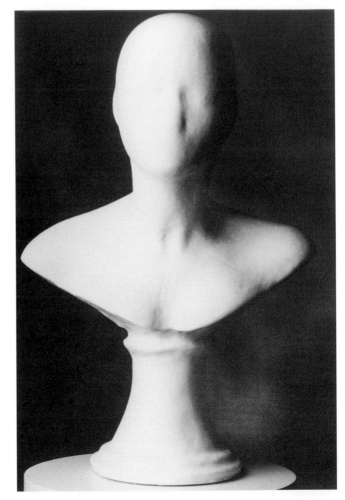

FIGURE 11.
Janine Antoni, *Lick and Lather* (detail).
Soap, 1994

What, then, *appears* to be and what *disappears* before our eyes constructs an internal tension to the work. Whilst we may recognize the works in their classical *bustness* they do not conform to the generic form in terms of materials or in terms of their 'askew' figuration. The materials are significantly dissoluble too, discontinuous in time. Consequently they do not celebrate the immortal, the durable, the ego or ideal. They are, however, a sophisticated narcissism – one which I will elaborate in a particular sense in this chapter – a narcissism exhibited as multiple *Doppelgängers*, which renders the artist and the work disjunctive to the unities of time and 'identity' and as categories known and understood.

Do the busts then: (i) compensate discontinuity in that they fill the space materially – are they *reparative*?[2] (ii) repeat such a discontinuity in their material impermanence – are they *nihilistic*? or (iii) construct a tension *between* reparation and nihilism as a dependent and indiscrete structure of narcissism? The busts also shift our visual-centric consideration of actions and objects to one that is also olfactory, albeit temporarily and partially, they doubly repeat a discontinuity. What *do* these pungent aromas, that admixture of cocoa and scented fats compel us to? – Simply look?

Does it act to remind us of a hunger, remind us of place, people, time or genre frozen and rewritten in our memories? Do we want to eat the work? Do we want to bite the work, break it, reshape it? If we do seize it, tear it, chew it, will we spit it out, take it in, draw what we 'want' from it and expel the rest? Will we love it, identify in some aspect with it and model ourselves after it, mimic it? Does it make us nauseous as in some anorexic nightmare of food in relation to the 'presence' of flesh; do we want to wash away the work along with any reminder of eating and sexual longing? If we incorporate something of the work, what is it we desire of it – comfort? Do we incorporate the work as a whole or in fragile parts? Hungry for more or not, will we make it disappear, fantasize the inevitability of it not being there, of being 'inside' or somewhere else?

The circuitous exchange between the fantasy of the power to make it disappear one way or another and the masochistic desire to disappear replicates the doubling effects of the drives[3] in an interdependent narcissistic relation, an assertion I will draw out in a psychoanalytic sense presently. This interdependent relation is produced between a spectator and works of art, between the producer and product of a work and between the dynamic and the somatic split-ego.

Narcissism also features in another more banal and restricted sense in the Janine Antoni *œuvre*. That is, owing to the privileging of the significance and malleability of materials, her work often engages with the so-called transgressive or feminizing 'position' of narcissism in relation to the particularity of materials used; textiles, hair-dye, lard, lipstick, chocolate, soap, dreams, the artist's body.[4]

These assertions into gallery spaces may be construed as a critique of gender from the 'other side', from a feminine position, although, arguably, such a critique is only possible if a gender is already adopted and considered in relation to an Other. This inevitability of gender, however fragile, is a difficult *place* to start, precisely owing to the assumption of its inevitability. Within such a logic the pre-given stabilizes and determines the discourse, however partially.

Janine Antoni's work is rather more mutable than illustrative, the materials, non-durable as they are, trouble the safe knowledge of place, position, sex and gender. In the busts' self-similarity and imperfection, I get a sense that their identity and their meanings always, in advance, evade us and will partially continue to do so.

Lingering a little while longer on the 'other side' of identity – on what I shall call *the desire to disappear* – contesting that such a desire be a *Zwang* (compulsion), I will be arguing that such a compulsion is neither a position (nihilism) nor the inverse or opposite of 'being' in its nihilistic 'appearance', as Jean-Luc Nancy has asserted in his introduction to *Who Comes After The Subject?*.[5] This desire, I suggest, is a recurring consequence of the recurring impact of the drives' conflicting aims on subjectivity; an internal resister to identity. Disappearance will not be predicated on an ancestry – an 'already there' which is then absented, but on a representation of the drives. The pivotal question for the rest of this chapter, then, will be *is there a drive or desire to disappear?* And, if so, does such a drive internally oppose or constitute a universalizing proposition for identity?

In advocating an impossibility of gender as position and subject, femininity and masculinity will be tropes read against the call for a wish to disappear *as* a desire. This call is written through a consideration of Sigmund Freud's conceptions of the death drive and masochism and Jean Laplanche's work on the drives as *other implants, enigmatically and unconsciously signified*.[6] Can narcissism be figured as a paradoxical 'structuring' of subjectivity, which, whilst constituting the fantasy of identity, simultaneously refutes such a category in a 'self-shattering'? The 'self-shattering' posited by Freud, by Laplanche and taken up and elaborated by Leo Bersani, seriously troubles identity even as fantasy. Leo Bersani's work on *self-shattering* enables us, here, to consider unconscious paradox and conflict as intergral to and impacting on a sense of identity as simultaneous critique: a super-ego and ego in conflict? In emphasizing unconscious conflict once again, I hope to argue for the need of a sustained re-theorization of a desire to disappear as *other* than the same as *or* opposite to omnipotent identity fantasies of self-presence; such a re-theorization I can only begin to sketch here.

In Freud's paper 'Repression', representation is configured as partially structured by and through the 'indirect and figurative' articulations of unconscious ideas, conflicts or wishes:

> The ambivalence which has enabled repression through reaction-formation to take place is also a point at which the repressed succeeds in returning. The

vanished affect comes back in its transformed shape as social anxiety, moral anxiety and unlimited self-reproaches; the rejected idea is replaced by a *substitute by displacement*, often a displacement onto something very small or indifferent.[7]

But what is the source of such anxieties if not *others*? Anxieties repeatedly represented in relation to the *appearance* and *disappearance* of others, through which signification is made possible?

In 'Beyond The Pleasure Principle', Freud conversely configures symbolization in his description of the child's repeated 'fort-da' game. Here vocalizations 'fort or o-o-o-o', translated as 'gone' in English, accompany the throwing away of a cotton-reel and 'a joyful' 'da' or 'here' accompany the drawing-back of a cotton-reel – as a process, broadly speaking, of symbolization. Symbolization in this account is drawn as a way of structuring the affects of *absence* or *disappearance* and *presence* or *reappearance* of parents or adults in relation to pleasure or unpleasure.[8]

This process of repression–symbolization is doubly compounded when the pairings of love–presence and loss–absence are not directly equivalent. Importantly, it is the dynamic relationship between doubles – for example, absence<>presence, love<>loss – which configure symbolization. The symbolic illusion of presence is not simply a cover for absence, nor is it a cover for a radical lack, but must be understood as radically and dependently double.

If, in the 'fort-da' game, anxiety and fear of helpless solitude is substituted or compensated for by symbolization, Freud also argues that – in relation to unconscious wishes, conflicts and ideas – anxiety or psychical excitation may be indirectly substituted for by symbolization. Alternatively, as drawn out in Melanie Klein's 'The importance of symbol formation in the development of the ego' (1930),[9] anxiety precipitates symbolization and may articulate the psychical conflicts between the drives and between wishes and the prohibition of wishes – between the demands of the super-ego and the demands of the libido. In a sense this is a process which provides the structure: for an illusionary mastery; for ego-formation; and for a reduction in, and tolerance of, anxiety.

Freud reproduces his arguments on symbolization and the fort-da game in a footnote,[10] where, in relation to a game, a boy plays with a mirror, 'making himself disappear'; here Freud draws a more explicit link between symbolization and the formation of the (split) ego. The *intersubjective* aspect of this process of illusionary ego-unity and 'mastery' through symbolization is emphasized and elaborated as a formative misrecognition by Jacques Lacan in his well-known paper on 'the mirror stage'.[11] This structuring is also coincident with the structure of, or replicated in, the Oedipal complexes. If (the fantasy of) meaningful signification is made possible through a process of repeating the very action that gives rise to anxiety, in order to reduce anxiety, what consequences does this process have for a conception and failure of a discourse on the positionality of identity and, of concern here, the positionality of disappearance?

Following Freud's definition of narcissism – in his paper 'Mourning and melancholia' – as a structure dependent on an intersubjective relation which is incorporated, we may understand symbolization as a retranslation of that relation and its affects:

> narcissistic identification with the object becomes a substitute for the erotic cathexis, the result of which is that in spite of the conflict with the loved person, the love relation need not be given up ... identification is a preliminary stage of object-choice, ... and one that is expressed in an ambivalent fashion – in which the ego picks out an object. The ego wants to incorporate this object into itself, and, in accordance with the oral or cannibalistic phase of libidinal development, it wants to do so by devouring it.[12]

Are we bound to configure 'identity' as a paradox here? A conflicting, devouring, incorporation of others constituted through a process of symbolization which doubles here/gone, I/not I, and drives in an interdependency with others? Is the activity of 'making oneself disappear' a representation of a drive with an impossible aim; disappearance as identity? Or is it the necessary repeating of *anxiety*?

According to this schema, symbolization is configured as radically double, uncanny, in that it operates through the double here–gone and not as positions taken up on one side of a double or another. A lingering melancholy, then, would be precisely the withdrawal from signification in a non-relation to others; a redoubling of symbolization itself. Melancholy may account for the sense of *loss* felt when the imaginary ego is perceived to have already disappeared, when it is also perceived to have once been an object; self-love. This melancholic redoubling may be figured as a 'self-shattering'; I will return to this presently.

Freud's paper 'The economic problem of masochism'[13] outlines three kinds of masochism: Erotogenic – which is sexually twinned with sadism; Feminine 'positionality' – an imaginary consequence of the Oedipus fantasy of castration and of penis envy or lack; and Moral masochism – also a consequence of the Oedipus complex, though as a re-sexualizing of morality and conscience, which themselves are desexualizations or 'overcomings' of the Oedipus complex. Melancholy, then, and the shattering, even disappearing, of identity refers us to a consideration of masochism.

In his paper Freud stresses that some form of conscience may very well 'vanish' into masochism. Now this vanishing is of interest here, as it may effectively be a repression, or even be replicated in a drive to disappear. We would then ask, *what is it* that desires to disappear, *what* or *who* wants to disappear, if not a subject or ego with an identity? The enigma of the relation between the super-ego and ego in masochism here is of key importance. Might one disappear into the other, move into it, fuse, without also absenting the subject (to unconscious discontinuities) or presenting identity?

Moral masochism is described by Freud as an unconscious sense of guilt, and is qualified psychoanalytically by Freud as a 'need for punishment'. He also attributes moral ego-masochism to the sadism of the super-ego, an incorporation of adult prohibition or, specifically, parental super-ego into the child, which compels us to ask whether subjectivity is predicated, in some form, on masochism. *Masochism may undermine our sense of unified identity, but more complexly is constitutive of subjectivity.*

Interestingly, the Sadism of the Super-ego and the Masochism of the ego 'supplement' and 'unite' for Freud, 'to produce the same effects': the first – anxiety, which Freud describes as an ego-response to the impossible demands made by its ideal – the super-ego. The second – the proposition of the *ideal*; others fantasized as unified and perfect models of ego-subjects. The third – defence; the conflict between the super-ego and ego are *defended* against in the ego with a *defensive* anxiety which Freud called 'conscience anxiety'. *Consequently, anxiety, guilt and defence not only effect 'identity' modelled on ideals, but are also constitutive of subjectivity.*

The imperfect semiotic exchange between imperfect subjects may *both* escalate and reduce anxiety, guilt and defence, they may have different measures of pleasure and unpleasure for the super-ego and the ego in partial conflict with each other and the id. Freud counters his account of moral masochism via the super-ego with the caution:

> this super-ego is as much a representative of the id as of the external world. It came into being through the introjection into the ego of the first of the id's libidinal impulses – namely, the two parents. In this process the relation to those objects was desexualised; it was diverted from its sexual aim.[14]

Is, then, a desire to disappear a consequence of the tension between the super-ego and the ego, or as a dynamic super-egoistic diversification of the id, which, being drive-led, acts as an unconscious splitting, doubling or seeming defusion of essentially fused drives?

Freud re-fuses the drives through sado-masochism and through the re-sexualizing of morality in moral masochism, concluding that even moral masochism has an erotic 'component'. The conflictual twists and turns in his paper are seemingly resolved by countering 'the subject's destruction of himself' with the relief of the fact that even this 'can not take place without libidinal satisfaction'. Is it simply the libido which is erotically satisfied if the subject is simultaneously destructed? What kind of subjectivity is posited in a pleasurable self-destruction? Is the ego simply at the service of the libido? Freud's 'evidence' of metapsychological 'conflict' resists the hypothesis that the drives are entirely fused. Strangely, however, it is a troubling ego-identity which defends against a super-ego identity and which partially constitutes the ego-identity. What, then, represents the impact of the id – the libido?

Leo Bersani puts it another way:

> the pleasure–unpleasure tension of sexuality – the pain of a self-shattering

excitement – aims at being maintained, replicated and even increased. The human subject is originally *shattered into* sexuality ... sexuality may be a tautology for masochism.

The concept of narcissism can be thought of as an extension of that definition.[15]

Freud's most original speculative move was to deconstruct the sexual as a category of intersubjectivity, and to propose a definition of sexual excitement as both a turning away from others and a dying to the self.[16]

If both sexuality and narcissism are understood as 'tautologies for masochism', a tautology which refutes sexuality as intersubjective at a level of 'origins', *does such a theory positivize such a tautology as an inverse kind of identity, nihilism as position and identity?* If so, it may be the id as configured *vis-à-vis* the super-ego that may refute such a closure, and, since the id also inhabits this tautological configuration, it undermines the possibility of such a closure. A recourse to 'origins' simply binds us to identity as prescription. Also, if moral masochism is a secondary form of masochism, how and why does the formation and impact of the super-ego come *after* the impact of infantile sexuality and auto-eroticism? If the super-ego is the heir of the Oedipus complex, why aren't parental demands and prohibitions also *enigmatically implanted simultaneously* to unconscious sexual messages in precisely the form of anxiety? Further, why aren't gender and sexual difference uncertainly or partially signalled, modelled as they are on 'imperfect' adult others? Sexual and gendered identity/identification as a consequence of an already discontinuous intersubjectivity would be, according to this account, *unsustainable*.

For the next part of this chapter it will be consequential to bear in mind the meaning of the word *Trieb*, or 'drive', in Freud's psychoanalytic theory[17] (as I have already outlined in note 2). Further, it is worth considering in what sense the drives come to configure unity or identity as object and aim, but also come to configure disavowal, disaffecting both object and aim. In emphasizing the aspect of Laplanche's general theory of seduction which has the source and the aim of the sexual drive as an unconsciously desiring other, we consequentially underline the circuitous movement between the source and aim of the drive as institutive of the process of seeming repetition or compulsion of the drives. This circuitous process must accommodate the *disappearance* of others to the structure which constitutes subjectivity and the fantasy of identity.

If the sexual drive is already split by the circuitous redoubling pressure of its movement, we are now left with the problem of accounting for the super-ego, which I see no reason for accounting for from the 'start', so to speak. If the redoubling of the drives compels us towards the fantasy of constancy, a constancy experienced both temporally and configuratively as a sense of unity, of 'I' and 'other', and as a curious fusion of drives, how can the death-drive figure as destructive, when its aim is precisely a unity?

Conversely, since the death-drive is *not* half the sexual drive, it is, according to the same doubling or splitting logic, the coming back, or the endless return of the sexual drive as it accrues values. The secondary aspect of the death-drive (secondary narcissism?) is a redoubling of the already split drive. To refigure the super-ego at this point, and taking account of the part of the dependency of disappearance to appearance in the narcissistic relation, the consequence of the absence of a significant other as the disappearance of the source and object of the subject's libido is a prohibition, in that *disappearance discontinues the unifying circuit of supply and demand. A kind of prohibitive super-ego not based on the signification of others' demands for sexual difference, but on the absence of such signification. This may be experienced or symbolized as a rupture of a circuitous process of signification, the tautology of meaning, or as a repetition of detachment – where detachment itself is symbolized as an appendage to the subjects' imaginary conception of 'their body'.*

Whilst, on the other hand, the representation of the nihilistic death drive follows the aim of lowering tension and anxiety, it also ruptures its aim and object as a single economy or position in its rupturing aspect. The redoubling process makes unity, identity or a 'zero tension' a doubly impossible aim. In order, then, to achieve anything approximating to a possible pleasurable economy of tension, the antagonistic rupture of the already redoubling drive will have to be partially repressed. The representative of the redoubling of the split drive may affect a sense of double loss; a melancholy, in that it splits from this process and circulates as an untranslatable repetition, unconsciously affirming a wish to die. The super-ego, then, would be as much an aspect of the *id figured as a symbolization of a signifying absence – a reservoir of loss*, as it is the internalization of the parental super-ego – parental prohibition as heir to the Oedipus complex. The drive to disappear would *aim* to repeat that absence, which may or may not come to be conflated with a sense of lack.

Drawing out Jean Laplanche's schemata for subjectivity now, we will turn to four of his key conceptions, some already referred to; enigmatic sexual signification, translation, the possibility of 'new experience' and afterwardness. For Laplanche, the representatives of the sexual drive are written as the impact of unconscious sexual signification of the adult world, implanted and metabolized as traumatic imprints on the body. This process of 'enigmatic signification' effects repression and drives; these enigmatic and sexually-emitted significers continue to collide with, or partially constitute, signification in a general sense; that is, signification is always and partially unconscious, enigmatic, and, I will add, discontinuous.

Laplanche draws out a complex temporal process of translation, re-translation and de-translation for the subject's psyche in order to give relative meaning to what always remains as an imperfect exchange of the wish to be understood. The process of enigmatic signification, which Laplanche describes as a 'primal' seduction – 'splits' self-preservation as instinct and the sexual drive, accounting for the structuring of the drives and unconscious through primal repression; thus, the drives are always psychical representatives of repression. Repression attempts to master or moderate oversignification, to reduce the traumatizing effects of helplessness in a conflicting and contesting 'strange culture' of others. It is, therefore, appropriate to account for a wish to cut off. We will cut off from time to time; shut our eyes, ears, mouth, sleep even; turn away from the consistent influx of otherness in any form. Absenting from conscious reflexivity and effecting a discontinuity in time, ego-bound identity, predicated on an identificatory relation to others, at times disappears.[18]

It is pertinent at this point to return to Janine Antoni's *Lick and Lather* (Figure 12) in order to argue it as a properly social product. That is, it is not an articulation of infantile or 'narcissistic' fantasies of omnipotence – nor does it simply have recourse to artistic genius which, arguably, configures the same fantasy. *Lick and Lather*, as a social product, does configure narcissism, as I have tried to show, but an interdependent and conflictual narcissism. This may be drive conflict, but a conflict which, none the less, takes account of the super-ego. The work to this extent is allegorical, in the way Craig Owens has argued.[19] The busts are, in part, a ruin or mutation of classical aesthetics whilst subscribing to it. The idealization and perfection of the genre 'classical bust' is, in *Lick and Lather*, reconfigured as impossible. It disappears through the act of rubbing or licking. This activity is also strikingly rendered in the marks across the materials, tracing the pleasure of oral libidinality on the one hand, and inviting bodily contact on the other. The spectator confronted with the evidence of the tongue and the fingers' marks across the surface of the artwork must

FIGURE 12. Janine Antoni, *Lick and Lather*. Installation, 1994

consider identification at the level of materiality in at least two directions. One, in the direction of repetition or mimicry; that is, since the materials continue to offer their own malleability, we may be tempted to touch. And two, collapsed into the activity will be not only a sexual content but also a reminder of the materials' familiarity in their domestic consumption. There is a double sensibility to *Lick and Lather*; it is not pure, the classicism is worn away with the soap, the failure with regard to the purity of genre is also the successful proposition of this installation. This failure is also one which renders questionable the notion of the artist as creator of both the artwork and herself. Identity as a concern fails to be important; it disappears. To this extent Antoni does not conform to a stark modernism.

Elizabeth Cowie's readings of Laplanche's writings on drives consider some consequences for a discourse of femininity.[20] We may draw on her work here, to consider some consequences for a critique or falling away of identity in a general sense. Cowie emphasizes the non-arbitrary transformable play of the drives in underlining four processes isolated by Freud in 'Instincts and their vicissitudes'. They are the 'Reversal (of the drive) into its opposite. The turning around upon the subject's own self. Repression. Sublimation'.

Following Laplanche, and revising the oppositional examples that Freud couples, e.g. sadism/masochism – Cowie moves from a consideration of the drive's aim as a movement changing from active to passive (sado-masochism) where the opposite's aims only coincide, to a consideration of another of Freud's schemes – scopophilia – where a 'preliminary' stage can be isolated as 'Oneself looking at a sexual organ = A sexual organ being looked at by oneself', which is 'the source of both the situations represented in the resulting pair of opposites, the one or the other according to which element in the original situation is changed'.[21] This stage is autoerotic, or erotogenically masochistic, according to Freud's formulation. Laplanche reformulates the conditions of oppositional pairings by adding another secondary stage, which in turn reformulates the first. The first is a turning around of the drive to mastery, to an auto-aggressive position – this is not sexual – followed by a self-aggressive position which is masochistic and may be sexual. That this, for Cowie, contests the conflation between femininity and the reversal of an active aim to a passive one, is a critical turn. Masochism, here, is primary.

For a further twist, this hypothesis refutes the correspondence between self-aggression and passivity, because 'no reversal of aim is necessary for this stage to be operative'. Auto-eroticism, here, is an intermediate stage, a kind of period where the acquisition of language and skills proliferate and are being tried. Importantly, then, these imperfect 'alien' bombardments are repeatedly assimilated as also sources of anxiety; they are perceived as ideals, remain partially enigmatic and are prohibitive. The residue of seductive and enigmatic signification, which is yet to be translated, is, therefore, repressed, forming unconscious desires and a drive to know, or 'translate' the enigmatic. That which will remain enigmatic – unknowable – will, paradoxically, function as the fixation for knowledge.

Cowie further splits the doubling process in relation to the reversal of the aim of the drive to that of passivity and its non-essential co-joining with maso-chism, which now can only be satisfied through an other object. This other could be the subject's own, or another's, body. The subject can be thought of as differentiated here. This re-theorization of the drives emphasizes the condition of integral paradox; a non-positionality of splitting and splitting as a condition of a drive for positionality.

In underlining the circuitous, the paradoxical and the integral rupturing of sadism and masochism, the assertion that they are twinned opposites is disputed, a dispute already made by Freud, but in coupling the source of the drive to signification, albeit in unconscious mode, the dispute conceptualizes the possi-bility that representatives of drives may divide, following diffuse aims. Since the diffusion and translation of the drives in their objects and their aims are not necessarily mutual, exhaustive or harmonious, they may be conceived of as proliferating and inherently antagonistic without being separate.

Freud's theory of seduction is elaborated in Laplanche's general theory as being an adult or other's sexual implant. Consequently, the bodily impact of *other* as 'sexuality' is the source of the drives, effects repression and is repressed. Repression is the process of disappearing which intrudes upon identities as we 'know them', but configures a subjectivity which is partially disappearing. In 'Repression', Freud articulates three 'phases':

(1) 'primal repression', which has the process of repression acting on the repre-sentatives of the drives, which are disavowed from consciousness, and to which the drives are fixated.

(2) *Nachdrängung*, 'after pressure', or repression 'proper', may be understood as a repulsion directed from another psychical agency, in that, for example, the aims of repressed wishes may be experienced as unpleasure by another agency. The desire or drive to disappear may disrupt, if not act as, discreet opposition to a desire to be and have identity.

(3) the return of the repressed, which, after having been through a process of metaphorization *vis-à-vis* e.g. displacement or condensation, may materialize as symptoms, dreams, slips of the tongue, jokes and so on. This 'return of the repressed' may be articulated as uncanny, an uncanny without origin or position referred to.

Finally, if the aim of the death-drive is sterile unity, a place or object of such an aim may be death *as* identity. The drives, in object and source, are partially also tautologically linked, and since there is 'only one libido', it is the Other who co-joins them. The identifiable aim of the death-drive is 'the Other' which is also the unifying 'crystallizing object' of the life-drive. This other is introjected as ego-ideal and as the fantasized possibility of being. Impossibly then, other *as* identity is also inevitable in a discourse of identity, a discourse which reduces its ruptures to self-sameness. Other than identity, on the other hand, in its psychoanalytic manifestation, must not forget the impact of the unconscious, the drives, repression for the *disappearing away from identity*.

Even whilst our devouring scopophilic consumption of ideal others constitutes identification and cautionary identities, the disunity of disappearance must counter the appearance of perfection in a 'shattering'. It is quite plausible to assert, then, that the object, aim and source of the drives and subjectivity are tautologically returned to 'others' which, once assimilated, are disavowed or detached from. The repeated circuit of exchange is disrupted temporally, discontinuous in its signification, that is; the enigma is the unconscious. The unconscious, therefore, signifies in that it affirms the 'I want' in the 'I want to disappear' – compels 'us' away from identity as we utter 'us'; it is quite other.

The busts in Janine Antoni's exhibition *Lick and Lather* are, amongst other things, a paradoxically material example of a discontinuity of generic form, disjunctive to the possibility of universal formal principles. They are, however, situated in reference to various historically accounted art practices, and to that extent do not conform nihilistically to a wish to practise entirely without relation or appearance. Their distortion, conversely, is a visible break within formal and strictly teleological unities. They are, to my mind, allegorical.

Notes

1 Janine Antoni, *Lick and Lather*, Sandra Gering Gallery, 476 Broome, New York, 8 February–12 March 1994.

2 For contrasting arguments for and against 'reparation' or 'redemption' see Melanie Klein, *Love, Guilt and Reparation and Other Works 1921–1945*, London: Virago, 1988, and Leo Bersani, *The Culture of Redemption*, New Haven, Conn.: Harvard University Press, 1990.

3 For Sigmund Freud the drive is configured as a dynamic process composed of four aspects: *pressure*; *source*, a bodily stimulus; *object*, that which enables the drive aim to be 'achieved'; and *aim*, to eliminate, or reduce to a minimum, unpleasurable tension or anxiety brought about by the somatic instinctual source.

4 On Janine Antoni's use of 'feminine' materials, see Jeffrey Deitch, *Post-Human Catalogue*, Torino: Castello di Rivoli, 1992.

5 Eduardo Cadava, Peter Connor and Jean-Luc Nancy, eds, *Who Comes After the Subject*, London: Routledge, 1991, pp. 1–8.

6 Jean Laplanche, *New Foundations for Psychoanalysis*, trans. David Macey, Oxford: Basil Blackwell, 1989.

7 Sigmund Freud, 'Repression' (1915), in *On Metapsychology: The Theory of Psychoanalysis*, trans. and ed. James Strachey, Pelican Freud Library 11, Harmondsworth: Penguin Books, 1984 pp. 139–58: p. 157.

8 Sigmund Freud 'Beyond the Pleasure Principle' (1920), in *On Metapsychology*, pp. 269–338.

9 See Juliet Mitchell, ed., *The Selected Melanie Klein*, Harmondsworth: Penguin Books, 1986, pp. 95–111.

10 *On Metapsychology*, p. 284.

11 See Jacques Lacan, *Écrits: a Selection*, trans. Alan Sheridan, London: Tavistock Publications, 1977, pp. 1–7.
12 Sigmund Freud, 'Mourning and melancholia' (1917 [1915]), in *On Metapsychology*, pp. 245–68.
13 Sigmund Freud, 'The economic problem of masochism' (1924), in *On Metapsychology*, pp. 409–26.
14 *Ibid.*, pp. 421–2.
15 Bersani, *The Culture of Redemption*, pp. 36–7.
16 *Ibid.*, p. 45.
17 Sigmund Freud, 'Instincts and their vicissitudes' (1915), in *On Metapsychology*, pp. 105–38.
18 In Paul Virilio's *The Aesthetics of Disappearance*, trans. Philip Beitchman, New York: Semiotext(e), 1991, 'Picnolepsy' (*petit mal* epilepsy) is a universal category for subjectivity and aesthetics, where cutting off from consciousness ruptures time and is compensated for narratively. Whilst very useful as a conception of temporality, it reduces epilepsy to the identity of 'the human condition' without differentiation.
19 Craig Owens, 'The allegorical impulse: towards a theory of postmodernism', in B. Wallis, ed., *Art After Modernism: Rethinking Representation*, Cambridge, Mass.: MIT Press, 1984.
20 Elizabeth Cowie, 'The seductive theories of Jean Laplanche: a new view of the drive, passivity and femininity', in John Fletcher and Martin Stanton, eds, *Jean Laplanche: Seduction, Translation, Drives*, London: Institute of Contemporary Arts, 1992, pp. 121–36.
21 *Ibid.*, p. 126.

Index

Works of art and literature are listed under the names of their authors. Page numbers in italics refer to illustrations on the pages cited.